Directions for the Road Ahead:

Stability in change among churches of Christ

DIRECTIONS FOR THE

ROAD AHEAD:

STABILITY IN CHANGE AMONG CHURCHES OF CHRIST

Editors: Jim Sheerer
Charles Williams

Editorial Committee:
Dr. Jim Baird
Jimmy Jividen
Dr. Howard Norton
Robert Oglesby Sr.
Dr. Don Vinzant

Yeomen Press
Chickasha, Oklahoma

Yeomen Press
110 Meadowdale Drive
Chickasha, Oklahoma 73018
(405) 224-2692

Printed in the United States of America
First Printing   March 1998
Second Printing   August 1998
Third Printing   March 2000
Fourth Printing   July 2003
Fifth Printing   April 2006

ISBN 0-9663531-0-2

APPRECIATION

We want to express our sincere appreciation to
LaNell Coppedge of Oklahoma Christian University
of Science and Arts of Oklahoma City, Oklahoma
and
Dana McMichael of Oklahoma State University of
Stillwater, Oklahoma for their valuable assistance
in proofing the chapters and offering grammatical
corrections.

Also we want to express our appreciation to the
editorial committee of Dr. Jim Baird, Jimmy Jividen,
Dr. Howard Norton, Robert Oglesby, Sr. and
Dr. Don Vinzant for their valuable help in
formulating the book, helping to select authors,
reading all the manuscripts and writing chapters.
Without these men, there would have been
no such book.

Contents

Preface

Howard Norton

This book grows out of strong desire to clarify and restate some distinctive biblical concepts that churches of Christ have tried to restore during the last two hundred years.

Some of us fear these unique doctrines and positions are in danger of being compromised or even forgotten. There are numerous reasons for this concern.

First, many people in churches of Christ have heard little or no teaching about the ideas dealt with in this book. Beginning in the 1960s, preachers and teachers began to de-emphasize Restoration themes; i.e., themes that our own Bible scholars had rediscovered and preached during the last two centuries or so. We readily admit that spotlighting other biblical concepts might have been appropriate for a while because some earlier spokesmen had focused too narrowly on doctrines that centered almost exclusively on salvation and the church.

In retrospect, some preachers and teachers overcorrected. In our zeal to teach and preach a wider range of biblical material, we almost quit teaching some of the most fundamental, biblical concepts that the Restoration Movement had rediscovered. When a certain preacher, for example, delivered a sermon on baptism a few years ago in one of the largest congregations in our brotherhood, a member of the congregation said he had been attending that church for fifteen years and, in all those years had never before heard a lesson from the pulpit dealing with baptism. Other preachers have had similar experiences in other places. It is unlikely that this scenario existed in a single church of Christ prior to the 1960s.

Second, some of us fear that certain biblical doctrines are in danger today because standing for them and teaching them puts the speaker out of sync with the mood of the present generation. Holding to these doctrines sets us apart and makes us different from other religious groups with whom we have many common beliefs.

I commented on this topic in an editorial in The Christian Chronicle in March 1995. "There is no question about it, we are a minority group. We are an out-group, not an in-group. Quite a number of doctrines push us from the inner circle. We believe, for example, that the Bible teaches baptism for the remission of sins. This doctrine alone separates us from virtually every other non-Catholic church in America. Roman Catholics believe that people must be baptized to be saved, but it is a rare Protestant group that will accept this truth. Quite naturally, then, some people in our fellowship are questioning this biblical doctrine. Why? Because holding this 'embarrassing' doctrine makes us different from most people around us....

"Gordon W. Allport, long-time psychology professor at Harvard and now deceased, published a book entitled The Nature of Prejudice in which he examines the behavior of out-groups insociety. He defines an in-group 'as any cluster of people who can use the term 'we' with the same significance.'"

"He also points out that, besides having an in-group, a person has a reference group. When a person's in-group is also his or her reference group, as usually happens, there is little dissonance. When, however, a person wants to identify with a reference group that is different from his in-group, Allport says, 'He may feel so intensely about the matter that he repudiates his own in-group. He develops a condition that Kurt Lewin has called "self-hate" (i.e., hatred for his own in-group).'"

"I fear that this is what is happening to some key spokesmen in our fellowship. Churches of Christ are their in-group; i.e., their heritage, their worship community, their source of spiritual identity, and financial support. They look to the larger evangelical community, however, as their reference group. They long for acceptance and approval from the evangelicals who, generally speaking, reject churches with Restoration roots because of their distinctive doctrines. Unable to receive approval from the evangelicals because of the in-group to which they belong, a kind of self-loathing develops; and churches of Christ become the enemy -- the cause of their discomfort."

Church leaders must make sure that the condition just described never keeps the local pulpit from providing the biblical teaching needed to guarantee that the local church holds to the teachings of God's word concerning salvation and the church -- regardless of their "embarrassing" quality.

Third, there is a danger that great Restoration doctrines discovered in the Bible will lose their power and influence unless the present generation hears them advocated with contemporary language and illustrations. Most of us admire such heroes of the faith as J. W. McGarvey and David Lipscomb. We enjoy reading their materials and following their arguments. Their materials, however, are dated and hold little attraction for today's typical reader. When we envisioned the present book, we made it our aim to invite authors who believed in the particular doctrine that each addresses. We also looked for people who would be able to present their finding with words and examples that communicate to our day.

Fourth, there is a danger that the Restoration Movement's gains in the realm of doctrine will suffer serious loss because of the heavy pressure on church leaders today to change the church. Churches of Christ are under attack on so many doctrinal fronts. Our traditional hermeneutic is under assault, and so is what we have believed and practiced traditionally with reference to the role of women. Many are questioning our understanding considering instrumental music in worship, the meaning of baptism, the relationship between the Gospels and the Epistles, the church's organization, the trustworthiness of the Bible, and the validity of our efforts to be nondenominational in a nation that is full of denominations.

In response to some of these circumstances, a group of concerned Christian leaders began meeting to discuss what we might be able to do in order to supply church leaders with some kind of assistance that would help them understand what is going on in our nation, in the church and in the larger religious world. We decided that one of the first things needed was a book that would address some of the topics that surface regularly among individuals and congregations throughout the nation.

Our mission, therefore, became one of providing a doctrinal handbook for elders and other church leaders that would help them deal intelligently with current problems facing the church. Almost immediately, we were suspected and even accused of developing a creed for the church. Nothing could be further from the truth. Our purpose here is not to provide a creed, but rather to provide a rationale and a reaffirmation of some distinctive topics that the Restoration Movement has championed because they are based firmly on the teachings of Jesus Christ and the inspired apostles.

We do not claim that each author agrees with every other author on all the topics treated in the book. The only way to find out what an author believes on topics he or she did not write is to ask the person. What we do hope to provide for our readers is a well-stated, biblical position on each of the sixteen topics included on the pages that follow. We hope readers will feel after reading a particular chapter that they have a better grasp of the doctrine that is being expounded. It is also our prayer that readers will use whatever good they gain from this book for the purpose of strengthening the body of Christ.

Our forefathers warned us repeatedly that we are never more than one generation away from apostasy. If we did not understand this when they first spoke the words, we now know the truth of what they were saying. Our challenge in churches of Christ is to avoid bowing either to the secular or the religious culture that surrounds us and devote ourselves to the task of finding what God said about the issues we face today. Then comes the greatest challenge of all: putting what He said into practice.

Introduction

Jack P. Lewis

The Psalmist affirms,

We will tell to the coming generation the glorious deeds of the Lord, and his might, and the wonders he has done..... He commanded our ancestors to teach their children that the next generation might know them, the children yet unborn, and rise up and tell them to their children, so that they should set their hope in God, and not forget the works of God, but keep his commandments (Psalm 78:4-7).

Knowledge of God's will is not inherited through the genes. The education task is an on-going one to be diligently pursued (Deuteronomy 6:7). Moses envisioned that children would rise up asking of the Passover observance, "What do you mean by this observance?" (Exodus 12:26). In time to come, children would ask of the stones at the Jordan River, "What do these stones mean?" (Joshua 4:21). On-going history is always the story of a new king arising who does not know Joseph.

The apostles were charged, "teaching them to obey everything that I have commanded you" (Matthew 28:20). Timothy was instructed to commit what he had learned to faithful men who would be able to teach others also (II Timothy 2:1-2), and Titus was to teach what is consistent with wholesome doctrine (Titus 2:11). Jude urges his readers "to contend for the faith that was once for all entrusted to the saints" (Jude 3). The on-going task of teaching is comparable to a relay in which the baton is passed from one runner to the next.

People do not live by bread alone but by every word that comes from the mouth of God (Deuteronomy 8:3; Matthew 4:4). It is a word not to be added to nor taken from (Deuteronomy 4:2;12:12; Revelation 22:18-19). Congregations move in fads, going from one emphasis to another; but any congregation that neglects to teach any part of God's Word will shortly find itself with people who do not know the beliefs and duties that have not been taught. Its neglect has planted the seed for departure from the Word of God.

The history of God's people is a story of cautions against forgetting (Deuteronomy 6:12), but also of cycles of departure and of return to the Lord. The book of Judges is built around six such cycles. The monarchy also proceeded in cycles with Jehoshaphat, Asa, Hezekiah, and Josiah remembered as the reforming kings of Judah. Josiah found the copy of the law in repairing the temple, a law authenticated by the prophetess Huldah and recognized as a law that "neither we nor our fathers have kept" (II Kings 22:8ff). The next cycle is the story of exile and return.

Though the kingdom envisioned in Daniel was a kingdom to stand forever (Daniel 2:44), its march through history was not an undeviating one. Jesus spoke of those who said, "Lord, Lord," but to whom he would say, "I never knew you" (Matthew 7:21-23). Paul warned the elders of Ephesus (Acts 20:29) and Timothy (I Timothy 4:1ff; II Timothy 4:3-4). The writer of the Epistle to the Hebrews admonishes, "Therefore we must pay greater attention to what we have heard, so that we do not drift from it" (Hebrews 2:1). The Epistle of John urges that we try the spirits to see whether they are from God (I John 4:1). The church in Ephesus is called on to "remember the height from which you have fallen" (Revelation 2:4), that of Thyatira to "strengthen what remains and is about to die," and that of Philadelphia to "hold on to what you have, so that no one will take your crown" (Revelation 2:11).

In our age, as in every age, the church is tempted to be a chameleon taking on the color of the background in which it finds itself. It is easier to be conformed to the world than to be transformed (cf. Romans 12:1).

xiv

It is widely agreed that the church today is in a state of perplexity. Whether the phase of the cycle is away from God or a return to Him will in the ultimate be judged by God. His ultimate purpose will not be frustrated. He is able to raise up children to Abraham from stones (cf. Matthew 3:9). He is able to take his kingdom from its possessors and give it to those who bring forth fruits (cf. Matthew 21:43). But in God's purpose, one would choose to be used as Peter, John, or Paul and not like Judas. He would prefer to be Timothy or Titus and not Demas. One is concerned whether the Lord will see my associates and me on the departure side of the cycle or the return side.

When I was a fledgling preacher, the book edited by J. H. Garrison entitled *The Old Faith Restated* (St. Louis: Christian Publishing Company, 1891) fell into my hands. Along with the Bible, I devoured its contents. More than a century has passed since that book was issued. It is time to restate doctrines that we all confess have not recently been preached or taught as they should be. A new generation has arisen that needs to hear.

Stability is a Christian virtue. We are not to be tossed about by every wind of doctrine (Ephesians 4:14). Timothy is admonished to hold to the standard of sound teaching that he has heard (II Timothy 1:13), and the writer of the Epistle to the Hebrews gives repeated admonitions to hold fast to "your confession" (Hebrews 3: 6; 4:14; 10:23). John warned that those who do not abide in the teaching do not have God (II John 9).

In the midst of a changing world there are constants. God (Malachi 3:6), Jesus (Hebrews 13:8), the universality of sins (I John 1:9), human need of a Savior (Acts 4:12), death and judgment (Hebrews 9:27; cf. I Corinthians 15:25), and the word of God (Isaiah 40:7-8) do not change. But also to be remembered is "The world and its desires are passing away, but those who do the will of God live forever" (I John 2:17).

These studies have not centered on the moral, spiritual and other matters that continue to face the church; but they should not be interpreted to imply a lack of concern about such questions. Substance abuse is everywhere. Commitment is a problem in every congregation. Despite the television programs, sermons and seminars on marriage and the family, the divorce rate continues to rise. Memphis, Tennessee has five mosques, establishments of the oriental religions, and masses of people with no religion. Doctrinal problems, spiritual problems, and moral problems are all a part of our assigned task of bringing every thought into subjection to the obedience of Christ (II Corinthians 10:5).

The approach the authors have intended is positive rather than negative. Issues, rather than personalities, are considered even where a name has been used to identify a contention.

It is hoped that these studies will be a stimulus to cause each reader to ask himself/herself, to what extent am I assuming that if I like a thing, the Lord must like it also? Remember that the ways of a person are right in his own eyes (Proverbs 16:2). The Lord warned, "Your thoughts are not my thoughts and your ways are not my ways" (Isaiah 55:8). What scriptural basis do I have for contending that what I want to retain is what the Lord wants retained?

It is also hoped that the studies will be a stimulus to each advocate of change to ask, what Scripture basis do I have for contending that what I want is also what the Lord wants?

If change is for the purpose of understanding truths of God not adequately understood before, than all truth-loving people should be advocates of change and should welcome change. Truth makes people free. If change is the dropping of practices or rules that moss-like have accumulated through the years, but which have no scripture to support them, change can set people free. If change is putting into practice duties that have been neglected, then change is only the recognition with Paul, "I have not yet attained, I am not yet made perfect" (Philippians 3:14). Every generation needs more abandonment of sin, more self-denial, more spiritual commitment and dedication.

In the tensions of these times, may we all keep before us the admonition of Paul, *"Do nothing from selfish ambition or conceit, but in humility regard others better than yourself. Let each of you look not to your own interests, but to the interests of others"* (Philippians 2:3-4).

1. The State of the Church Today

Glover Shipp

It was a little white structure with a bell tower. Located at a country crossroads, the London, Oregon church building was the only meeting place of any kind in the upper end of the Willamette Valley. There were perhaps fifty members. They were farmers, miners, loggers, etc.

This was the congregation in which I grew up for my first twelve years. My great-grandfather and grandfather were elders. My grandfather and grandmother both taught Bible classes. Grandpa was the regular song leader.

Lighting was furnished by kerosene lamp. Heating was provided by a pot-bellied wood stove. Air-conditioning consisted of opening the windows. Facilities were two little shacks at the back of the property. Classes all met in corners of the auditorium until about 1939 when four classrooms were constructed.

That small congregation had few financial resources, but emphasized missions and gave half or more of its contributions to domestic and foreign evangelism. With its encouragement and a little monetary aid, my father began preaching, which he continued to do, both on the West Coast and overseas, for fifty years.

The London church was devout and studious. Learning the word was a serious matter. There were many a midweek Bible bee or memorization contest, to sharpen our knowledge. The men of the congregation always knelt in prayer and expected even the boys to do the same. Horseplay during the services was anathema. We knew we were there to worship our God and learn more of His way for us.

1

The London church could sing. Oh, how it could sing! My grandfather had been a musical entertainer in his youth, so he saw to it that both the adults and children learned to read music and sing hymns properly.

A Different Time and World

That was a different time and a different world for churches of Christ. It was in a rural setting, operating on a seasonal cycle. Education was limited, with few having gone beyond the eighth grade. My father was the only member who had ever taken college-level courses.

We Knew What We Believed and Could Defend It

Yet, we knew what we believed. We accepted the Bible as God's revealed Word and were well acquainted with the New Testament. True, the Old Testament tended to be neglected, but doctrine about Christ and the church was firmly planted in our hearts.

We knew what we believed and could defend it strongly, sometimes even belligerently. We were the New Testament church. We taught the one and only way into the Kingdom, by way of the five steps of salvation -- hearing, believing, repenting, confessing and being baptized in water for the remission of sins. Through that sequence, we were added to the Lord's church. Our preachers and debaters could chart the process graphically and logically.

In fact, all of our doctrine was logical, arrived at through deductive reasoning. We believed that the Bible taught by command, example and necessary inference.

Baptism for Remission of Sins

For instance, we affirmed that baptism was commanded by Christ and His apostles. Baptism was a burial in water for the remission of sins. Therefore, baptism was essential for remission of sins, or salvation. Or, baptism was a new birth (John 3: 3-5). Through this new birth, we entered the Kingdom and were added to the church. Therefore, only those who were born of water and the Spirit were to be considered members of the church.

2

Individuals in the New Testament were buried in water for the remission of sins. Therefore, to be saved, it was necessary to be baptized in water for the forgiveness of sins. Here we see the use of command, example and necessary inference all used in arriving at a doctrine.

The Lord's Supper

We believed in the essentiality of observing the Lord's Supper weekly through much the same mental process: the Lord instituted His memorial feast to commemorate His death until He comes again. The early church celebrated the Lord's Supper. The church in Troas observed the Supper on the first day of the week. Therefore all churches were to observe it each first day of the week. Here we again see our argument based on command: "This do in memory of me." An example: The church in Troas met together to break bread (the Lord's Supper) on the first day of the week. A necessary inference: We are the church today, meeting on the first day of the week. Therefore, we must partake of the communion every first day of every week.

Inspiration and Inerrancy of Bible

By the same process, we believed in the inspiration and therefore the inerrancy of the Bible. We argued: all scripture was inspired of God. The New Testament was scripture. Therefore, the New Testament was inspired and inerrant.

We carefully distinguished between the old Covenant given through Moses and the New Covenant given through Christ. We believed that the Old Covenant was done away with by Christ and therefore was not to be followed in any way today. This mentality backfired to some extent, because many Christians concluded that the Old Testament was therefore of no practical value and need not be studied. Some members would object if much time were spent on Old Testament studies, despite the fact that Paul told Timothy that every scripture was inspired of God and profitable to the Christian (II Timothy 3:16), and that Peter affirmed that the Old Testament prophets were inspired by God (I Peter 1:10-12; II Peter 1:19-21).

3

Autonomy of Local Church, Governed by Elders

We believed in the autonomy of the local church which was to be governed by elders. We arrived at these conclusions through reasoning that there is no hierarchy of authority over the churches; only Christ is its head. In the early church, each congregation was to have elders. Therefore, local churches today were to be autonomous and governed by biblically-qualified elders. We did not consider the possibility that in a city such as Rome, with many house groups, there may have been but one body of elders in the city. We did fail in some respects with this position, for we largely kept to ourselves as local churches, encouraging neighboring congregations only in a limited way and often competing with them for members.

Mission Programs

We practiced missions because the Lord gave the church His Great Commission. That commission is still binding. Therefore, all congregations were to be involved in mission activity. Relatively little mission work was done brotherhood-wide in those decades, with relatively few being directly involved in worldwide missions. But still we believed in the Great Commission. I recall vividly a poster on the front wall of our little London church building. Published by B. D. Morehead, it pictured each of our overseas missionaries, perhaps twenty five in all. That poster had a profound influence on my life, turning my heart toward world evangelism.

The Grace of Giving

We gave of our means, even though limited, on the first day of the week, because this was what the apostle Paul ordered the Corinthian church to practice. Since churches of today were to practice what the early church practiced, we too were to give on the first day of the week. Since tithing was part of the Old Law, our giving was to be according to our level of prosperity and not precisely ten percent of our income. We may have had only a dollar or half-dollar to give, but we gave it willingly.

4

A Cappella Singing

We accepted the doctrine that our singing was to be *a cappella* - that is, by voice only. We argued that music in the New Testament was singing - the fruit of the lips in praise to God. The early church sang psalms, hymns and spiritual songs in their worship, without musical accompaniment, instruments not being officially used in worship until the eleventh century. Since we were not to add to, or detract from, New Testament doctrine, and since historically instruments were not used in the early church, we believed that we had no authority for their use. We gave to God only the fruit of our lips (Hebrews 13: 15), not the fruit of a mechanical instrument

The One Body

We understood that Christ died to purchase His body, the church. There was but one body. Therefore, the church was His only body and salvation could only be realized through membership in the church.

That church, we firmly held, was the church of Christ, which had been restored to its original plan, organization and doctrine as revealed in the New Testament. This meant, in essence, that our teaching and practice were accurate and complete. However, upon closer investigation, some among us realized that much remained to be restored. We seldom, if ever, taught on the Holy Spirit. We taught doctrine almost to the exclusion of grace and individual holiness or piety. We mentioned the kind of love Paul describes in I Corinthians 13, but often failed to practice it, being harsh in our dealings with others, especially those who disagreed with us doctrinally.

Salvation Only In The Church

Despite our inconsistencies, we preached that salvation was found only in the church of Christ, which could date its history to the very first congregation, founded by Christ in Jerusalem in A. D. 33. Only later did we discover that this date may not have been accurate, since dating discrepancies over events in ancient times may have meant that the church began in A. D. 28, 29 or 30, rather than 33 A. D.

5

Biblical Name

We used only the "church of Christ," because we believed that this name was biblical, gave honor to Christ, showed the world that we were the bride of Christ and wore His name, and served as a universal identification sign for the church. A traveler could know, almost without exception, that a church building labeled "Church of Christ" would be the true church and could be visited safely. We knew that there was no one identifying name in the New Testament for the church, but that many descriptive titles are given to it. However, we selected one of these, to the exclusion of all others and, in a sense, sectarianized it through exclusive use of it.

Readiness to Defend the Church

We were ready to defend the church at all costs. This gave rise to countless public debates and reams of arguments on paper. We discussed almost every detail in the New Testament with whatever sectarian preacher who was willing to debate us. After all, we were set for the defense of the Gospel (Philippians 1: 17).

Many of our debates and discussions, however, were among our own. We debated one cup versus many in the Lord's Supper, divided classes on the Lord's Day, kitchens, food served in meeting places, premillenialism and cooperation among churches on mission and benevolence projects, including nation-wide radio, children's homes and other programs.

A Divided Body

Whether or not we were willing to admit it, we were not one body, but many, each pretty much refusing fellowship to the others. This was especially true for the Disciples of Christ, which we considered no longer a true New Testament church and the Christian Church, known also as Churches of Christ/Conservative Christian Churches, about which we had serious doubts.

Humble Roots

As a general rule, we were to be found meeting in rural settings or in out-of-the way locations, "across the tracks" from the more affluent areas of towns and cities. We were of the lower or lower-middle classes, with limited resources. Few leading citizens associated with us. And we were a constant target for ridicule -- "those folks who believe they're the only ones going to heaven."

Rapid Growth

Yet, we grew. In fact the media reported in the 50's and 60's that churches of Christ were "the fastest-growing religious group in the United States." We greatly increased our domestic and foreign outreach in post-World War II years. Along with our growth, we upgraded in the location and quality of church buildings. We were "somebody" and slowly came to be accepted by our communities and by other churches.

How It Is Today

Today, however, congregations of earlier generations would be dismissed as totally out of touch with our modern world. Today, we are much more sophisticated than they. We have left the farm and have become urbanites. We have been to college. We are doctors, lawyers, journalists, accountants, school teachers, computer-literate professionals. Many of us are even "professional" students, laboriously collecting multiple graduate degrees.

More Sophistication

Today, our churches, too, are much more sophisticated. Our meeting places are replete with comfortable, air-conditioned auditoriums. Pews are padded. Lighting can be adjusted to every situation. Speaking systems are at least supposed to operate efficiently. Our churches have many of the newest marvels of our day -- FAX machines, computers, Internet capability, and projectors of all kinds. We have many well-equipped classrooms, a large family life center and adjoining kitchen, sports facilities, conference rooms, a chapel, etc.

Highly Educated Specialists

Our preachers are no longer humble men with a fire in their bones for evangelism. Rather, they are highly-educated specialists in one aspect or another of ministry. They are expected to be the church's professionals, ministering to the members and their friends and relatives. They no longer live on a shoestring, as did their predecessors of past generations. Rather, their salary and benefits generally are handsome. Yet, many jockey for position in the brotherhood, seeking that "divine call" to a larger church and higher salary.

Most of our members are educated and demanding. They expect quality messages delivered in an entertaining and provocative manner. They expect to be fed and with little effort on their part to be made to feel good about themselves.

Loss in the Spiritual Realm

In the hurry and scurry of everyday life, something has to give. Often, it is in the spiritual realm. Today, few besides preachers and class teachers do any serious Bible study on their own. Relatively few are truly active in the church. And very few win souls to Christ. In most congregations this comes to about five percent of the members actively attempting to win others to Christ.

We find it difficult to schedule time for Christian matters, because our agendas are so very full of business and other secular considerations. Both parents work outside their homes in most cases, so by evening they are too tired to do much besides watch television.

A fall-out of our frantic life-style is a decrease in general Bible knowledge and its application to our lives. We even come to classes and worship with empty hands and spiritually-starved hearts. Because we are "too busy" to absorb God's Word, we become spiritual illiterates. Therefore, we are easy prey for other influences in our lives.

An Uptight People, Dying Spiritually

We are uptight, frustrated and hassled, dying spiritually. So we blame the preacher, Bible teacher, or church for not providing the spiritual diet that we say we need. There may be truth in some of our criticism, because many classes have turned into discussion circles, rather than periods of serious Bible study. And those who guide the sessions may have little depth of Bible knowledge, or spiritual maturity. At best, in some churches the diet served is milk, perhaps even skimmed milk, rather than solid meat of the word (I Corinthians 3:1-3; I Peter 2:2).

Rejection of Authority

Coupled with our ignorance of the word is a pervading rejection of authority at all levels, including spiritual. The scriptures are no longer considered binding or even relevant. For some, the Gospels contain principles, not commands. The writings of Paul are "love letters" and not doctrine to be followed. The Bible is not completely accurate, say some, having been polluted down through the centuries by translators.

Since we argue that the word is not binding on us today, there is no reason for us to submit ourselves to the authority of Christ, or of elders in local churches. If the local shepherds admonish or discipline us, we immediately rebel, claiming that they have no right to do so. Instead of accepting their role as pastors and bishops of the flock, we launch a campaign to discredit them, move on to another congregation, or drop out entirely.

A Right To Own Opinion

Or, we may drift on to another religious body. We have bought into the idea that everyone has a right to his or her own opinion (See Leudtke, Chapter 14, and Guiness, page 26). We believe that every opinion is equally valid. Then we conclude that every church has a right to its own doctrine, that all doctrines are valid and that all churches have their particular attractions. We therefore shop through the religious "mall," searching for the church that makes us feel good.

9

The doctrinal uniqueness of the church is no longer accepted, appreciated, or for many, understood. As a result, we have begun to drift. We have lost our identity. For some of our folk, this means that the church is no longer relevant. Any church -- or no church -- will do. .

Choice the Operative Term

In our contemporary world, "choice" is the operative term. We can choose among hundreds of cereals in the supermarket. We can pick our own personalized automobile from hundreds of styles. There is no longer any "brand" loyalty in our society. We can choose to marry, or to have a live-in "significant other." We can choose to divorce. We can choose to abort a fetus. Sports teams can choose to move to another city, with loyal fans left frustrated. Individual athletes can choose from among many teams. We then carry this mentality of many options over into religion. We pick and choose what suits us, rather than what suits the Lord.

Mania for Change

Compounding the situation is the current mania for change. Generational change has always been with us, but our present age sees change taking place at a rate never before known. Here are some examples.

A leading computer technologist observed, when the first 640 K computers came out in 1985, that he could not see anyone ever needing more memory than that. Today, computers have hundreds of times more memory. Tony Alley, a computer specialist at Oklahoma Christian University of Science and Arts, observed that within months, or even weeks after a new computer model or application is released to the public, it is already obsolete.

A quarter century ago, global communication was problematic. Long distance phone calls often required tedious delays; and when a connection was made, one had to shout over the line. Letters could take months to arrive at their destination. Today, we have satellite telephone connections that are clear and instantaneous, FAX machines that send entire manuscripts on their way in minutes, and now, the Internet, which processes communication in a matter of seconds.

My first plane flight, as I recall, was on a Douglas DC-4, in 1949. It took about six hours from Los Angeles to Dallas, with three stops. The same route today can be covered in just over two hours, non-stop. Or, one can travel from New York to Paris, Miami to Rio, or Chicago or Moscow, all flights non-stop, safe and relatively comfortable.

Companies are adopting artificial intelligence on a grand scale. Major industries in Japan have robots that can not only assemble cars, but can also patrol corridors, direct traffic and monitor appliances in a home. Organizations are downsizing, and in the process, terminating many jobs, thus creating the need for retraining. Employees may be shifted anywhere in the world. Companies are merging and re-merging daily, with some going bankrupt.

Society's norms are also changing rapidly. What not many years ago was only mentioned in secret is now "dished" out daily on the television screen, for all to see. No topic appears to be taboo. And our church families are absorbing all of this. It has been observed that the church today is "more a mirror of society than a light to society." This suggests that we are becoming more secular and materialistic as time passes, rather than having a sense of being different from the world.

Change and Local Congregations

The mania for change affects congregations. Many of the members, especially younger ones, do not understand why churches should follow the same routine week after week, year after year, while everything about them is in a constant whirl of change. They crave innovation, excitement and adventure.

The desire to feel good triggers a parallel desire to hear only positive words from the pulpit and classroom. Like Israel in Old Testament times, they want their prophets to speak only smooth things and to prophesy illusions (Isaiah 30: 10).

The urge to feel good calls for entertainment in worship and church work, more than serious exhortation and humble praise lifted to God. To accommodate the wishes of the members, song books are closed, "praise teams" of worship leaders (each equipped with a state-of-the-art microphone) lead the worship, sermons are more "how to" discourses and are filled with anecdotes and illustrations. Every effort is made to present a carefully orchestrated and professional worship hour. Members see professionalism every evening on television, so expect the same kind of lights and sounds, bells and whistles, that character-ize the media.

"Shopping Center" Churches

If members do not find such slick quality in their congregation, they think nothing of shopping around, even among other church groups, until they find one that satisfies them (See Smith, page 208). However, the moment a crisis arises in that church, they are "out of there." Church growth specialists catalog some larger groups as "shopping center" churches, offering everything for every taste. The seeker can find whatever he or she wants. But this kind of seeker may soon drift off to another "shopping center," to try its offering. Guiness observes:

> "One-stop shopping" is a theme common to all megachurches. The biggest offer not only spiritual attractions, but such features as moving theaters, weight rooms, saunas, roller rinks and racquetball courts. (Dining With the Devil, page 12)

Other Church Models

Other models, apart from the "shopping center" church, include the "tunnel church," with members constantly entering while others are exiting at the other end; the "little cottage " church composed of a small flock of house-church attendees; and the "catacomb" church, in which members wither away and die. All of these exist today, but our mania for modernity tends to drive us toward the "shopping center" style, with something for everyone.

Four Poles of Attitude

Within the church itself, four poles of attitude can be seen, according to Foster (Will The Cycle Be Unbroken?, p. 90-96). These are conservatism (holding fast), intellectualism, liberalism (moving on) and pietism (personal spirituality based in great part on feelings).

Four Poles Described

As Foster describes it, conservatism "places much importance on doctrinal precision and correctness, and views the Bible as a legal document to which all must strictly adhere" (Ibid., p. 92). This mentality generally takes a low view of human nature.

On the contrary, liberalism has a high view of human ability, says Foster, "Yet also has a wide view of the grace of God that allows for imperfections and failures" (Ibid., p. 90). It tends not to consider the Bible as a code of law, but rather, as a set of broad principles, or as a collection of "love letters."

The third pole of mentality in the church today is pietism, which stresses the importance of good works -- connecting with and caring for others -- and living a godly life directed by the Spirit (Ibid., p. 92).

The final pole is intellectualism, which handles scripture in a careful, highly scholarly manner. This view places great stress on the meaning of words (especially in the original languages) in historical documents and hermeneutics. This position requires a high view of human capacity to reason (Ibid., p. 93).

Mutual Distrust

All of these groups tend to distrust the others. As a result of this and of pushing their own conclusions and agendas, they create a climate for fracturing the body of Christ.

Because of this, some schedule lectureships and workshops aimed at opening the door to communication with other religious bodies. And some schedule programs that deal with "how to live in a much reduced faithful brotherhood." There are instances of congregations radically changing their names to be more acceptable to the community, while others are considering changing their name so as no longer to be identified with the mainstream of the churches of Christ. Some reach out to embrace kindred spirits in the larger evangelical world. Others withdraw into a shell of exclusiveness. And, of course, there are various positions in between these two more extreme ones.

Various Camps of Christians

Today we face, not a dichotomized division of the church, as occurred generally in the latter part of the last century over instrumental music, church societies and other matters, but rather, a fracturing into various not-clearly-defined camps. As Foster points out, these may include fundamentalists, neo-conservatives, conservative moderates, pragmatists, post-modern conservative moderates and intellectual post-moderns (Ibid., pp. 93-96).

Loss of Doctrinal Distinctives

One reason for the fuzziness we feel regarding what members of the church now believe and where they stand is the loss of our doctrinal distinctives, or rather, the loss of appreciation for why they are distinctives. We still baptize. We still celebrate the Lord's Supper. We still sing *a cappella*. We still have elders in most congregations. But we sense that many of our number no longer understand or appreciate why these and other such points are distinctive to who we are as a group. We still follow the forms, but may no longer have much regard for the functions. It is something like Halloween. Centuries ago, on "All-Souls Day" jack-o-laterns were placed in windows to ward off the spirits of the dead. For the same reason, masks were worn. Today, we no longer believe in any of that and have forgotten the original function, but still practice the forms.

We live in a day of relativity, when only a third of Americans believe in the existence of absolute truth, in contrast to two-thirds thirty years ago (Colson, p. 330). When the existential, not the historical, governs the thinking of our nation, how shall we make a certain doctrinal sound, if we too are existential in our thinking? While this shocking shift has been taking place all about us in regard to truth, we have tended to remain content with our own church world.

Rip Van Winkle Syndrome

Don Vinzant, a student of church growth and challenges facing the church today, suggests that we are suffering a Rip Van Winkle syndrome. As the fabric of our culture unravels and our nation finds itself groping through moral decline, loss of faith in all authority and a "me-first" mentality, we awaken as from a long slumber, no longer recognizing our world or having a clearly-enunciated answer to its present ills. Some of us are answering questions that no one today is asking. In the process, we are failing to even acquaint ourselves with the real concerns of others.

Can it be that we somehow have missed the mark, not necessarily in doctrine, but in application of it to society? Have we found ourselves standing outside of the world's stream? Do we even want to stop it from its mad whirl so we can get on? Do we deal in relative trivialities rather than the basic ills of society? Do we tinker with our style of worship and make other attempts to polish up the face of the local body, so as to be seeker-friendly, but not address the seeker's real needs?

Somehow, we have lost our sense of identity, as it relates to both the word of God and the ongoing crisis of today, and have yet to find a new one, as observed by long-time minister J. Harold Thomas. We have yet to find how effectively to be the church separated from the world, but at the same time be in its market-places with a vital message that it can understand. (See Niebuhr, *Christ and Culture*, for more on the tension between the church and today's cultural stresses.)

A Crucial Time for the Church

We stand at a crucial time in our history. Our net growth is minimal. We have done fairly well among our own kind, but on the whole have not been able to cope with deteriorating neighbor-hoods, inner cities, vastly different religious faiths and diverse ethnic groups. There are shining exceptions, such as in Miami, Houston, Dallas, Memphis and Los Angeles, but on the whole, we must all admit that our record is less than impressive in many areas of our nation and world.

Are we then watching the decline and death of a movement? Is the church which we affirm to have direct links to the first century church to disappear? All that we have said may indicate this, but there is another side of the matter to consider.

The Other Side of the Matter

For instance, there is our Lord Jesus Christ. If we truly are members of His body, then nothing can permanently destroy us. He announced that the church is His, and "the gate of Hades will not prevail against it" (Matthew 16: 18). These words, says Charles Colson, "should be posted over the entrance of every church building in the land" (One Body, p. 67).

Giving the Church Back to Christ

We have a proprietorial attitude toward the church, especially our own congregation. We believe that if we do not accomplish certain things, the church will not prosper. One preacher was heard to say that it was the greatest day of his life when he turned the church back over to Christ, rather than fretting constantly over it. We are neither the owners nor officially-appointed guardians of the faith. We are His servants, to do His will at all costs (Romans 12:2; I Corinthians 6:20; Ephesians 2:1-10; 3:10-11).

All Resources Available

This being the case, we have all of the resources of the universe at our disposal, even "the cattle on a thousand hills" (Psalm 50:10). Our Lord tells us to ask and it shall be given unto us (Matthew 7:7-8). The apostle Paul reminds us that we have the riches of Christ to use for His glory (Ephesians 3:16-21). There is no excuse for spiritual failure, when we are backed by heaven and know that Christ has already won the victory for us (Romans 8:37; I Corinthians 15:57).

Yes, we do have resources beyond counting. Considering only our own personal financial worth, as a largely middle-class body, we have the ability - and at times the heart - to give impressive contributions to the Lord's cause. What a change from the 1930's when giving fifty cents or a dollar was a sacrifice for many.

Speaking of heart, we open our hearts wide in times of disaster. Flood, hurricanes, tornadoes, earthquakes, fires, medical emergencies, terrorists acts -- when we hear of a real need, we respond magnificently.

No one really knows how much we are able to give, but it has to be a sizable sum, more than we imagine. We are a blessed people, with many of us earning more than average incomes. We number something like one and a fourth million, meeting in twenty five thousand to twenty eight thousand congregations world wide.

Extensive Mission Work

Our mission efforts are extensive, growing steadily and reaching well over one hundred forty countries. We are engaged in dozens of international campaigns each year, along with being committed to radio, television, publications, translations, medical, children's and educational missions.

Excellent Educational Institutions

We operate educational institutions in many nations. These range from pre-school to college levels. They include a number of training programs for national evangelists. In the United States alone, we count some twenty-one degree granting institutions of higher learning, more than sixty non-degree training schools and more than seventy-five academies. We are more highly educated than ever in our history. Our preachers, elders and deacons are better educated and more capable than in past decades. Many of our Bible class teachers are professionals in public or private schools. More and more congregations operate their own Christian academies or weekday day care/Bible study programs.

A Caring People

We show a greater social awareness than ever in recent history. We pour our hearts, money and time into caring causes of all types. We have ministry systems and small caring groups in place. Some churches have professional counselors on the staff, along with youth, college, involvement and other ministry specialists.

Comfortable Facilities

Local congregations meet as a general rule in comfortable and well equipped facilities that are strategically located. We use current to fairly current electronic equipment such as phone mail, FAX machines, computers and E-mail. Some congregations are on the Internet and have their own Home Page.

Serious About the Word

For the most part, churches still take the Word of God fairly seriously and practice the basic tenets of the faith found in it. We have a long history of Bible awareness and even proficiency in its use.

Conclusion

All in all, then, much good can be said for the church today, despite our recent near-stagnation in growth in the United States and our present tendency to stray away from loyalty to the church as the blood-bought bride and body of Christ, and our doctrinal distinctives.

Never have we faced more opportunity, except perhaps in the first century, for evangelism, growth, international campaigning, missions and other facets of the church's international mission to the lost. Our Lord has truly lavished on us His richest blessings, despite our many shortcomings. Let all of us magnify Him for the love He has poured out on us and let us renew our allegiance both to Him and His bride, the church.

In this book, our writers explore in more detail many of the facets involved in our present dilemmas as a body. Read these chapters prayerfully, applying the principles found in them to your own situation in the church local and worldwide.

Questions

1. Describe the church as you remember it during your childhood.
2. Do you believe that Christians in your grandparents' day had a broader knowledge of the Bible than the average church member today? Why do you answer as you do?
3. Is today's generation better equipped to give a defense for their faith than those of two generations ago?
4. Were the rules commonly used interpreting the scriptures thirty years ago different from those used today? If so, in what way?
5. In your estimation is the message being preached today as distinctive and clear as it was in the past?
6. What Bible subjects were most often preached on when you were a child? What are the subjects most preached on today?
7. In comparing the outreach of the church during the 1950s with that of the 1990s, what conclusions do you reach?
8. What agendas or priorities do you see the church setting today?

9. Is the church losing it's identity in this generation? Why do you answer as you do?
10. Do you believe that a climate is being built to foster unity in the church today?
11. What are the pressing needs of restoration in the church today?
12. Describe the "Rip Van Winkle Syndrome."
13. Do you believe that the "church growth movement" has taken the matter of church growth out of God's hands?

2. Hermeneutics, Culture and Scripture

F. Furman Kearley

Introduction

The purpose of this study is to examine the essential principles for the study and interpretation of the Bible. These can lead to the unity of those who truly desire to know and to do God's will. We must subjugate our own wills to God. Jesus said in John 7:17, "If any man wills to do his will, he shall know of the teaching, whether it is of God, or whether I speak from myself."

Interpretation Is Hermeneutics

Webster's *New World Dictionary*, 3rd College Edition, 1988 defines hermeneutics as "The art or science of the interpretation of literature." Hermeneutics then is the process of studying the Bible and making application of the ancient message to the modern audience. For example, Paul's letters to the Corinthians dealt with specific problems in that local congregation, including the use and abuse of spiritual gifts. The task of exegesis would be to explain clearly what Paul's message meant to the Corinthians in the first century. The task of hermeneutics would be to differentiate between the miraculous circumstances and the cultural circumstances of the first century and to teach a contemporary audience what principles should apply today.

Demystifying Hermeneutics

Hermeneutics relates to understanding as grammar and syntax relate to speaking or writing. The ability to communicate is inborn. Every normal baby is born with the ability to understand language and to speak language. Actually, a baby must understand or practice hermeneutics before it is able to respond in meaningful speech. The baby must understand and associate the sound, "mama," with the particular woman who is its mother. Likewise, the baby must come to associate all of the sounds we call words with the particular objects those words describe. Clearly, understanding or hermeneutics comes before meaningful language does.

Critics have tried to mystify hermeneutics and affirm that it is impossible for any two people to understand the Bible alike. They have charged that "our distinctive Restoration hermeneutics is not in the Bible." They have alleged that this hermeneutic is an artificial creation by men imposed on the Bible. This author emphatically denies that charge. The ability to understand language is a natural, inborn gift from God. We call it common sense.

The principles of interpretation (hermeneutics) are not strange, mystical nor artificial. They are natural to every normal child in every language and society. The art and science of hermeneutics is analogous to the art and science of grammar and syntax. Grammar and syntax as we study them in school are the result of the process of scholars analyzing the spoken language and arranging the various aspects of the language in a systematic way in order to unify the language for native speakers and in order to teach foreigners. Hermeneutics in its formal aspect analyzes the way people think, reason and understand. This is done in order to fulfill the command of Jesus, *"Judge not according to appearance, but judge righteous judgments"* (John 7:24).

Common Sense Interpretation

The God who created the minds of all humans is also the God who inspired the Bible. It is not only reasonable, but it is affirmed in scripture that God addressed His word as it is to the minds of human beings as they are. God communicated His instructions with the intent and purpose that humans could, should and must understand them and obey them in order to be saved. No special man-made principles are necessary to understand the Bible. The common sense God has given to each person enables

21

him or her to understand God's word if we will to do His will (John 7:17).

One understands his mother's command, "Go and take a bath," in the same way as one understands the Holy Spirit's command, "*Repent you, and be baptized everyone of you in the name of Jesus Christ unto the remission of your sins....*" (Acts 2:38).

The teacher teaches the history of America and its government in the same way as he teaches the history of Christianity and its government.

Gary Collier quotes Alexander Campbell on this point:

> *The words and sentences of the Bible are to be translated, interpreted, and understood according to the same code of laws and principles of interpretation by which other ancient writings are translated and under-- stood* (Gary Collier, "Reading the Bible Like Jesus," Image Magazine, p. 9).

Moses Stuart wrote:

> *Nearly all the treatises on hermeneutics, which have been written since the days of Ernesti, have laid it down as a maxim which cannot be controverted, that the Bible is to be interpreted in the same manner, i. e., by the same principles, as in all other books. . . from the first moment that one human being addressed another by the use of language, down to the present hour, the essential laws of interpretation became, and have continued to be, a practical matter. The person addressed has always been an interpreter, in every instance where he had heard and understood what was addressed to him* (Quoted by John Allen Hudson in *How to Read the Bible*, pp. 10, 11).

The proper use of common sense hermeneutical principles did not cause Israel to misunderstand Moses and his law and to go into captivity. It was their stubborn rebellion and refusal to understand and obey God's teachings through the prophets.

Christ and His apostles spoke so people could understand. Their refusal to understand and obey had nothing to do with hermeneutics. It was because they refused to submit their own wills to God's will. The mob cried for Christ to be crucified not because they did not understand Him but because they understood Him too well, and they refused to leave their sin.

The Bible Can Be Understood By All Alike

A critic of the Restoration plea and standard common sense hermeneutics has a chapter in a book entitled, "Decoding the Bible." He affirms that because he is from the northwest he cannot understand the Bible the same as other Christians from the south. Such is a ridiculous view toward the Bible if one intends to take it seriously as the foundation for Christian faith and practice.

The Bible clearly teaches that all readers can and are expected to understand the Bible alike. Paul wrote to the Christians at Colossae commanding, "*When this epistle has been read among you, cause that it be read also in the church of the Laodiceans; and that you also read the epistle from Laodicea*" (Colossians 4:16). Clearly, Paul wrote intending and expecting that his epistles to the Colossians would be understandable both at Colossae and at Laodicea. He also expected that his epistle to Laodicea could be understood by those at Colossae.

Modern human beings do not understand the Bible alike for several reasons. They are basically the same reasons that Israel did not follow Moses and the Law and the Jews did not accept Christ and the Gospel. They did not understand the word of God because they withstood the word of God.

The Bible affirms that it can be understood. Paul told the Ephesians, "*By revelation he made known unto me the mystery; (as I wrote afore in few words, whereby, when you read, you may understand my knowledge in the mystery of Christ)*" (Ephesians 3: 3, 4 KJV). Paul, inspired by the Holy Spirit, affirmed that the Ephesians could understand the message by which he wrote by inspiration.

In Ephesians 5:17 Paul charged, "*Wherefore be you not foolish, but understand what the will of the Lord is.*" It is obvious that Paul wrote his epistles to churches and individuals expecting them to understand his letters as we expect those to whom we send letters to understand what we write.

The entire Bible was written for mankind with the presumption that those who heard it and read it could understand it and obey it. Moses, in Exodus 24, read the book of the covenant to the people. They responded, "*We will do everything the Lord has said, we will obey*" (Exodus 24: 7 NIV).

God would not give us His will in a form not understandable by us. Titus 2: 11-13 affirms, *"For the grace of God has appeared, bringing salvation to all men, instructing us, to the intent that, denying ungodliness and worldly lust, we should live soberly and righteously and godly in this present world."* God's instructions can be understood by believing, penitent people who want to do God's will and not their own. Jesus said in John 7: 17, *"If any man willeth to do his will, he shall know of the teaching, whether it is of God, or whether I speak from myself."*

That God expects His word to be understood is emphasized by the fact that He will hold us accountable to it and judge us by it. Jesus said in John 12: 48, *"He that rejecteth me, and receiveth not my sayings, hath one that judgeth him: the word that I spake, the same shall judge him in the last day."*

How To Understand the Bible Alike

Hear, read and study. Correct understanding begins with careful listening, close reading and prayerful study. The lack of reading and study is the main reason people do not understand the Bible alike. Twenty percent of Americans, according to a Gallup poll, have never read the Bible except for isolated quotes in literature. Over eighty percent have never read the entire Bible through even one time. Over seventy percent of Americans have never read the New Testament through one time. Only eleven percent in 1990 claimed to be daily Bible readers, and we all know that even reading one's Bible through and being a daily Bible reader is not sufficient to be a careful, prayerful student of God's word. The only way we will ever understand the Bible alike is to study it prayerfully and carefully with love for God, Christ, truth, heaven, one another and fear of hell.

Believe and study the Bible, not the doctrines and commandments of men. In Matthew 22:29 Jesus said of the Sadducees, *"You do err not knowing the scriptures nor the power of God."* To the Pharisees Jesus said, *"You have made void the word of God because of your tradition. You hypocrites, well did Isaiah prophesy of you, saying, 'This people honoreth me with their lips; but their heart is far from me. But in vain do they worship me, teaching as their doctrines the precepts of men'"* (Matthew 15:7-9).

Through the centuries people have added human doctrine to human doctrine. They have perverted the Gospel of Christ, have added to it, have taken from it and exalted the opinions of

24

men as authority. They have convoked councils, written and adopted creeds and have made the doctrines of men the foundation of their beliefs and churches.

Adults have learned the Bible through the sermons of men and not through personal Bible study. Parents have taught their children with a little Bible mixed in with the doctrines and commandments of men. Most people study the Bible through the colored glass of human doctrines, traditions and opinions. Too few drink from the pure waters of life. So long as God's truth is studied through human religious systems, God's truth will not be understood.

Rightly divide or handle aright the Word of God. Paul charged Timothy by the Holy Spirit, "*Study* [give *diligence, expedite*] *to present yourself approved unto God, a workman who needs not to be ashamed, handling aright* [*rightly dividing*] *the word of truth*" (I Timothy 2:15). The basic natural common sense principles of interpretation are stated and illustrated in the Bible, contrary to the claim of some critics that the Bible does not tell us how to interpret it. The Bible teaches us to study and to avoid the doctrines, commandments and traditions of men, and it teaches us to handle aright or rightly divide God's Word. As we proceed we will note that the Bible teaches and exemplifies other essential principles of interpretation including distinguishing between the old and new covenants (Hebrews 8).

Rightly dividing includes noting the grammatical differences in past tense and present tense and in singular and plural. Jesus argued for His pre-incarnate existence on the basis of the present tense verb (Matthew 22:31-33; John 8:56-59). Paul indicated that theological significance was contained in the singular form of the word, seed, as opposed to the plural, thus intending God's prophecy to apply to Christ (Galatians 3:16; Genesis 22:18).

Principles Of Exegesis

Sound hermeneutics must have as their foundation sound exegesis. One must understand what the author meant as he wrote to the original audience before application (hermeneutics) can be made of first century principles to the twentieth or twenty-first century. The Bible likewise teaches and illustrates these principles. Also, the great majority of scholars from all religious traditions teach and agree upon the basic principles of exegesis. Note the most fundamental and wisely agreed upon principles of exegesis.

First, establish the text or have the accurate Greek, Aramaic or Hebrew text as the basis and an accurate English translation made from it. This is the field of textual criticism and most scholars are agreed that the results of centuries of textual criticism have provided us an accurate text in the biblical languages. Comparison of the best English translations will enable one to understand more clearly the original text and meaning (See "The Value of Comparing Translations" by F. Furman Kearley in Gospel Advocate, October, 1989, pp. 14-16). People certainly cannot understand alike unless they are considering the exact same statement. So much misunderstanding of the Bible takes place because of superficial consideration of the text.

Second, understand the words of the Bible according to the definition as used by the author in the original autograph. This requires word study, careful Greek and Hebrew word study. Tragically, many are not willing to invest the time and energy necessary to understand the original words as used by Moses, Jeremiah, Jesus or Paul. The controversy over the mode of baptism is easily settled if people will accept the definition of *baptidzo* as given by standard and widely accepted Greek lexicons. The division comes because many have exalted their opinions and desires above the plain meaning of the word in the Bible.

Third, understand the grammar and syntax of the Bible. In normal human communication we fail to listen closely enough to note the nuance of words and the grammar and syntax of the statement. In the Bible, however, the communication of the Holy Spirit through human agents is perfect. Any misunderstanding is on our part and not on the part of God, Christ, the Holy Spirit or the apostles.

Fourth, understand the historical background or the situation in which a Bible book was written. Dr. W. B. West, Jr., longtime dean of Harding Graduate School of Religion, often said, "We must sit where they sat." If we would understand Paul's letter to the Romans, we must transport ourselves by historical study back to Corinth in the sixth decade of the first century and to Rome where his audience lived. We must know as much as we can about the first century when Christ and His apostles lived, when the church was established and when the New Testament was written.

Jesus and Paul urged their audiences to understand the words, the grammar, the text and the historical situation (Matthew 22:41-46; I Corinthians 10:1-13; Galatians 4: 21-31; Romans 15:4).

Fifth, study the historical foreground. This technical term in the field of exegesis or Bible study means to study the people and situations that came soon after a book was written and to see how the earliest readers understood and applied the teaching.

The most widely used application of this principle is the study of the church of the second and third centuries and the literature by these early Christians that has survived. These make clear the practice in the worship assemblies of the early Christians, the observance of the Lord's Day or Sunday and the observance of the Lord's Supper in the assembly and many other important matters. Dr. Everett Ferguson is an outstanding scholar among us who has made excellent and beneficial application of this methodology (See his outstanding work in using historical foreground in his article, "The Breaking of Bread," Gospel Advocate, June, 1991, pp. 552-55). The New Testament exemplifies the observance of the first day and the partaking of the Lord's Supper in the assembly. The evidence from the second and third centuries confirms this as the certain and universal practice of the church and provides strong evidence for the Lord's Day assembly and observance of the Lord's Supper.

Sixth, study each passage carefully in its broader context and especially in its immediate context. The context determines the exact meaning of words and sets the framework for the meaning of a statement. Proof-texting often results from taking a passage out of its context. Clear understanding results when a passage is studied in its original context.

Seventh, determine whether the language is literal or figurative. This again is a natural common sense process. Often children hear the figurative before they understand the literal. Parents may say, "I love you to death!" As the child matures he understands that the word, death, is used figuratively and also literally, and he is able to distinguish these functions without even knowing the words literal or figurative. In a similar manner, we understand that Jesus does not really mean to hate one's parents when he uses that phrase in Luke 14:26 but to love less than we love Him.

Eighth, do comparative study of the best translations and best commentaries. These will help us to accomplish all of the preceding aspects of Bible study more thoroughly and accurately. It will help us to check that we have not gone off in an aberrant direction. Again, this is a common sense approach.

Ninth, be sure that the interpretation of any particular passage is in harmony with all other Bible teaching. God is perfect and His instructions do not contradict themselves.

Many other details could be noted concerning principles of interpretation both of the Bible and of normal human communication. These suffice to lay the foundation and to indicate that the same principles we use in daily communication are the ones to use in Bible study. Now let us look at specific aspects of understanding God's will for our lives.

Commands

How do we determine God's authoritative demands for Christians today? Most everyone concerned with this discussion acknowledges that the Bible is the authority for Christian faith and action. Tragically, however, the many denominations and factions among Christendom have resulted because people could not agree as to what in the Bible constitutes God's demands we must obey. It is amazing that probably over ninety percent of Bible scholars can agree on what the original author meant in his message to the original audience. The problems come when we try to decide what the biblical statements mean in terms of our faith and obedience today.

The New Testament Is Covenant Literature

The Bible is covenant literature. The Old Testament describes the Patriarchal Covenant or Testament (Genesis 1 - Exodus 19) and the Mosaic or Jewish Covenant or Testament (Exodus 20 - Malachi). The New Testament is so designated by Jesus and Paul because it sets forth the will, the testament or the covenant that God has given for His people through Christ (Hebrews 8:1-13).

Some want to reject the idea that anything in the New Testament has any authority or any force of law. They want to emphasize that the New Testament is primarily composed of "love letters." To deny the force of law to the New Covenant or Testament is to deny its benefits as a testament as well. If the demands have no force, then the promises have no force. Jesus said, *"If you love me, you will keep my commandments"* (John 14:15).

Many critics of standard principles of biblical interpretation have ridiculed a classical sermon of the Restoration Movement. This sermon emphasizes that the New Testament contains facts to be believed, commands to be obeyed and promises to be received. Again, the rejection of these matters is due to a failure to understand the nature of a will.

In any ordinary will the facts to be believed are the details of the possessions and goods that are being left for distribution. The commands to be obeyed are the commands concerning the distribution of these possessions to the beneficiaries according to the will of the testament maker. The promises to be received are the treasures and heirlooms bequested to the beneficiaries.

Frequently in history a last will and testament has been in the form of a "love letter" written to heirs detailing the wishes of the letter writer concerning possessions.

The New Testament is a loving covenant, but it is also a legal covenant. We must learn its facts, know and obey its commands if we would hope to receive its promised blessings.

The standard way to establish authority is by commands from the one in authority. Psalm 119 uses at least ten different terms such as word, law, testimonies, statutes, judgments, precepts as synonyms of commandment. Also, a command may be expressed by an imperative, a hortatory subjunctive (let us), a plea, or in various other ways. However, a plea from the Holy Spirit is just as authoritative as an imperative. Romans 12:1,2 is an example.

The command to be baptized is expressed several ways in the New Testament. Yet, many in the denominational world and now some in the fellowship of the churches of Christ have rejected that command. They deny baptism is essential to the remission of sins, to put on Christ and to enter into the kingdom of the Lord. This simply illustrates that people who are self-willed refuse to acknowledge the most simple and even direct imperative commands (Acts 2:38).

The New Testament teaches by narrative (the facts to be believed), by command (the commands to be obeyed), by example (approved precedents) and by necessary inference. Great criticism has been leveled at the importance and use of approved examples and necessary inference. Some have denied that authority may be established by these.

Examples - When Do They Bind?

No responsible teacher in the Restoration Movement has ever contended that any and every example by itself alone is binding. None has ever contended, for example, that assemblies must be in an upper room. What has been taught about examples is that any approved example in the New Testament sets forth a way that is right that cannot be wrong. If we believe the Bible, then we believe that if we do a Bible thing in the way the Bible thing was practiced in the New Testament, we can all agree and be united in this. Since it is an approved example, it is a way that is infallibly right and cannot be wrong. We would not divide over doing Bible things in Bible ways.

New Testament authority is at times established by certain examples as they are established in the form of judgments or case law. Psalm 119 repeatedly mentioned judgments as authoritative from God. Technically today a Supreme Court decision is the law of the case, but by necessary inference the example of a case becomes a precedent and essentially a law of the land in authority. An individual may proceed against the Supreme Court decision until he is brought before the court. However, wise lawyers advise clients to follow the Supreme Court decision as if it were the law of the land not just the law of the case.

Paul dealt with the problem of a man who was committing adultery and incest. He commanded the church to have no company with him in order to lead him to repentance and to make clear that the church did not approve of the shameful conduct. This example or case law becomes binding on every congregation and every Christian by extension; this exemplifies God's will for all cases of such sinful conduct by wayward Christians.

Every example is instructive but not necessarily binding, or we may say the Bible teaches by examples, but every example is not a binding example. Examples are only binding when they are combined with a background commandment or principle and constructed in God's word so as to imply authority. This leads us to a necessary inference that this is an obligation upon us.

Necessary Inferences

Nothing has been attacked by critics of hermeneutics more than the principle of necessary inference. Some seem to deny that necessary inference even exists, and they demand that matters determined by necessary inference never be allowed in tests of fellowship. For further discussion of some of these points see J. D. Thomas, *We Be Brethren; Heaven's Windows*, pp. 107-130 and *Harmonizing Hermeneutics*, pp. 46ff; Thomas B. Warren, *When Is An Example Binding?*; Everett Ferguson, "The Lord's Supper and Biblical Hermeneutics," Mission, September, 1976, p. 59.

If one is speaking in Nashville today and relates a personal experience that occurred in Tokyo yesterday, then the audience must necessarily infer that the speaker flew from Tokyo to

Nashville. If one says he once had tonsils and appendix, the listeners must necessarily infer that he had an operation that removed these. Much of what we learn in ordinary conversation does not come by direct declarative or narrative statements. It comes by inference and much of it by necessary inference.

The Supreme Court decision striking down the separate but equal doctrine and declaring segregation to be unconstitutional was the law of the case. However, by necessary inference that this ruling would be upheld in all similar cases, many school boards began to move to integrate.

Sunday Is The Day

That Sunday is the day for Christians to assemble and worship is a conclusion drawn by necessary inference. This is required by the Lord and cannot be set aside by leaders of the church nor by civil authorities acting in opposition to the church. This is the conclusion universally and historically of almost every religious group in Christendom. Christians of the second and third centuries violated the demands of the Roman persecutors and held their assemblies on the Lord's Day in spite of the threat of death and knowledge of the fact that the persecutors had killed thousands of others. Why did the Christians not just worship at home secretly? Why did they not change the day of their worship frequently to confuse the Romans? It was because they under-stood that the assembly of Christians on the Lord's Day for worship was a mandatory requirement of God (See "Sunday" by Everett Ferguson in *Encyclopedia of Early Christianity*. New York: Garland Publishing, Inc., 1990 pp. 873-875; W. Rordorf, *Sunday: The History of the Day of Rest and Worship in the Earliest Centuries of The Christian Church.* Philadelphia: Westminister, 1968).

How do we know Sunday is the day that God requires Christians to assemble? The answer is by necessary inference. The New Testament states that Jesus arose on the first day of the week; showed Himself alive to many on the first day of the week; the church was established on the first day of the week (John 20; Acts 2; 20:7; I Corinthians 16:2). No other day has special signifi-cance for the Christians according to the New Testament. Early church history demonstrates that Christians braved slave owners' wrath and persecutors' torture to assemble on the first day of the week.

Christendom has rightly concluded universally and for two millenniums that Sunday is the day based on the compelling accumulation of evidence that necessarily infers that Sunday is the day. A command exists to observe the Lord's Supper. We are charged not to forsake our assembling together (Hebrews 10:25). We have examples of the importance of the Lord's Day and of assemblies on the first day of the week. These are sufficient to lead those dedicated to the Lord to honor him on the first day of every week as a matter of conscience.

The same evidence for an assembly on the first day of the week gives evidence of observing the Lord's Supper on the first day of every week, but Christendom has held the day but refused to practice the central event, the observance of the Lord's Supper on the first day of every week.

At the very minimum, the New Testament example concerning assembling and observing the Lord's Supper on the first day of the week is an approved example. This establishes a way that is right that cannot be wrong. No one can accuse us of committing sin if we assemble each first day of the week and observe the Lord's Supper. This is clearly what the New Testament Christians did and what the Christians of the first three centuries did. It is a safe way, a way that is right that can not be wrong.

I also believe that it is necessarily inferred that this is the only day, the only time authorized by God for Christians to set a mandatory assembly and observe the Lord's Supper. The example is missing of early Christians and churches ever observing the Lord's Supper on any other day. One is treading on dangerous ground who neglects the Lord's Day and the Lord's Supper.

Civil Disobedience Is Established by Necessary Inference

Another illustration of an example that has been considered binding to the point of death by Christians through the ages concerns civil disobedience. In this illustration the civil disobedience I am discussing is where it becomes necessary for Christians to disobey the civil authorities in order to obey their consciences and practice Christianity.

Virtually universally Christians have believed and practiced civil disobedience for sake of conscience, even though there is no explicit command in the New Testament demanding that we violate civil law in order to live in all good conscience. Romans 13:1-7, Titus; 3:1, I Peter 2:13-17 command and demand that Christians obey civil authorities even though civil authorities were pagan and personally wicked.

32

We do have clear illustrations of Christians engaging in civil disobedience for conscience sake. In Acts 4:17-21 the leaders of the Sanhedrin threatened Peter and John and charged them not to speak or teach in the name of Jesus. Peter and John responded that no matter what they charged them, it was necessary for them to speak the things which they saw and heard. Another example is found in Acts 5. The Sanhedrin reminded the apostles that they had charged them not to preach Jesus. Peter and the apostles answered, "We must obey God rather than men" (Acts 5:29). Throughout Christian history we have repeated this statement as if it were a command. However, in context it is not. It is simply an example. Never is there a command or an exception clause commanding Christians to practice civil disobedience.

We conclude that it is essential for Christians to practice civil disobedience in order to live in all good conscience and to obey God. This conclusion is the result of necessary inference we must draw from the combined implications of general commands to faithfulness and loyalty and specific examples (Matthew 6:33; Revelation 2:10; II Corinthians 11:16-33).

Circumstantial evidence sets forth evidence drawn from several circumstances that leads a jury to necessarily infer the guilt of someone. Necessary inference is part of every day communication. It is the good use of common sense. Of course it can be misused by fallible humans but successful life cannot be lived without making necessary inferences (Jimmy Jividen, "Should Fellowship Be Broken Over Inference?" Gospel Advocate, June, 1990, pp. 21, 22; Hugo McCord, "Necessary Inferences," Gospel Advocate, August, 1991, pp. 47, 48; "How the Bible Teaches," Gospel Advocate, June, 1995).

The Principle of Silence

By "the silence of the scriptures" we mean that the scriptures do not speak specifically about the action, practice or belief under consideration. Differences concerning what this means or how to interpret the silence of the scriptures are at the heart of division of Christianity into denominations.

Particularly, it is a focal problem in the major division between various segments of the Restoration Movement. Those who introduced instruments of music and the missionary society affirmed that whatever the scriptures do not specifically forbid is permitted. They affirmed that the silence of the scriptures about a topic meant it was left in the realm of opinion. Thus, people could do as they pleased in that area. They pleased to use instruments and missionary societies and, therefore, added them and led to the division of the Restoration Movement.

Interestingly that same element divided over the same issue in the 1950s and 60s. The independent churches of Christ separated from the liberal Christian churches (Disciples of Christ) over restructure. The Disciples of Christ affirmed that since the scriptures did not forbid a hierarchical organization or denominations superstructure, that they could form a world wide organization over all the churches. Their only basis was the scripture is silent and, therefore, this silence permits hierarchical organization according to the liberal Disciples of Christ.

In this case, independent Christian churches affirmed that since the Bible exemplified autonomy of congregations and did not authorize a hierarchical superstructure organization, it was sinful and wrong. They insisted that silence prohibits or forbids hierarchical organization.

Churches of Christ reject the use of instruments and the missionary society and affirm that the silence of scripture is a most important principle in the interpretation of scripture. We affirm that silence is a natural principle of interpretation. This silence can be, depending upon the context of generic commands verses specific commands, both permissive and prohibitive. It can both forbid or approve certain matters in practice or doctrine.

Silence is a natural principle. Silence is a major aspect of the natural principles of interpretation. If silence were not a clearly natural and understood part of communication, parents would have to spend hours to give a child the simple command, "Go play in the back yard." The command, "Go play in the back yard," is both permissive and prohibitive; it both allows and it forbids. By play, the child understands that he can swing, slide, play in the sand box, color, chase bugs or anything he wishes to do. However, previous instruction may have made clear that play does not include swimming in the swimming pool or climbing the tree with no adult present. In other words, play allows many different activities, but it may have been preconditioned and limited by other teaching.

Properly understood the word "play" would not mean dig up the rose bushes or pull up the garden plants. Thus, the word "play" allows a certain latitude of activity chosen by the child but forbids other activity that is beyond the meaning of the word "play."

The term "back yard" is specific. Play is generic within preset limits of the term "play." Back yard is a specific back yard. The mother does not have to name all of the places where the child is not to play because she has named the place to play. She does not have to say, "Do not play in the neighbor's back yard or do not play in the street." Since back yard is specific it has the specific limits of the surveyor's marks.

If the principle of silence were not a natural principle of communication, each time the mother said, "Go play in the back yard," she would have to name all of the other possible places in the world where a child could play and say, "Do not play there." She would have to name all of the other kinds of activities the child could do and say, "You are not to do those, you are only to play." We must naturally understand that silence is permissive and permits as much latitude as the generic command. It is also prohibitive and limited to the strictures of the specific command. Otherwise, it would be necessary for us to speak a volume the size of a dictionary every time we gave a command.

In the highly technical, targeted and limited warfare conducted against Iraq, the principle of silence was very important. The pilots were briefed concerning their mission. Each was told, "Go bomb sites X, Y and Z." By this command they understood they could go and take any evasive route they chose to get to their target. Even that was limited in that they could not go into air space not previously approved. Specifically, they were to bomb targets X, Y and Z. The commander did not have to tell them all of the other sites in Iraq not to bomb. By silence they understood they were to bomb those three and no more lest there be political ramifications for attacking a civilian site.

Passages affirmed the principle of silence. In I Corinthians 4:4 the apostle Paul told the Corinthians, *"Now these things, brothers, I have in a figure transferred to myself and Apollos for your sakes; that in us you might learn not to go beyond the things which are written."* To go beyond the things which are written is to act without authorization, to add to God's word.

I Peter 4:11 affirms, *"If any man speaks let him speak as it were oracles of God."* This passage has long been used as the biblical foundation for the Restoration motto, "Speak where the Bible speaks and be silent where the Bible is silent." In matters of Christian doctrine and practice we are to speak what God has spoken, no less or no more.

Paul instructed the Galatians not to leave the Gospel of Christ and not to listen to a perversion of it. He stated, *"But though we, or an angel from heaven should preach unto you any gospel other than that which we preached unto you, let him be anathema"* (Galatians 1:6-10). To add to God's word or to take from it or to disregard the silence of God's word is to alter, pervert and preach another Gospel.

Jesus told Peter and the apostles, *"Whatsoever you shall bind on earth shall be bound in heaven; and whatsoever you shall loose on earth shall be loosed in heaven"* (Matthew 16:19; 18:18). God's revealed will from the apostles by the Holy Spirit binds what God wants bound and has loosed what God wants loosed. Man is not to alter God's word in any way.

Moses affirmed in Deuteronomy 4:2, *"You shall not add unto the word which I command you, neither shall you diminish from it, that you may keep the commandments of Jehovah your God which I command you."*

Surely, these and other passages teach us to honor the silence of God, to know, exalt and obey exactly what God has said and all he has said. We must refuse to add to God's Word any human commandments or practices not authorized by God's specific or generic commands (See the example of Balaam, Numbers 22:18;24:13).

Biblical examples illustrating the principle of silence. A specific command plus silence affirms no priests are to come from Judah. In Numbers 3:2 God commanded Moses to appoint Aaron and his sons to keep their priesthood. He did not list all of the other tribes and forbid them to be priests. The Jews through-out history, however, understood that priests were to come only from the family and descendants of Aaron. Jeroboam defied this and appointed strangers as priests (I Kings 12). For this he was condemned, and he and his nation cursed.

The Hebrew writer understood the silence of God concern-ing priests from any other tribe to prohibit them. By inspiration he argues, *"For he [Christ] of whom these things were said belongs to another tribe, from which no man has given attendance at the altar. For it is evident that our Lord had sprung out of Judah; as to which tribe Moses spake nothing concerning priests"* (Hebrews 7:13,14).

Uzziah tried to usurp the function of priest. The inspired record of 2 Chronicles 26:16-21 reports that he trespassed against Jehovah because he went into the temple to burn incense. Azariah and eighty priests withstood him and said, *"It pertains not unto you, Uzziah, to burn incense unto Jehovah, but to the priests the sons of Aaron."* God authorized priests of Aaron and his family. This was a specific mandate. God's silence about priests from any other tribe was authoritative. God's silence forbade anyone else from being a priest.

Strange fire. The case of Nadab and Abihu, the sons of Aaron, clearly illustrates the validity of the principle of silence. Numbers 10:1 in the NIV states that they *"took their censers, put fire in them and added incense; and they offered unauthorized fire before the Lord, contrary to his command."* The KJV and ASV say *"strange fire."* The NIV rendering of unauthorized fire makes very plain the problem. God had given a positive command to use fire from the brazen altar in the courtyard. He had said nothing pro or con about other fire. He had been silent. However, since He had commanded a specific fire, to use any other fire from any other place was unauthorized and thus sin (See also David's sin by his unauthorized method of moving the ark of the covenant, I Chronicles 13:1-14;15:1-15; Numbers 4:15 and article, "Lessons from the Ark," by Scott McDowell, Gospel Advocate, October 3, 1985, p. 58).

The chart of law and incidentals. Still an outstanding illustration for determining God's will is the chart of law, inclusion, exclusion and expedients or incidentals. The case of Noah and God's command to build the ark is classic. Critics have tried to ignore this, but they have never been able to answer it nor any of the other illustrations of these principles.

God commanded Noah, *"Make you an ark of gopher wood, rooms shall you make in the ark, and shall pitch it within and without with pitch. And this is how you shall make it: the length of the ark 300 cubits, the breadth of it 50 cubits, and the height of it 30 cubits"* (Genesis 6:14,15). The command was to build an ark with rooms, pitch, specific dimensions, a window, a door and three stories.

The command was to build it of gopher wood. This is inclusive and automatically excludes pine, oak or any other kind of wood. The command included a door but was not specific about its size or decoration.

The command mentioned nothing about tools, where to build it, how to get the wood or other matters. These were incidental or in the realm of expediency. Noah could use his best judgment concerning the tools available to him, where to have his ark yard and many other matters. God's silence both permitted Noah a wide area of judgment in the area of incidentals or expedients but also excluded certain actions on his part.

In Numbers 19:2 God commanded Israel to offer a red heifer. The command included all that was necessary to raise, feed and prepare the heifer for sacrifice. It automatically excluded a black heifer and the male of the species. The command left to the realm of expediency how to obtain the heifer (except other commands that said not to steal), raise or feed her.

Dr. Bill Humble exposed the inconsistencies of the conservative Christian church in their criticizing our use of the argument from silence. Yet, they follow the same argument with respect to the Lord's Supper. He says, "There must be many practices not mentioned in scripture, neither commanded nor forbidden, which the independents never would accept. Consider, for example, the Lord's Supper.

"The Lord commanded the bread and fruit of the vine and said, 'Do this in remembrance of me.' We and the independents would agree this is scriptural and must be obeyed, but couldn't we make the Lord's Supper a little more meaningful for today's world?

"While the bread is the communion of the body of Christ, it may be difficult for some Christians to see the body of Christ in bread. Wouldn't flesh, actually animal flesh, be a more graphic reminder to the body and blood of Christ? Behold the Lamb of God slain for our sins! Why wouldn't little pieces of roast lamb on the Lord's table make his presence and his death more real to some? Suppose then, that in addition to the bread and the cup, we add cubes of roast lamb to the Lord's Supper to deepen its meaning.

"Because the Bible is silent and does not forbid this, would we be at liberty to do it? Would our independent brethren accept roast lamb on the Lord's table? Surely not. But here is my challenge: if these brethren will tell us on what basis they would reject roast lamb at the Lord's Supper, I think they will discover the silence of the scripture forbids instrumental music in precisely the same way it forbids the lamb on the Lord's table" (Dr. Bill J. Humble, "The Silence of the Scripture," Gospel Advocate, March 5, 1987, p. 138).

Without understanding and applying the principle of silence and the law of inclusion, exclusion and expedients, the obeying of God's command to assemble would be impossible. He has commanded us to worship and not to forsake the assembly (Hebrews 10:25; John 4:23,24). Automatically included in a command to assemble is a place, a time and a purpose.

The Lord has left the place completely in the realm of expediency and incidentals. It may be a public place, a borrowed place, a rented place or a bought and built place.

He has specified by necessary inference that the assembly be on the first day of the week and include prayer, singing, teaching, the Lord's Supper and giving (I Corinthians 11:17 - 16:4; Acts 20:7). This automatically excludes any other day and any other activities. Incidental would be all other factors necessary to make the assembly possible and comfortable and accomplish the things that are to be done in the service.

The organization of the church also illustrates the importance of understanding the authority of God's silence. God has commanded and illustrated in the New Testament that each congregation is to be autonomous and to have elders and deacons. The Bible is silent about any kind of hierarchical organization or offices of power and authority over and beyond the local congregation.

Concerning Christian music, the command is to sing (Ephesians 5:19; Colossians 3:16). The purpose is to teach, admonish and praise (James 5:13). Intelligible, verbal communication set to some type of music is essential to accomplish these commands. Thus included in the command is the composition of songs, both words and music, and making these available for the congregation to use in some way. Excluded is singing in a foreign language or singing in any kind of gibberish that does not teach or admonish or praise. Incidental is whether the words or music are presented on a blackboard, on handwritten paper, or photo copy paper, in a book or in some other manner.

Instrumental music is a different kind of music than singing. It is playing. Instrumental music cannot fulfill the command anymore than gibberish can. At best, instrumental music could only be an accompaniment but in most instances instrumental music interferes with and hinders the understanding of the words to teach, admonish and praise.

The question of instruments of music might be a more open one if it were not for the historical foreground. Historical foreground is the evidence from the early Christians immediately after the command. In the foreground in the New Testament we never find the use of instruments mentioned or approved in conjunction with Christian singing. In early church history, not only were instruments not used, but they were opposed by the early Christians (See Dr. Everett Ferguson, *A Cappella Music in the Public Worship of the Church*, 2nd ed., Abilene, TX, ACU Press, 1988).

In matters so important as our eternal salvation, we should follow the way that is safe, that cannot be wrong. All acknowledge that Christian singing is to emphasize verbal communication for praise, teaching and admonishing. All recognize that instruments of music are not necessary but rather have been questioned by scholars in the church of the early centuries as well as Calvin, Knox, Wesley, Spurgeon, Campbell and others of more recent centuries. To introduce instruments of music is to introduce division. To leave off instruments of music is to follow a way that is safe, that cannot be wrong. Also it builds unity because it does not offend the conscience of those who are opposed to it and drive them away.

Truly, we need to honor the silence of God and recognize the principle of silence as an essential element in human communication. As such it is also an essential element in understanding the Bible and applying the commands of God to our lives. Let us then obey the commands of the New Testament, follow the approved examples and be guided by the necessary inferences.

Questions

1. What is the distinction between hermeneutics and exegesis?
2. To what extent may people living in different cultures understand the Bible alike?
3. Did the culture of the first century affect the formation of New Testament doctrine? If so in what way?
4. When people failed to submit to Christ and His teaching, was it because of their inability to understand His will?
5. If Christ and His apostles spoke so people could understand, what is the main reason for people failing to understand the Scriptures?
6. Did Paul expect the Ephesian Christians to understand what he wrote them? (Ephesians 3: 3; 5: 17)
7. List five important principles of exegesis that aid in understanding the scriptures.
8. How are God's commands for Christians today determined?
9. When are examples binding on Christians?
10. What principle is used in determining the day that God requires Christians to assemble?
11. In what way does the principle of silence determine the kind of music God wants in worship?

3. The Role of Women In the Assembly of the Church

Nancy Ferguson

Many are concerned about the role of women in the church today. Some think that all women should be totally under the control of men, even in the business world and in social situations. Others think that there should never be any differences between the roles of men and women; they should be equally entitled to do anything, anytime, anywhere. Most people probably fall somewhere in between these two extremes.

The purpose of this chapter is to examine what the Bible teaches about the role of women in the assembly of the church. There are many unanswered questions that fall outside the scope of this study. However, if we understand the biblical teaching concerning women in the assembly, it will also help our understanding of women's role in other areas.

We should all be disturbed by the superficiality of some of the arguments being used in support of women's leadership role in the assembly of the church. We should also be concerned by some arguments used to suppress women. There are many things women can do for the Lord, but there are limits.

It is argued that if women are capable of taking a role of leadership in the assembly, they should be allowed to do so. However, the question is not whether women have the requisite abilities and are physically, mentally, and emotionally able to do so, but whether it is part of God's plan. Not all gifts are to be exercised in the assembly (I Corinthians 14:18-19, 26-33).

It is also argued that it has been done successfully in the past, even in our own Restoration Movement. However, the fact that something has been done before does not make it right. Even the worst sin does not seem so bad after one has done it again and again and built a comfortable relationship with it. A clear conscience is not necessarily the proper guide.

Often we look at scriptures such as those dealing with the silence of women and interpret them only as cultural aspects of their time, not to be taken seriously now. On the other hand, today's customs must also be examined to determine which are in accord with scripture. It is inconsistent to dismiss some practice in biblical times as "*merely the custom of the time*" and then to accept uncritically whatever is considered socially correct today. Cultural aspects of our time should not become the norm for our religious practices. God's truths are the same yesterday, today, and forever, and we must not be swayed from God's will in any matter of the culture of the times.

Some have simply said, "*It's a good idea to use women in leadership roles in the assembly.*" But is the idea good only in the minds of people, or does God think it is a good idea? One can always find a way to rationalize what one wants to do, but that does not make it right. King Saul made this mistake in I Samuel 15 when he told Samuel, "*I did obey the Lord!*" (verse 20). Instead of destroying everything as commanded, he had kept alive some of the best to sacrifice to the Lord. This was not what God intended. God wanted Saul to obey Him precisely, not to do what Saul himself thought would be a good idea. "*To obey is better than sacrifice*" (verse 22). To do something as an act of service to God does not justify it, if God has not authorized it.

The criterion for what is done in the assembly of the church is not what gives us a feeling of uplift or what pleases us, but what God wants.

Galatians 3:28 tells us: "*There is neither....male nor female*" in Christ. This is often quoted to show that women can do anything and everything men can do. However, this passage cannot be taken alone or out of context. The context is baptism and incorporation into God's people. Ethnicity, social condition, and gender still exist, along with their attendant characteristics and responsibilities. These things are not obliterated, but God does not consider them in receiving a person into Christ. Women receive salvation as fully as men do. When a woman clothes herself with Christ in baptism, she becomes a saint, she becomes a priest, as surely as a man does. "*Priest*" and "*preacher*" are not equivalent terms. As a priest in the new covenant, one offers spiritual sacrifice and has direct access to God without having to go through another person.

Nowhere does the Bible say that women are inferior to men or less capable. Nowhere in the Bible are women excused from following God's commands. Women have the same responsibility to study the Bible and obey God's commands as men do; they cannot hide behind their husbands or anyone else. Nor can they gain their spirituality from the spirituality of another. However, there are God-given differences between male and female, and God has given each a special sphere. That God placed man as head of the family does not mean woman is inferior. Submission has nothing to do with quality, but is based on God's order in the world. The woman's place in the world is unique--a man cannot do what she does. Similarly, God has given men some things to do that in certain situations women are not to do.

Most of the commands in the Bible are given to all Christians. For example: I Peter 1:13-16: *"....Be holy in all you do."* Philippians 4:4-6: *"Rejoice in the Lord always.....In everything, by prayer and petition, with thanksgiving, present your requests to God."* Romans 12:1-2 uses the generic term, *"brothers"* that includes *"sisters;"* *"Therefore, I urge you, brothers, in view of God's mercy, to offer your bodies as living sacrifices, holy and pleasing to God--which is your spiritual worship."*

Some commands, however, are given specifically to men, and some specifically to women. An obvious example of both is in Ephesians 5:22 and 25: *"Wives, submit to your husbands as to the Lord." "Husbands, love your wives, just as Christ loved the church and gave himself up for her."* Paul gives Titus specific commands concerning what is to be taught to the older men, the older women, the younger women, and the young men (Titus 2:1-8). Some of the commands addressed only to men will be noted in the further discussion.

Most commands addressed to women concern their modesty in dress and their roles as wives, homemakers, mothers, and doers of good deeds (I Timothy 2:9-15; 5:9-14; Titus 2:3-5; I Peter 3:1-6). When one looks carefully at these things women should do, one realizes that there are many important and time-consuming commands to be obeyed, some of which cannot be done by men.

Sometimes women think that they are left out of active involvement in the church, and sometimes men have generalized from statements of scripture to claim absolute authority for themselves. Actually, the only explicit restrictions on women's role in the church occur in contexts dealing with the assembly of the church, which is the emphasis of this chapter. The qualifications of bishops in I Timothy 3 and Titus 1, of course, exclude women from this position. Otherwise, we find women very active in serving and teaching roles in the church. We are familiar with Priscilla teaching

Apollos (Acts 18:26), Phoebe as patroness and servant of the church at Cenchrea (Romans 16:1), the women at Philippi who worked along side Paul (Philippians 4:3), and the daughters of Philip who prophesied (Acts 21:9). The list can be lengthened extensively. The church may have failed to utilize its woman power and failed to give due acknowledgment to the work done by women. Our concern should be to follow the scriptures-- encouraging neither men in an unauthorized suppression of women nor supporting women in imitating the worst aspects of male attitudes.

The two passages which make the strongest limitation on women's activities are I Corinthians 14 and I Timothy 2. Both are in the context of the church meeting in group assembly.

"En Ekklesia"

If we examine the phrase *"en ekklesia,"* which literally means *"in church"* or *"in assembly,"* we find that it means *"when the church meets together as a church."* The church as a whole may be involved in some activity but not be in assembly; that is a different usage of the word *"church."* To illustrate: In Acts 5:11 *"Great fear seized the whole church"*; and that fear was not limited to the time when the members were meeting. But in Acts 11:26 we read, *"For a whole year Barnabas and Saul met with the church (en ekklesia);"* that is, they assembled together with them. To illustrate further the usage in a secular setting: the word *ekklesia* is used in Acts 19:32 to refer to a secular meeting during which a riot occurred. However verse 39 refers to another, special, particular meeting: *"If there is anything further you want to bring up, it must be settled in a legal assembly [en ekklesia]."*

An obvious example of the meaning *"in assembly"* is I Corinthians 11:18:*"When you come together as a church [en ekklesia]...."* Other examples are: Colossians 4:16: *"After this letter has been read to you, see that it is also read in the church [en ekklesia] of the Laodiceans;"* and Hebrews 2:12: *"He says, 'I will declare your name to my brothers; in the presence of the congregation [en meso ekklesias] I will sing your praises.'"*

The following verses use *en ekklesia*: Acts 7:38; 11:26; 19:39; I Corinthians 4:17; 6:4: 7:17; 11:18; 12:28; 14:19, 28,34,35; II Corinthians 8:1; Ephesians 3:21; Colossians 4:16; II Thessalonians 1:4; Hebrews 2:12. The following verses do not use that Greek phrase, but a comparison of them will help understand the concept: Acts 13:1; 14:27; 19:32; I Corinthians 1:4, 5,12; Colossians 1:18,24.

Thus there is a time when the church meets together as a church. Whatever is done at that special time must be according to God's will. In this assembly (*en ekklesia* according to I Corinthians 14:33-35 and *en panti topo* in I Timothy 2:18-12), when the church comes together as the church, women must remain silent. As Christians we are always in the presence of God and must always follow His will, but when we assemble together as a church we approach God in a special way. When we approach any king, we must do so on his terms, not ours. So, when the church meets together as a church, we must be careful to follow God's will, whatever our personal preferences might be.

According to I Corinthians 11:17ff., there is an assembly for the purpose of taking the Lord's supper. There can be other purposes for the assembly as well.

First Corinthians 14 is obviously an assembly context as shown in the following verses: *"But in the church I would rather speak five intelligible words to instruct others than ten thousand words in a tongue"* (verse 19); *"So if the whole church comes together ...."* (verse 23); *"....When you come together, ..."* (verse 26); and others. It is in this setting of the church assembled that the prohibitions of verses 34 and following are given:

> Women should remain silent in the churches [en tais ekklesias, *"in the assemblies"*]. They are not allowed to speak, but must be in submission, as the Law says. If they want to inquire about something, they should ask their own husbands at home, for it is disgraceful for a woman to speak in the church [en ekklesia].

The nature of the speaking (laleo) and the being silent (sigao) is evident from the use of the same words in the preceding verses (27-30) about the speaking of tongue-speakers and prophets. The language there refers to the public speech used to bring God's word in a message to the assembly (prophecy or preaching) or to address God in prayer (speaking in tongues [cf. verses 2,14]), and to the silence that is the opposite of such speaking.

Because of the pairing of the terms for man (husband) and woman (wife), some interpreters want to limit the word for women (*gunaikes*) to *"wives;"* but it would be unprecedented for a single woman to have a public role a married woman could not have. Often when verses 34 and 35 are quoted, the discussion stays on

45

the periphery--*"But what if a woman doesn't have a husband? Then this can't apply, so it must be invalid."* Paul, however, is dealing ith a general situation. The point is not whether a woman has a husband, but that she must be in submission.

The proscription is not limited to Corinth (so is not dependent on some special circumstance there, although that is what would have required the instructions, even as the problem with tongue speakers was the occasion for the teachings in the chapter as a whole), but the instructions are those observed *"in all the assemblies of the saints"* (verse 33b; cf. 11:16).

I Timothy 2 may not have been recognized as so obviously an assembly context. Nevertheless, there are definitely some pointers to this as the setting for the instructions here. Two of these deserve our attention here. Lifting up hands (I Timothy 2:8) was the normal posture for public prayer in the synagogue and early church. Furthermore, the Greek word *topos, "place,"* among its many meanings, had a technical usage among Jews for the temple or a synagogue, and this usage was continued among Christians in reference to places of meeting of the church. (See Everett Ferguson *"Topos in I Timothy 2:8,"* <u>Restoration Quarterly</u> 33 [1991] pp.65-73.) According to this usage, I Timothy 2: 8, *"in every place"* (en panti topo), would refer to every place of meeting of the church, corresponding to *"all the assemblies"* in I Corinthians 14:33. The men are the ones to pray in these meetings. At such times the women are not permitted to teach. The prohibition of teaching (I Timothy 2:12) is not absolute for every situation. Elsewhere in the Pastoral Epistles the older women are commanded to instruct the younger (Titus 2:3f). The operative principle in I Timothy 2 is for the woman not to exercise authority in the assembly. The public meeting of the church would be the place where her teaching would violate the principle of submission (I Timothy 2:11). However, if the membership of the church in a particular place is composed entirely of women, then their speech would not be in violation of the principle.

Anthropos and Aner

We need to notice the difference between the two Greek words for man, *anthropos* (mankind) and *aner* (male). Although this difference is not absolute, it is significant. One example is in I Corinthians 11. In discussing the Lord's Supper in verse 28, Paul says, *"A man (anthropos) ought to examine himself...."* All Christians, both men and women, should engage in this self-examination. However, in verses 3-16, where males and females are being contrasted, the word *aner* is used exclusively.

The difference is also evident in I Timothy 2. In verses 1-7 the word translated *"men"* is uniformly *anthropos*, and it is clear that all humankind is intended. Verse 4 states that God *"wants all men [anthropos] to be saved."* Verse 5 again uses *anthropos* to say there is *"one mediator between God and men, the man Christ Jesus."* But in verse 8, where the phrase *en panti topo* indicates the church assembled, the word for man is *aner*, thus indicating the role of males in the assembly of the church. Verses 9-12 discuss women's place in the assembly. It is the men, the males, who are to lead in prayer in the same assembly in which the women are to learn in submission.

Let me emphasize again that this study is concerned with what the Bible says about the activities of women in the assembly of the church, when the church members meet together as a church. It should be recognized that there are other times when Christians may be together in the same place at the same time, but not be the church assembled. There may be activities that are part of the church, i.e., sponsored by the church, but still not the assembly of the church. It is possible that at these times spiritual things will be discussed, prayers will be offered, and women are not prohibited from speaking. There are activities connected with the church, but outside the assembly of the church, in which women can function as leaders.

Roles and Responsibilities

We may not understand why God has given certain authority and responsibilities to men and not to women. Women, too, have been consecrated in Christ. Women, too, are included in the term *"the holy ones"* or *"saints."* So why can't they do everything men can do? Why should men have any authority over them?

It is not the first time in God's dealing with humans that He has made selections concerning roles that persons are to fill in His service. Compare the parallel in Numbers 16. Korah and those with him challenged the authority of Moses and Aaron and said: *"You have gone too far! The whole community is holy, every one of them, and the Lord is with them. Why then do you set yourselves above the Lord's assembly?"* (verse 3).

Moses replied: *"Isn't it enough for you that the God of Israel has separated you from the rest of the Israelite community a̶͟ brought you near himself to do the work at the Lord's tabe͟*

47

and to stand before the community and minister to them? He has brought you and all your fellow Levites near himself, but now you are trying to get the priesthood too. It is against the Lord that you and all your followers have banded together...." (verses 9-11).

Korah and his followers had been consecrated to do holy service to God. But there was one area reserved for someone else, and it was that which they demanded. They failed to see that it was not Moses who made the restrictions, but God. They did not rebel against Moses, but against God and His plans.

Why is there a limitation on women's activity in the assembly? The relevant passages offer some indications. The assembly exemplifies the church as the people of God. Hence, there should be a representation of God's appointed order. Paul gives doctrinal reasons for his statements about male-female relations: the divine order of headship (I Corinthians 11:3-10), the relationship of Christ and the church (Ephesians 5:25-33), and the introduction of sin into the world (I Timothy 2:11-15). The church is described as a family or household (I Timothy 3:15). In the family, the husband is given the responsibility of leadership within a relationship of mutuality that goes back to God's arrangements at creation (Ephesians 5:21-33). In the same way, in the family of the church, where all have mutual responsibilities, leadership is given to the men (I Timothy 3:4-5). In all instances there is appeal to a natural order derived from creation. This assigns a particular function to a woman. Women have often been more spiritually minded than men, but in the public affairs of religion the man is assigned a distinctive role.

Women and Culture

It is often argued that for women to remain silent was a matter of culture in New Testament times. Almost everything in the Bible can be found to have some connection with the culture of the time a given passage was written. Proper application of the teaching of scripture requires discernment of what is merely cultural and wh~~---~~ ~~\se~~ cultural matters is given a doctrinal basis. The ~~r~~ the head covering in I Corinthians 11 is based on ~~derations~~ (verses 6, 13-15), but the relations of men ~~f~~ which the head covering was a cultural expression, ~~stinctions~~ and principles that belong to the doctrine ~~ses~~ 3, 7-12). Wearing a veil was for a woman of ~~cultural~~ sign of authority. There is no comparable,

48

generally recognized sign today. Women in our culture do not wear a veil, and if they did no one would recognize it as a sign of authority. The sign may be different, or even missing, but the principle is the same. The order of creation is not *"cultural,"* it is a fact of which we need to be reminded by God's sign of authority. Silence of women in the assembly may function as such a sign of the created order. Moreover, it is a characteristic of the biblical revelation for practices known to the people to be adopted as part of divinely authorized conduct. The Christian cannot simply dismiss a teaching of scripture because it is found to have a basis in the culture at the time.

If one accepts the divine inspiration of the scriptures, one cannot dismiss women's silence in the assembly as being only culturally dictated, because Paul bases his reasoning on doctrinal considerations.

I Corinthians 11 is often cited to indicate that it is all right for a woman to pray and preach in the assembly. Let us look at that passage and its context more closely. In 10:14-22 Paul compares idol feasts and the Lord's Supper. In verses 27-30 he discusses a social situation: dinner in the home of an unbeliever. In 10:31-11:1 he talks of proper behavior in all aspects of life - following the example of Christ. He continues in 11:2 to encourage the Corinthians to hold to the teachings he has given them. Paul begins the passage in 11:3-16 by making a point of the divine order of God, Christ, man, woman: *"...the head of every man is Christ, and the head of the woman is man, and the head of Christ is God"* (verse 3). Although this passage includes worship, not all worship, prayer, and teaching have to take place *en ekklesia, "in church,"* which is not mentioned here. The passage does not exclude the assembly but may not be limited to it. Wherever and in whatever situation a woman prays or prophesies publicly, she must still be reminded that she is *"under authority."* She must conduct herself in such a way that others can recognize that she is under that authority. This does not mean she is inferior to man any more than it means Christ is inferior to God. But God does have an order of authority. Perhaps Paul has been talking in general terms in verses 3-16, but in the next section he turns to the specific setting of the church assembled as he says *"when you come together as a church"* (verse 18). This is the first mention of the assembly in this passage.

Throughout history God has used what we might consider insignificant things as signs to remind us of important truths. For example, when the Israelites crossed the Jordon River, God commanded them to take up twelve stones from the dry river bed and to set them up *"to serve as a sign among you....These stones are to be a memorial to the people of Israel forever"* (Joshua 4:6-7). God forbade the use of yeast (leavening) during the period of the Passover. That was a sign to His people. Yeast was allowed at other times but the lack of it at a certain time was a special sign meant to remind God's people of something important. Its lack was so obvious that even the children noticed and were curious. When the children asked, *"What does this mean?"* they were told the mighty works God had done for the Israelites (Exodus 12). God even provided a sign as a reminder to Himself: *"Whenever the rainbow appears in the clouds, I will see it and remember the everlasting covenant...."* (Genesis 9:16). Something natural, even ordinary, is given a greater meaning.

God has chosen insignificant things like rocks, yeast, and the rainbow to remind us of significant truths. It may not seem important to us whether it is a man or a woman in the pulpit, but God says for the women to keep silent in church. Paul's language is rather strong in I Corinthians 14:37: *"If anybody thinks he is a prophet or spiritually gifted, let him acknowledge that what I am writing to you is the Lord's command."* Every time a man instead of a woman speaks to the assembled church, the divine order is thus demonstrated. The different functions assigned men and women in the assembly are a sign of the created order.

It must be noted that I Corinthians 11:3, *"....the head of every man is Christ, and the head of the woman is man, and the head of Christ is God,"* was written to Christians. Thus these lines of authority are relevant only within the body of Christ, within the parameters of the church (cf. I Corinthians 5:9-12). They do not regulate the larger world of business and society, even though as Christians we naturally want to extend our spirituality in all areas of life.

The Old Testament was written that we might know God and understand better what He wants of us. When we read it, we often see parallels that help us today. Is there a parallel between women who want to speak in the assembly and Eve in the garden?

Genesis tells us that Eve lived in the beautiful Garden of Eden, where only one thing was denied her. She could eat the fruit from any of the trees except the one in the middle of the garden. It alone was forbidden to her.

Although we may not understand why God put that restriction on her, we know that He did. It is easy for us to see that Eve should have obeyed whatever God commanded.

Unfortunately, Eve believed the lie when she was told, *"God didn't really mean it when He said, 'Don't eat.'"* As the serpent urged her to think about that one tree, it seemed to take *"center stage"* in her misguided mind. It did not matter that she could eat from every other tree in the garden; she had to have that one certain fruit, the forbidden thing.

Eve decided (with encouragement from one outside the fellowship of God) that the fruit of that tree was good and pleasing and desirable. Perhaps Adam just wanted to keep his wife happy, so he did not restrain her, but went along with her and also ate of the fruit.

Women and Leadership in the Church

God has given woman the right to full membership in His body; she is sanctified by Christ's blood and must obey all of the commands the same as any other Christian. However, as in the Garden of Eden, God has laid down a certain restriction. In the assembly of the church, when the church comes together as a church, she is to be silent. All areas of service open to men are open to women except authoritative leadership in the church. Women are not to speak authoritatively either to the assembly (i.e., by preaching, I Corinthians 14) or for the assembly (i.e., by leading the congregation in prayer, I Timothy 2), nor serve as elders (I Timothy 3; Titus 1). In the eyes of many, that denied role seems to have become *"center stage."* It does not seem to matter how many areas of service to God are open to women, some long for the one thing that is restricted.

Unfortunately, today the world (i.e., anyone outside the fellowship of God) is telling us that it is good and pleasing and desirable for women to do anything men do. Even fellow Christians are telling us, *"God didn't really mean it when He said, 'Be quiet in church.'"* Perhaps men want to please the women; consequently, they do as Adam did by allowing the new Eves to lead them.

Although there are disagreements among Bible student about the exact interpretation of these passages, there is o' definitive statement that we cannot ignore: I Corinthians 14:37 t' us it is the Lord's command. We may not understand why God commanded that this restriction be placed on women, but He did. If we have the same submissive attitude toward God that Christ had, *"Not my will, but yours,"* then we will be willing to obey whatever God commands, even if we don't fully understand why, or even if we don't completely agree that it really is the best way.

The attitude of our hearts is extremely important. A Christian should not put himself or herself forward and demand anything of God. If we who are women insist upon our *"rights"* to do what we want to do, we lose sight of certain truths. God has commanded that all Christians should be in submission not only to Him but also to each other (Ephesians 5:21). The prayers of Christ Himself were heard *"because of his reverent submission"* (Hebrews 5:7). No less must we reverently fear God and follow His will and authority. If Christ had insisted on His *"rights"* and had not submitted Himself to God, we would have no hope whatsoever.

Although it may be scriptural for a woman to speak in public situations other than the assembly of the church, it may not be expedient. We may compare Paul's discussion of eating meat offered to idols in I Corinthians 10 as causing someone to violate his or her conscience. Moreover, it may give the wrong impression to those who do not understand the distinction between *"as a church"* and other meetings.

It may also be scriptural for women to do certain things in the assembly, such as pass communion plates, a non-authoritative serving role; but it may not be expedient in a given situation. The practice may tear down the church instead of edifying it. Everything must be done with a loving attitude.

Some may ask, *"But if a woman is denied a public speaking role in the assembly, what then can she do?"* The answer to that question is found in another question, *"If a man is not the one who is leading the congregation in a public way, what can he do for the Lord?"* When you answer the second question, the first has also been answered. A woman must obey all the commands of God as surely as any man does, and that includes the Great Commission. However, if we think that the only, or even the best, way to fulfill that command is in speaking before the church assembled, then our view is too shallow, and we are sadly failing in carrying out that command. Women, as well as men, can and should be doing more to tell others about God and to bring the lost to Christ.

Perhaps we need to examine the doctrine of what should be done in the assembly--we seem to be in an era of *"anything goes."* We need to re-examine God's plan for how we approach Him when we come together *en ekklesia*. Maybe the question of women's leadership role in the assembly is based as much on an inadequate understanding of the biblical doctrine of the assembly as on a misunderstanding of the role of women.

Questions

1. What arguments are being used to say that women can and should have a leadership role in the public assembly of the church? How would you answer these arguments using the scriptures?
2. What criteria should be used in determining what is done in the assembly of the church?
3. How is the assembly different from other functions of the church? List some occasions when Christians could be together but not be the church in assembly. Would it be permissible for women to talk about spiritual things at these times?
4. What is the meaning of *"silent"* in I Corinthians 14: 34? Does It include singing, congregational responsible readings, etc.?
5. What are some indications that I Timothy 2 is talking about the public assemblies of the church?
6. What parallels are there between Korah and his followers (Numbers 16) and those who say there should be no distinction between the roles of men and women in the assembly?
7. What parallels do you see between the story of Eve in Genesis 3 and the women's movement today?
8. What was King Saul's mistake in I Samuel 15?
9. What is the created order in regard to husband and wife according to Genesis 2-3? How is this used in the New Testament in regard to relations between husbands and wives?
10. Consider the Christian men who are not preaching, leading prayers, etc. in the assembly. What can they do to serve the Lord? Since the scriptures only limit women's activities in the assembly of the church, is there any reason why women cannot perform for the Lord these same services which are done outside the assembly?
11. What significance does culture have in interpreting scripture?
12. What commands are given specifically to women?
13. What religious activities of women are mentioned in the New Testament?

4. What Kind of Music Does God Want?

Milo Richard Hadwin

Thousands of churches of Christ through out the world worship God in song without the accompaniment of instrumental music. Many articles, books, sermons, and debates have presented reasons for believing it is a sin to use instrumental music in such worship. There may always have been some members who disagreed, but who chose not to discuss the matter. These may have felt intimidated, considered the matter unimportant, or preferred not to argue about it. Others may not have considered the use of instrumental music in worship to be sinful, but, because of a preference for a cappella music, did not wish to push for change.

However, in recent years a seemingly increasing number of members, including preachers, have disagreed publicly. Many factors may have contributed to this. Less preaching and teaching on the subject may have produced a generation less able to make a well-informed judgment. Some may choose not to investigate the subject on the assumption that it is "trivial." Some fear they will lose their young people if instrumental music is not allowed (Those who take that position surely must already have decided its use is not sinful).

There are "Christian Churches" or "Churches of Christ" who use instrumental music but who agree with the non-instrumentalists on almost all other matters. It would be wonderful if disagreement over instrumental music could be resolved and unity could be achieved. Some who desire such unity may have been influenced by the arguments of the pro-instrumentalists. Some of these may now believe the use of instrumental music in worship to God is not sinful. Others may simply believe the case against instrumental music is too weak to be allowed as a barrier to fellowship.

Undoubtedly, more factors are involved in leading some to object to prohibiting instrumental music in worship. However, the basic question that must be answered is, "Is it a sin to use instrumental music in worship to God?" A bibliography at the end of this chapter will list books that cover the subject in breadth and depth. This chapter will attempt to cut to the heart of the question and break new ground in an effort to answer it. (Breaking new ground in this instance means uncovering old ground that has been forgotten or unnoticed.)

The religious environment of the twentieth century tends to cause the modern mind to be prejudiced in favor of instrumental music. Only a minority of people oppose its use. Those who do so are often perceived as being eccentric or strange. So it may be important to put the matter in a larger historical perspective. When this is done, the prejudice should disappear, and the matter can be decided on its own merits.

The View Supported In This Chapter

For many centuries before the church began, Jews and pagans used instrumental music in worship to God. For several centuries after the church began, neither Jews nor pagans who became Christians used instrumental music in worship to God. Although professing Christians disagreed on virtually every doctrine in the Christian system, one belief and practice that was universal was that the music offered to God in worship was to be singing unaccompanied by instrumental music. Nothing less than a command of God would have been sufficient to account for such a radical reversal in belief and practice. Such commands are found in Ephesians 5:18-20 and Colossians 3:16-17. Christians in our time who have believed instrumental music in worship to God to be wrong have taken these commands to sing as meaning to sing only, unaccompanied by instrumental music.

It is the position of this chapter that God meant to say precisely that in those passages. The New Testament is not silent concerning instrumental music, contrary to what often has been presumed. It is argued here that the earliest Greek-speaking readers of the Greek New Testament understood the words *psallo* and *psalmos* as used in these passages explicitly to exclude and forbid the use of instrumental music. This, and this only, accounts for the universality of the teaching and practice of the church on this matter. The meaning was clearly understood as embedded in the words used in these commands. It was only among people centuries later who lost sight of the meaning of the words or the authority of scripture that instrumental music was introduced. But among Greek-speaking people, even into this century, instrumental music has been excluded from worship to God. God used language in the New Testament that clearly prohibited the use of instrumental music in worship to Him, and Christians who do so are violating the will of God.

Support for This View

In the Old Testament God commanded the Jews to use instrumental music (e.g., 2 Chronicles 29:25; Psalm 150). It was used in worship in the temple, and its use permeated the life of the Jewish people even in the time of Christ (Matthew 9:23; 11:17; Luke 15:25). Instrumental music was also used throughout the pagan world in its worship. Against this background it is startling to learn that when Jews and pagans entered the church they stopped using instrumental music in worship. This is historical fact. There is no unambiguous evidence of any church that even claimed to be Christian using instrumental music in worship to God for almost a thousand years after the church began! Not only did they not use instrumental music, but those who wrote on the subject condemned its use.

The research of James McKinnon is especially helpful at this point. As a Roman Catholic he wrote with no bias against instrumental music. In 1965 he completed his Ph. D. dissertation at Columbia University on "The Church Fathers and Musical Instruments." In 1987 he edited *Music in Early Christian Literature*. This volume was designed to include all of the essential literary evidence concerning Christian music from the New Testament to approximately 450 A.D. In the abstract of his dissertation, McKinnon spoke of two facts: "There is the fact that early Christian music was vocal, and there is the patristic polemic against instruments." Concerning the latter he noted:

The most important observation one makes about the numerous patristic denunciations of instruments is that they are always made within the context of obscene theatrical performances, orgiastic banquets and the like, but not within the context of liturgical music. Evidently the occasion of speaking out against instruments in church never presented itself. One can only imagine what rhetorical outbursts the introduction of instruments into church would have elicited from Fathers like Augustine, Jerome and Chrysostom.

Later McKinnon made the point in this way:

Now a close reading of all the patristic criticism of instruments leads to the remarkable conclusion that there is not a single quotation which condemns the use of instruments in church!............... If it had ever occurred to any Christian communities of the third or fourth centuries to add instruments to their liturgical singing, indignation over the action would certainly be prominent in patristic literature (p. 262).

After twenty two years of further study and reflection, McKinnon still spoke of "that chorus of denunciation directed against pagan musical customs, concentrating with special fervor on musical instruments" (*Music*, p. 1).

An additional observation of McKinnon in "The Meaning of the Patristic Polemic Against Musical Instruments" in the Spring, 1955 issue of *Current Musicology* is important. He said that:

Many musicologists, while acknowledging that early church music was predominantly vocal, have tried to find evidence that instruments were employed at various times and places. The result of such attempts has been a history of misinterpretations and mistranslations (p. 70).

A final comment from McKinnon in the same place is particularly striking:

If the casual reader of patristic denunciations of musical instruments is struck by their vehemence, the systematic investigator is surprised by another characteristic: their uniformity. The attitude of opposition to instruments was virtually monolithic even though it was shared by men of diverse temperaments and different regional backgrounds, and even though it extended over a span of at least two centuries of changing fortunes for the church. That there were not widespread exceptions to the general position defies credibility.

It is the conclusion of this chapter that there is only one basis on which it does not defy credibility. That will be stated shortly.

Unanimity on Form

Virtually every point of Christian doctrine was disputed in the first centuries of the Christian faith. But one point on which there was unanimity, uniformity, and universality was that the form of music employed in Christian worship was singing unaccompanied by instrumental music. Every effect must have an adequate cause. Surely nothing less than the most powerful and demanding cause could account for pagans and Jews, who for centuries had employed instrumental music in their worship, to suddenly cease their use on becoming Christians, and for centuries more to employ nothing but singing in the music they offered to God. So striking is this fact that it created a new term in our language, "a cappella," a term that refers to singing without instrumental accompaniment, "according to the chapel (church)." What cause could have been powerful enough to have made such an astounding change?

Some have suggested that unaccompanied singing was simply a Christian reaction to the pagan use of instruments. But McKinnon has said: "The truth remains that the polemic against musical instruments and the vocal performance of early Christian psalmody were--for whatever reason--unrelated in the minds of the church fathers" (*Music*, p. 4). Before that he noted:

> What one observes there are two separate phenomena: a consistent condemnation of instruments in the contexts cited above, and an ecclesiastical psalmody obviously free of instrumental involvement. It is puzzling to the modern mind that the church fathers failed to forge an ideological link between the two--leaving this apparently to the *a cappella* partisans of the nineteenth century (pp. 3-4).

And strangely, one might add, to the instrumental partisans of the twentieth century. Simply stated, as strong as Christian opposition was to pagan use of instrumental music, this was not their reason for singing without instrumental accompaniment.

The more common current explanation for the early Christian exclusion of instruments is the perpetuation of the presumed synagogue practice of singing without instrumental accompaniment. This is an inadequate explanation for more reasons than space here allows. Two will be given here. First, there is no historical proof concerning first century synagogue practice regarding music. The case rests basically on fourth century sources that are increasingly challenged. Some argue (and with some good reasons) that no music was employed in the synagogue. It was strictly a place for scripture reading and teaching. Certainly in all the New Testament references to the synagogue, this is all that was recorded as having been done there. Second, there is no statement by anybody in the first centuries of the church's existence that synagogue practice had anything to do with its exclusion of instrumental music. This explanation is hypothetical, speculative, and contrary to the evidence.

So what reason is powerful enough to account for the dramatic and immediate change in Jewish and pagan practice regarding instrumental music on their becoming Christians? Only a belief that the use of instrumental music in Christian worship was sinful could have abruptly changed such a deeply ingrained and centuries-long practice. And only a command of God could have produced such a belief. Do such commands exist? Twentieth century opponents of instrumental music base their opposition on commands contained in Ephesians 5:18-20 and Colossians 3:16-17. An examination of the evidence indicates that the earliest writers who professed faith in Christ based their practice on these commands as well.

Five different writers who lived as adults in the second century gave reason why they sang in worship to God. In each case they either explicitly quoted these commands or stated that their reason was because they had been "instructed," it was the "will of My Father," or they had been "commanded," with evidence that these biblical commands were in mind. (Notice the word associations with these commands.)

Justin Martyr wrote around 150 A.D.:

> We have been instructed that only the following worship is worthy of him, not the consumption by fire of those things created by him for our nourishment but the use of them by ourselves and by those in need, while in gratitude to him we offer solemn prayers and hymns for his creation and for all things leading to health (Apology,1,13).

Between 120 and 140 A.D. the writer of 2 Clement 9.10 said: "Let us therefore give him eternal praise, not from our lips only, but also from our heart, that He may receive us as sons. For the Lord also said, 'These are My brethren, which do the will of My Father.'"

About 180 A.D. the writer in Book VIII of *The Sibylline Oracles* wrote:

> But joyful with pure minds and cheerful soul, With love abounding and with generous hands, With soothing psalms and songs that honor God, We are commanded to sing praise to Thee, The imperishable and without deceit, All-Father God, of understanding mind.

In *Against Marcion*, Tertullian wrote: "The command to 'sing to the Lord with psalms and hymns,' comes suitably from him who knew that those who 'drank wine with drums and psalteries' were blamed by God."

About 190 A.D. Clement of Alexandria listed eight musical instruments used by ancient peoples and said:

> We, however, make use of but one instrument, the word of peace alone by which we honor God, and no longer the ancient psaltery, nor the trumpet, the tympanum and the aulos, as was the custom among those expert in war and those scornful of the fear of God who employed string instruments in their festive gatherings, as if to arouse their remissness of spirit through such rhythms. (*Paedagogus*, Book 2, Chapter 4).

The essay in which this statement is made is especially important because it contains the first known argument by a professed Christian writer against instrumental music and in favor of Christians worshiping without instrumental accompaniment. As Clement developed his argument, he quoted Colossians 3:16-17 at the center of his case. This deserves some attention and will be returned to shortly.

A Common Argument

Perhaps the most common argument in recent times against instrumental music has been that there is no authority for its use in Christian worship. It has been said that Colossians 3:16-17 and Ephesians 5:18-20 give us authority for singing, but nowhere does the New Testament authorize the use of instrumental music in worship by Christians. This has been dismissed by some as being an argument from silence. It is said that the New Testament does not explicitly forbid the use of musical instruments. It is argued that "where there is no law there is no transgression" (Romans 4:15). But a law does not necessarily have to explicitly condemn to exclude. For example, in instituting the supper to be observed by his disciples, the Lord had them eat bread and drink the cup. He said, "do this." In spite of its potential theological significance, roast lamb is rightfully to be excluded from that supper. In view of such a consideration, those who use instrumental music must still answer the question, "By what authority are you doing these things?" (Matthew 21:23).

Perhaps the most common argument in recent times for instrumental music has been that authority is found in the Greek words *psallo* and *psalmos*. *Psalmos*, which is commonly translated "psalm," is used in both Ephesians 5:19 and Colossians 3:16. *Psallo* is used in Ephesians 5:19 where it is frequently translated "make melody" or "make music." Elsewhere it has usually been translated as "sing." Pro-instrumentalists have often argued that *psalmos* is a song sung with instrumental accompaniment and *psallo* means to "sing with instrumental accompaniment." If this were what the words meant in Ephesians 5:19 and Colossians 3:16, the issue would be settled and opposition to instrumental music would be impossible. But is that what those words meant?

Pro-instrumentalists have cited many lexicons in support of the view that *psallo* means "to sing with instrumental accompaniment." These citations have been of the meaning of the word in classical Greek or possibly in the LXX (Septuagint, a translation of the Hebrew Scriptures done about 250 B.C.). It must be understood that meanings of words can vary from place to place and often change with the passing of time. Words such as "bonnet" and "lift" have different meanings in the United States and England. Hundreds of words in the English language have changed meaning since the KJV was translated in 1611. Teenagers in recent years have given new meanings to words such as "cool," "neat," and "bad." It is important to know what words in the New Testament meant around that period of time--and not more

61

than 250 years earlier, unless continuity of meaning can be demonstrated.

The standard lexicon for New Testament Greek studies is the latest edition of the Bauer-Arndt-Gingrich lexicon. In its comments on the meaning of *psallo*, it says the original meaning of the word was "'pluck,' 'play' (a stringed instrument)." Then it says that the meaning in the LXX "freq. means 'sing,' whether to the accompaniment of a harp or (as usually) not." Then it says this process of change in meaning continued until *psallo*, in Modern Greek means "sing" exclusively. In defining *psalmos*, no mention is made of instrumental music. It says it is a "song of praise."

Possibly the most fascinating effort to prove that *psallo* includes the use of instrumental music is based on Romans 15:9. The argument goes like this: Christians are commanded to *psallo* in Ephesians 5:19. *Psallo* translates the Hebrew word, *zamar*, in Romans 15:9 (quoting 2 Samuel 22:50; Psalms 57:9; or 18:49). *Zamar* means "to play on a musical instrument (or sing so accompanied)." *Psallo* translates *zamar*, so it meant the same thing as *zamar*. Therefore, it is acceptable for Christians to use instrumental music in worship to God.

The problem with this argument is that *zamar* does not mean "to play on a musical instrument (or sing so accompanied)." How can one arrive at this conclusion? Both *Gesenius' Hebrew-Chaldee Lexicon to the Old Testament* and a Hebrew and English Lexicon of the Old Testament by Brown, Driver, and Briggs gave as the first meaning of *zamar*, "to sing" or "of singing to." There is good reason for this: One can insert the word "sing" in place of *zamar* in all 46 occurrences of the word in the Piel (a Hebrew verb form), and the sentences make sense. The same cannot be said for the word "play" as in "play on an instrument."

Gesenius gave as a second definition of *zamar*, "to play on a musical instrument [or to sing so accompanied]." He gave Psalms 33:2 and 71:22 as instances. Brown, Driver, and Briggs (BDB) gave as a second definition, "of playing musical instruments." They provided as additional instances, Psalms 144:9; 98:5; 147:7; and 149:3. BDB prefaced their two definitions by indicating the word means "make music in praise of God." It is clear that this broader dimension was required by the presumption that their second definition is true.

However, Karl Barth in his eight-page article on *zamar* and related words in the *Theological Dictionary of the Old Testament* cited all of the instances provided by Gesenius and BDB. He demonstrated that they drew an improper conclusion. The instances that led to forming an improper second definition involved *zamar* followed by a preposition followed by an instrument. Barth showed from the use of the word in the language from which it was borrowed and the parallelism of the Hebrew text that there is no basis for assigning the meaning of "play" to the word *zamar*. This leaves "sing" as the exclusive meaning of *zamar*. It is true that one could *zamar* <u>with</u> instruments, and one can "sing" with instruments. But "sing" still means "sing," and *zamar* still means "sing." A word that translates *zamar* must therefore be a word that means "sing."

Independent study of *zamar* in the Hebrew or in a careful English translation will produce the same conclusion. It becomes clear that the simple word "sing" (or some equivalent expression involving exclusively some form of vocal articulation) consistently makes sense in the various contexts. The words with which *zamar* is associated in the Hebrew parallelisms are striking. Often it is paralleled with words that clearly involve vocal articulation such as "telling," "declaring," and "giving thanks." Especially noteworthy in this regard is Psalms 71:23 where *zamar* is done with the lips. The most frequent paralleling--with *shir*, which always means "sing"--is particularly impressive. This is especially so in Psalms 57:7 where *zamar* and *shir* are in parallel with two identical words (a word simply repeated).

Barth and the contexts where *zamar* is connected with an instrument prove that the meaning is <u>sing</u> "with the accompaniment of _____." *Psallo* is used in the Septuagint to translate *zamar* in these instances, and the instrument is specified by a dative phrase. This is the precise construction in Ephesians 5:19 and justifies the translation "<u>sing</u> with the accompaniment of your heart." "Heart" stands where an instrument would be in the Old Testament passages.

It is certain that the word *zamar* means only "sing." It has absolutely no instrumental associations of itself. The instrument must be stated if the word is to be understood within a context of instruments, for the word always and only means just "sing." A defender of instrumental music has argued that *psallo* in Romans 15:9 is the fulfillment of prophecy that predicted *zamar* would be done among the Gentiles. He said: "What *zamar* meant at the time the prophecy was given was what *psallo* meant when it was fulfilled." If that is true, it has been established that *psallo* has absolutely no instrumental association at all, and it means exclusively to "sing." There is certainly no authority for the use of instrumental music in *psallo*.

This brings us back to Clement. Clement quoted Colossians 3:16-17 in the course of his argument against instrumental

63

music and in favor of vocal music. This is especially significant since this passage contains the word *psalmos*. If that word meant "a song sung to instrumental accompaniment," Clement's argument would have been destroyed. But Clement felt no need to explain anything about *psalmos*. The word clearly and obviously had no instrumental association in his own mind. Otherwise he would have been using a scripture that required or permitted instrumental music to sustain his opposition to it!

The words *psallo* and *psalmos* were continually used by writers from the second century onward in contexts where opposition to instrumental music was being expressed or unaccompanied singing was being advocated. For example, in about 325 A.D. Eusebius wrote the first history of the church. But he also wrote a lesser-known commentary on the Psalms. In commenting on Psalms 91:2-3 he said:

> Of old at the time those of the circumcision were wor-
> shipping with symbols and types it was not inappro-
> priate to send up hymns to God with the psalterion
> and kithara,................ We render our hymn a living
> psalterion and a living kithara, with spiritual song. The
> unison of voices of Christians would be more accept-
> able to God than any musical instrument.Accordingly
> in all the churches of God, united in soul and attitude,
> with one mind and in agreement of faith and piety, we
> send up a unison melody in the words of the Psalms.
> We are accustomed to employ such psalmodies and
> spiritual kitharas because the apostle teaches this
> saying, "in psalms and odes and spiritual hymns."

Several things are noteworthy in this passage from Eusebius. First, this writer, intimately acquainted with the history of the church from its beginning, matter-of-factly and unselfconsciously reflected the contrast between the ancient Jewish practice of using instruments with the universal Christian view of their unacceptability. Second, Eusebius said the reason they sang unaccompanied by instruments was because of the command of Paul in Ephesians 5:19 concerning "psalms and odes and spiritual hymns." His statement is nonsense if "psalms" (*psalmos*) even permits instrumental music, much less requires it.

It is clear that in classical Greek the word *psallo* included the idea of "play" on an instrument. It is clear that in the LXX the word sometimes retained its classical meaning and sometimes was used to translate the Hebrew word *nagan*, "play." But it is also clear that the word was already shifting its meaning more than 250 years before the New Testament was written and sometimes, if not usually, meant "sing." Both the lexicons and the contexts in which *psallo* appears attest to this. But the best and most recent Greek scholarship (including Kittel's *Theological Dictionary of the New Testament*) says that in the New Testament the word meant "sing." The indication is that the word had lost its instrumental association altogether.

That this should have happened need not seem either surprising or unlikely. The same kind of thing happened with our English word "lyric." Its root is in a musical instrument, the lyre. Yet today it means "the words of a song, as distinguished from the music." So if one says that a certain person is a lyricist, the presumption must be, unless additional information is provided to the contrary, that the person writes only the words of songs.

It is the conclusion of this chapter that this is precisely the way in which *psallo* and *psalmos* were used in the New Testament. This is evidenced by the way those who heard it at the earliest period of time responded to it and used it themselves. *Psallo* meant to "sing only" (that is, without instrumental accompaniment) unless additional information was given to the contrary. This is not to say the lexicons are "wrong" to say *psallo* means "sing." They are simply ambiguous and less than precise.

To illustrate the point, the millions of people today who sing in worship without instrumental accompaniment use the word in three ways. When the song leader in their assemblies says, "Let us sing," he means "sing only," and those present understand it that way. They would consider the will of the song leader to have been violated were someone to start accompanying the singing with a musical instrument. Yet in a non-worship setting, the word could be used differently. If one of these people were the director of an opera house and signed a performer to "sing in an opera production," his will would have been violated if the performer refused to sing when the instruments of the orchestra began to accompany him. Or in a social gathering if one of these people asked a talented singer to sing a song, it might be regarded as immaterial whether the person merely sang or was accompanied by a piano. The same person could even tell someone to "sing with the piano" without jeopardizing his ability to mean "singing only" in another context when he just says "sing." "Sing" has different meanings in these settings, and the one who uses the word has no difficulty making these distinctions.

In the first century and beyond, the word *psallo* among pagans continued at times to be used in its classical sense of "play" on an instrument. When those who professed to be Christians used the word to refer to its meaning in the LXX, they properly attributed to it, where appropriate, the classical meaning of the word. But when the word was used alone in contexts with application to Christian worship, the word was used clearly and consistently in the sense of "sing without instrumental accompaniment." And *psalmos* was viewed as a "song without instrumental accompaniment."

This point has been illustrated in the case of Clement and Eusebius. But some have argued that Clement did not oppose the use of some instruments. This is based on a statement he made following his quotation of Colossians 3:16-17. He said, according to the translation of William Wilson in the *Ante-Nicene Christian Library*, "And even if you wish to sing and play to the harp or lyre, there is no blame." (It is worth noting that while Wilson translated *psallo* as "play" here, Simon P. Woods in *The Fathers of the Church* ed. by Roy Joseph Deferrari translated it "chant psalms.") Wilson's mistranslation of the statement may have contributed to misunderstanding Clement at this point. The word "harp" should be translated "cithara" (see McKinnon's translation in *Music*, p. 33). This is important because earlier in the same essay Clement allegorized the "cithara" (which Wilson at that point incorrectly translates "lyre") showing he was not advocating the literal use of the literal instrument. He also, earlier in his essay, explicitly condemned the literal use of the lyre. An examination of the context shows that Clement was not making an exception for certain instruments, but was engaging in the rather bizarre allegorical exegesis commonly employed in the early centuries. (See the introduction to McKinnon's work on *Music* for a brief discussion of this).

The argument being used in this chapter is not that instrumental music is wrong because writers in the early centuries said so. They are not authoritative for doctrine; only the Bible is. But to understand the words used in the Bible, one sometimes has to go to the literature of the period to see how the words were used at the time. Meanings of words are determined by their use in context. This is how lexicons come up with their definitions. (See *Linguistics and Biblical Interpretation* by Peter Cotterell and Max Turner published by InterVarsity Press, for a good discussion of this.)

It is clear from the writings of those who professed to be Christians in the centuries immediately following the writing of the New Testament, that those Greek-speaking people who read the Greek New Testament saw no instrumental association in the words *psallo* and *psalmos*. In fact, the contexts in which they used those words indicate they believed those words as used in the New Testament excluded instrumental music. If those words did exclude instrumental music, then its use is explicitly condemned in Ephesians 5:18-20. Certainly these words provide no authority for using instrumental music in Christian worship. The fact that the Greek-speaking church never used instrumental music and opposed its use is further confirmation of those points.

Questions

1. Why do you think instrumental music is being increasingly discussed in the church today?
2. What factors might lead to a prejudice for or against instrumental music in worship to God?
3. What did the Old Testament teach regarding instrumental music?
4. What was the status of the use of instrumental music during the time of the earthly ministry of Jesus?
5. What was the status of the use of instrumental music in worship by those who professed to be Christians for the first few centuries of the church's existence?
6. What is wrong with the argument that Christians did not use instrumental music because pagans used it?
7. What is wrong with the argument that Christians did not use instrumental music because it was not used in the synagogue?
8. What evidence indicates early professed Christians used the commands of Ephesians 5:18-20 and Colossians 3:16-17 as a basis for their singing to God?
9. In what way does the Hebrew word *zamar* contribute to the understanding that *psallo* means only to "sing"?
10. What does Clement's use of the word *psalmos* indicate about its meaning?
11. How does the quotation from Eusebius contribute to our understanding of the meaning of *psalmos*?
12. In what way can writers of the second century help our understanding of the New Testament?
13. On what basis can it be argued that Ephesians 5:18-20 explicitly condemns the use of instrumental music in worship to God?

5. Are You on God's Praise Team?

A Look at Public Worship

Robert Oglesby, Sr.

In the church's current turmoil, why has so much focus been on worship? Jesus clearly told the woman at the well that God was interested in our worship (John 4:20-27). Likewise, the Psalmist exhorted God's people to "Praise the Lord" (Psalm 117:1,2). If heaven has this much interest in worship, why shouldn't we?

God is interested in all kinds of worship. Jesus referred to private prayer when he said we should enter our inner chamber to pray to God "in secret" (Matthew 6:6). Daniel, in the midst of danger down in Babylonian captivity, went to his house three times a day to pray privately (Daniel 6:10).

Even though we recognize the importance of private devotion, the problem area always seems to be those times when the church assembles to worship. Even David's psalms speak not only of private praise, but of praising God in the "midst" of the congregation (Psalm 22:22; 26:12; 68: 26).

With the air of change sweeping over our society, some feel the Sunday morning gathering of the whole church represents the best time to work a change agenda for the church.

Having asked, "Why so much focus on worship?", we now ask the opposite question, "Why not focus on worship?" We have nothing to lose if what we have been doing is truth. Truth not only will stand the test, but abrasive attacks will merely polish it to a brighter finish. With nothing to lose, we have everything to gain if we discover some Biblical truth. Also, it may reveal any imbalance we have sincerely, but mistakenly, enshrined in our traditional understanding of scripture. Looking again cannot hurt, and it might help.

As we embark on our quest, we need to ask some key questions.

Our first question is, "What kind of worship does God want?" In our rush for change, we may easily lose sight of the fact that it is God and not man who is to be pleased in worship. The apostle Paul said, "Am I seeking the favor of men or of God?" (Galatians 1:10). The implied answer to Paul's question is that pleasing men is not important. Another obvious inference is that some worship does not please God. Bypassing this implication is easy for the modern mind which is tuned more for "political correctness" than for pleasing God. If we have any doubt that God must be pleased, we should ask Cain about his sacrifice that God rejected (Genesis 4:5). Likewise, we might ask Nadab and Abihu about the "strange fire" they offered God and the death sentence they received in reply (Numbers 3:4).

Paul specifically told the Corinthian church that he "did not commend them" (I Corinthians 11:22) because they were not properly observing the Lord's Supper. Jesus chided the Samaritan woman at the well because the Samaritans sincerely, but incorrectly, worshipped "what they did not know" (John 4: 22).

So our pertinent question is, "What kind of worship does please God?" Once again, our Lord's words to the Samaritan woman are helpful. He said God seeks worship done in spirit and in truth (John 4:24). This is the only kind of worship God accepts.

It makes sense that God, who is Spirit, would want to be worshipped by man's spirit. This is a recurrent theme of scripture. Jesus agreed with Isaiah who said, "These hypocrites honor me with their lips, but their hearts are far from me" (Matthew 15:7,8). David emphasized emotion in worship when he wrote, "Make a joyful noise unto the Lord" (Psalm 100:1). James made the same point about feelings when he said, "Is any cheerful? Let him sing praise" (James 5:13). Psalm 42:1,2 describes the spirit we should bring to worship when it says, "As the deer longs for flowing streams, so longs my soul for thee, O God. My soul thirsts for God, for the living God."

On the other hand, Jesus also said worship must be "in truth"; that is, it must be done according to divine instruction. Worship guided by nothing but emotion can drift off into a formless fog of feelings. The Lord's corrective to this tendency is to specify that we should also be guided by truth. This principle is evident in the Bible. Moses on top of mount Sinai was told to build the tabernacle "according to the pattern shown to him on the mount" (Hebrews 8:5). Since every part of the tabernacle foreshadowed some truth about man's worship of God, Moses was not left free to improvise in making that worship tent.

In the light of these general instructions, we must re-examine our worship. Some feel that our historical emphasis on the rational side of worship has left us without the emotional part of our worshipful nature being fed. They insist that we stand, like the prophet Ezekiel, in a worship valley full of dry, rational bones (Ezekiel 37). Their solution is to go to the other end of the spectrum and exchange our rationalistic worship practices for warm emotion. The tension builds when others become concerned that such an emphasis may cause us to disregard the restraints truth places on us. Fortunately, God has given us a clear mandate. He does not want worship which is an either-or proposition. He wants worship to be in spirit AND in truth.

If God is the one to be pleased by worship, the next question is, "What approach will please him?" Some conceptualize worship as a list of rational items to be done. They check those items off in their mind as a pilot runs through his preflight check list. Once the check-off list is complete, they assume that they have therefore worshipped God acceptably. Others conceive of worship as a dynamic and fluid experience which has no form. In the enthusiasm to avoid mechanical legalism in worship, it is possible to fall into the formless, feel-good ditch of emotional experience on the other side of the road.

A better conceptualization of worship would be to think of approaching God on broad avenues which He has asked that we use. Reading the New Testament carefully will reveal the exhorttations God gives us about worship.

Let Us Sing

As Jesus mentioned the need for truth in worship, we should note that there is a "truth" side to singing. First of all, we can clearly establish that the early church sang in its public worship. Although Ephesians 5:19 introduces the subject of singing in a context of Christian living, the reflexive pronoun suggests a reciprocal singing to "one another." Colossians 3:13 uses the same word to describe forgiving "one another." Surely Paul was not urging the Colossians to forgive themselves, but to forgive someone other than themselves. Singing to someone else would require some kind of public worship. Likewise, Colossians 3:16 indicates that in singing, they were "teaching and admonishing." In order to teach and admonish others, there must be some kind of assembly with others present.

The New Testament emphasizes the "spirit" side of singing also. Paul wrote to the Corinthians to remind them that he would "sing with the spirit and with the understanding also" (I Corinthians 14:15). Singing was never intended to be a ritual done by rote, without feeling. Ephesians 5:19 teaches we should be filled with the Spirit when we sing, and we should "make melody" to the Lord with all our hearts. Paul told the Colossians to have "thankfulness" in their hearts when they sang. Singing by its very nature is a wonderfully expressive avenue of approach to God. At the same time, singing is designed by God to create heart melody in the person doing the singing and a response from the other worshippers as well. Clearly, God's intention was that singing should be an active participation experience and not just passive entertainment.

Let Us Pray

The apostle Paul's desire was that in every place the men should pray, but he insisted that their hands should be holy and without anger or quarreling (I Timothy 2:8). Paul emphasized that prayers in public worship should be done with spirit and understanding (I Corinthians 14:15). God wants the intellectual side of man involved in offering prayers to the Father, but He does not want mindless "vain repetitions" (Matthew 6:7) even if they are eloquent. Prayers were never intended to be intellectual rituals devoid of feeling. Bits and pieces of eloquent phrasing do not an acceptable prayer make. In prayer, God wants us pouring out our hearts to Him.

Let Us Read The Scriptures

The reading of scripture has always been important in worship. Exodus 24:7 describes Moses reading the book of the covenant in the hearing of the people. In Deuteronomy 31:9ff Moses commanded the reading of the law at the feast of booths when all the men, women, and children of Israel appeared before the Lord. Luke 4:16-21 describes the custom in Jesus' day of having someone stand in the synagogue, read the scripture, and then sit down to teach. Paul exhorted the young preacher, Timothy, to "Give attention to the public reading of scripture" (I

Timothy 4:13). The Thessalonian church was charged that Paul's letter be read to all the brethren (I Thessalonians 5:27). Colosse was told by Paul to read his letter to them, and then to trade letters and read the letter to the Laodiceans too (Colossians 4:16).

Again, as an avenue of worship, reading falls under God's general rule that it be done with understanding. Ezra the scribe gathered together the exiles returned from Babylon and read them the book of the law. Nehemiah 8:8 says Ezra read it clearly and gave the sense so that the people understood the reading. Not always do we do our reading of God's book with the spirit and understanding. All in all, public readings may be the weakest part of our public worship. With no advance preparation, men often limp through the reading, just calling words and not capturing the feeling of the inspired author or his intended meaning.

Let Us Partake Of The Lord's Supper

The early church thought communion was an important part of its worship. Even a casual reading of the New Testament documents reveals that Jesus instituted something very impressive in that upper room the night of his betrayal. His disciples heard Jesus say, "This is my body." They likewise heard him say, "This is my blood." None of them could ever forget this memorial meal. His exhortation to, "Do this in remembrance of me" (Luke 22:19), no doubt lingered in their minds long after he was gone. A quick reading of I Corinthians 11 shows that even though the church at Corinth was not doing a good job of observing the Lord's Supper, they at least knew it should be a part of their public worship. Likewise the church at Troas is pictured by Luke as gathering together for an assembly in which Paul preached and the bread was broken (Acts 20:7).

There was a certain truth about this meal. The bread and fruit of the vine were prescribed elements of the celebration, as Matthew 26 and I Corinthians 11 make clear. Apparently this observance happened on the first day of the week when they came together for worship. This is certainly what Troas did. The testimony of the second century documents supports this pattern as an every Sunday celebration in the centuries after the close of the New Testament. The meal's purpose continued to be something done in remembrance of Jesus (I Corinthians 11:26).

As always, there was a spiritual side expressed in this avenue of worship. God intended that it be more than an empty ritual. In the supper, they were told to examine themselves and to eat the meal "discerning" the Lord's body, lest they bring "judgment" (I Corinthians 11:29) upon themselves.

Let Us Give

According to I Corinthians 16:2, we know the church at Corinth assembled on the first day of every week. Paul exhorted them to give at that time as they had been "prospered." Paul also admonished them to give "bountifully" (II Corinthians 9:6). The apostle reminded them that he had also given this same instruction to other churches, such as those in Galatia (I Corinthians 16:1).

Giving under the old covenant had an emotional dimension to it as well. One can only imagine the emotional impact of Jews bringing a living lamb to the priest as a sacrificial gift to be offered for their sins. One can almost touch the emotions each Jewish household must have felt as they huddled inside their homes on Passover night to eat the lamb which would cause the destroyer to "pass over" them (Exodus 12). For this reason, we can see why giving in our worship should be more than a routine, pass-the-basket ritual. It should not be done grudgingly, because it is "cheerful givers" (II Corinthians 9:7) whom God loves.

Let Us Teach and Preach

King Zedekiah, when he was besieged inside the walls of Jerusalem, asked the prophet Jeremiah, "Is there any word from the Lord?" (Jeremiah 37:17). When God's people gather for worship, they need to ask that same question. The New Testament paints a vivid picture of the assembled church listening avidly to the teaching and preaching of God's word. Paul's message to the Troas church was so important it lasted until midnight (Acts 20:7). The church at Antioch also gathered together to be exhorted (Acts 15). Although God's message is a rational one which appeals to man's understanding, Paul would add that it also arouses our emotions and makes us aware of the "terror of the Lord" (II Corinthians 5:11). When God's family gathers, the most logical thing for us to do is to read and explain the commands, promises, and blessings of God.

73

Other Matters

Having described the early church's public worship, we realize that we have had to piece this picture together from many inspired sources, because no one New Testament passage describes completely what was done in the Lord's day worship. Now we must turn to some matters of concern for the church today. The clash of our modern culture, variations in biblical inter-pretation, and personal preferences create questions not covered in the general picture we have sketched thus far.

The Role of Women in Public Worship?

Some have surmised that most of the limitations placed on women in public worship are based not on God's eternal will, but on the culture of New Testament times. If this is true, then much of the New Testament may be discarded at our own discretion. We must be cautious in taking this approach to Bible interpretation, because once we start to walk that path, the way is steep and slippery. Unless we are careful, we may wind up without a real guide for our lives. So with some misgivings, we ask ourselves if the role of women in worship is a scriptural matter or simply a cultural one.

In I Corinthians 11:3ff Paul sketches a chain of relationship, which places God, Christ, man and woman in a certain order. The apostle mentions a woman praying or prophesying but makes no comment about that except to say that she should have her head veiled when she prays. In Corinthians 14, Paul returns to the question of who should speak and when. At this point Paul addresses the question of whether or not women should speak in the assembly of the church. His command is that they should keep silence in the churches, because they are not permitted to speak, but should be subordinate, as even the law says (I Corinthians 14:33,34). The reference in chapter 11 to women praying or prophesying is puzzling in the light of what Paul says in chapter 14. Whatever Paul means, he definitely puts some kind of limita-tion on what women can do in a public worship service when the whole church is assembled together. That conclusion is difficult to evade.

I Timothy 2:11-15 is another passage in which Paul talks about women in worship. Clearly Paul addresses women's role when he says while the men are praying, the women are to learn in silence with all submissiveness. Paul further defines the meaning of silence by saying this means he does not permit a woman to teach nor to have authority over a man. Although this may have some cultural elements in it, the apostle definitely argues his point from scriptural grounds. He points out that Adam was formed first in creation, and that Eve was the one deceived. The implications are clear that if men are praying and women are to be learning in silence, Paul must be describing some kind of public worship. How could the woman teach or show authority over a man if no men were present?

Admittedly, this kind of teaching is not "politically correct" in today's world, but the Bible does say it, and we must wrestle with its implications for worship. We must come to grips with the fact that Paul meant something by the distinction he described between the roles of men and women. Obviously, nibbling at the edges of public roles and testing the boundaries will establish a trend line. We must be cautious about starting down a road which promises to erase the differences God put in place. No one is scheming to oppress women in the church; rather, we are all struggling to determine what God is asking us to do. We must be careful not to use test cases which question the details of interpretation so minutely that we miss God's overwhelmingly obvious point that men and women have different roles in the church.

What About Special Types of Singing?

Solos have become a special interest question in our worship. Some have based the acceptability of solos on the thought expressed by Paul in the first Corinthian letter. He said some came to the assembly with a "hymn, a lesson, a revelation, a tongue or an interpretation" (I Corinthians 14:26). Since we already know that Christians of the first century were encouraged to mutually participate in the singing, we have to question whether or not this one reference is enough to set that aside. Obviously, it can mean something other than the practice of solo singing in the church worship. It might be nothing more than a Christian bringing a new hymn to teach the church. Instead of looking for loopholes from congregational singing, we should consider where this new direction will lead us. The New Testament statements about singing (Ephesians 5:19 & Colossians 3:16) suggest we should all participate in the kind of singing which speaks to God and to each other. To be sure, we have for years had groups singing different parts of a song. For example, the sopranos and altos sing a line and the bass and tenor respond by echoing that same line. In those cases, however, all the worshippers are still actively involved in the process of singing. When we turn toward solos, we are changing a basic direction from participation by all and moving toward performance by a few. These two are very different concepts of worship. In the first, the full congregation is a part of the action. In the second, they become an audience which passively listens to a worship performance by someone else.

The "Praise Team" is another subtle shift in our practice. The rationale for a small group of singers is that they can lead and make the singing better. So instead of having one song leader, we may have four, eight, or more. With microphones on each part of harmony, the claim is made that the congregation will be enabled to sing better because they can hear their own part of the harmony. Again the trend line of this practice is subtle, but clear. At first, some teams remained seated and let their voices do the work. In practice, many have quickly moved to the point that these special singers now stand. Exactly why it is necessary to stand is not clear, especially when it is only the sound of their voice that we need to hear. Also, when they stand, the element of "performance" once again rears its head. Of course, once we start walking that trend line, it is easy to see that we can wind up with a chorus singing for us in worship. This is hardly full participation by all worshippers. It is almost inevitable that special singers with special skills will want to introduce harder music than the average worshipper can sing. Likewise, the printed music may be unavailable for all, so it will be an easy step to relax and allow the special group to do most, if not all, of the musical part of the worship. Somewhere in this mix, congregational singing will die a slow, natural death. That tendency has always been one of the big objections to choirs, and the praise team show promise of being merely a gentler, more palatable way to depart from congregational singing. It is a more finely tuned approach, but the principle of departure from the full participation by all singers is essentially the same.

Some may point out that we manage to worship in prayer with a prayer leader doing all the praying. In such cases, our participation consists of listening and saying "Amen" at the close of the prayer. The difference here is that I Corinthians 14:16 describes prayer being done in exactly that manner; that is, with one praying and the others saying "Amen." To the contrary, singing was urged on the Ephesians and the Colossians as something everybody did. The New Testament worship picture is not of one person singing and all others listening, but of everyone teaching, admonishing, and speaking to each other in song.

No discussion of singing would be complete without at least giving the issue of instrumental music an honorable mention. This may sound like ancient history to some. Others will say this issue does not need to be discussed because it does not now occupy the center stage among things being discussed in our brotherhood. The controversy over whether we ought to have instrumental music in our worship, however, is part of our recent religious history. We have no desire to resurrect the ghosts of controversies past, but this issue always seems to be in the wings of the theater, waiting for its cue to come on stage. After all, if we are trying to improve our singing, the next logical step for some will be to add instruments to the mix.

Some would say, "Why not?" Let's look at the reasons why we should not take this path.

About a hundred years ago, some in the Restoration Movement decided that instruments could be put into worship either as an aid or an addition. Traveling different hermeneutical roads, the movement split.

The New Testament evidence is clear and uncontroverted. In the New Testament we read exhortations to sing (Ephesians 5:19; & Colossians 3:16), as well as examples of how early disciples (Matthew 26:30 & Romans 15:9) did sing. The word "Psallo" used in such texts is defined by Greek lexicographers as singing without instrumental accompaniment. It is true that in earlier times this word carried the meaning of "plucking" something, such as the strings of a harp. By New Testament times, however, the word had shifted its meaning so that it meant only singing. If indeed there was plucking to be done, the passages describe the instrument as being the strings of the heart, which we use to "make melody."

Honest men differ on how to interpret these facts, but we should remember that they are facts, and not fancy. No instruments were ever mentioned in connection with New Testament church worship. Of course, the silence about instruments could be accidental. It was certainly not a cultural aberration, because the first Jewish Christians not only had instruments in their own religious background in Judaism, but they were also surrounded by them in the secular world and in pagan religion. Their culture provided them encouragement to use instruments, but they did not use them. The silence about instruments in New Testament worship is deafening.

The New Testament silence about instruments in worship is even more amazing when we tie it to the succeeding centuries of church history. If the a cappella interpretation were not really important, we would expect to see that restriction fade quickly with the passing of years. Instead we search in vain for instruments in church worship through more than six hundred years of church history. The non-instrument position was so well established in people's consciousness that the very word "a cappella" meant singing "in the style of the church." If instruments in worship were either approved or a matter of indifference, the historical evidence does not support that interpretation. The voice of early church history does not refute a cappella singing, but rather reinforces it.

Once again when we step back and look at instruments, we see that history has established a trend line in worship. Where instruments are introduced into worship, the participation in singing of many worshippers tends to decline. It seems doubtful this is what God had in mind.

What About Clapping?

The practice of clapping has been introduced into worship and has stirred some opposition. It may be that some object simply because we have not traditionally done it, and its unfamiliarity makes them uncomfortable. It is easy to believe that our uneasy feelings suggest a lack of scriptural approval.

People did clap their hands in the Old Testament. Psalm 47:1 says, "Clap your hands, all people! Shout to God with loud songs of joy." Figurative language pictures even inanimate things such as the "floods" (Psalm 98:8) and the "fields" (Isaiah 55:12) clapping their hands.

The New Testament record, however, is a different matter. We look in vain for even a slight mention of clapping in worship by Christians. With no specific guidance from New Testament documents, we are left to work with general principles. Clapping in our society usually means approval and affirmation. When honoring or affirming our appreciation, we often applaud. No doubt many congregations have applauded someone who did notable Christian service. Is a baptismal service a suitable occasion for clapping? Only the context of each society can determine that. As always, good taste is difficult to legislate, but decorum should permeate our public worship.

Clapping during the singing of a song is a more troublesome matter to clarify. Clapping has rhythmic value, but adds nothing to the meaning of the song being sung. Perhaps clapping is objected to because of its association with religious groups who believe in present day miracles on command, latter day revelations apart from the Bible, and TV evangelists who glibly tell audiences to "give God a hand." Clapping seems innocent enough, but we ought to be very careful before we thoughtlessly incorporate every cultural expression into our worship. Although this may identify us more closely with our culture, we must remember the New Testament model leans toward the use of the word "Amen" as a means of affirmation. "Amen" tends to be an approval of the message, not the messenger, no matter how polished his performance. Obviously, decorum in worship would suggest we should not uncritically import all the expressions of approval used in other settings. Although some things may be culturally acceptable at entertainment events, they are decidedly out of place at worship. Surely there are limits we must observe.

What About Lifting Up Holy Hands?

Should we lift up holy hands when we pray? The New Testament specifies no precise posture for prayer. David, Daniel, and Jesus all give us examples and encouragement to kneel before our Maker. (See Psalm 95:6, Daniel 6:10, and Luke 22:41.) In the parable of Luke 18, both the Pharisee and the publican stood to pray. Lifting up holy hands in prayer is something Paul mentions in I Timothy 2:8ff. Lifting the hands can be nothing more than a figurative way of saying we ought to pray. The context of Paul's remarks suggest he is instructing us more about the hands being "holy" than he is binding the "lifting" of hands upon us. Jesus' parable of the Pharisee and the publican in Luke 18:9ff approves the publican who would not even lift up his eyes to heaven. The inference is that the Pharisee did lift his eyes to heaven. Admittedly, some of the early church fathers indicate that it was the practice of some to raise their hands in prayer. Once again, lifting the hands reminds us of the practice of some religious groups who rely more heavily on the direct intervention of the Holy Spirit for guidance than on the reading of God's inspired word. Such an association makes it difficult for some to accept the lifting of hands. Even so, no matter what our preference, we must be cautious about being dogmatic in demanding a particular posture in prayer.

What About the Use of Drama in Worship?

Amidst a sea of change in the church, new expressions of worship have risen. The use of drama to convey the message is one of those new expressions. Perhaps it is incorrect to call it new, because God's teachers have often used drama. Samuel had the task of revealing to King Saul that God had rejected him from being king over Israel. After delivering his message, Samuel turned to leave, and Saul grabbed Samuel's robe and tore it. Seizing the dramatic moment, Samuel took advantage of the non-verbal action and reinforced God's point by saying, "The Lord has torn the kingdom of Israel from you this day" (I Samuel 15:27,28). When some of the disciples were urging Paul not to go to Jerusalem because of the danger, the prophet Agabus made the same point by dramatically binding himself hand and foot, and then telling Paul this is what was going to happen to him (Acts 21:11). We should also remember that at the Passover meal Jesus made his point about humble service by washing the feet of the disciples during a dramatic moment in the upper room (John 13). We must realize, that the Lord's Supper is a continuing drama which is played out in our worship every Sunday.

We ought to remember, however, that in these biblical examples the teacher reinforced the drama with clear words of teaching. Characteristically, the message was not left unspoken nor ambiguous; to the contrary, the words and drama worked together to convey the same message. If we dramatize, we can certainly do no less. Surely we must recognize that drama is at best the handmaiden of preaching, but it cannot replace preaching as God's chosen method to deliver His message.

What About Different Worship Styles?

For years we have been accustomed to having multiple worship services in order to accommodate larger crowds, but both services usually had the same style of worship. Due to the influence of the church growth movement, another purpose has been added for having more than one worship period. In our efforts to appeal to the unsaved outsiders, church growth theory suggests we ought to have a "user friendly" service; which is to say, one in which strangers would be comfortable. Now some churches accommodate not only the outsiders, but also church members who prefer a different worship style. For this reason, some churches have made a conscious effort to make the two periods different.

One service is for the long-time church members. It has been given titles, such as "traditional" or "heritage" service. Things in it are left very much as they have traditionally been done. The same songs and the same order of worship are used to keep the worship experience within the comfort level of veteran church members.

The other service, however, is designed to be sensitive to the needs of outsiders and those members who desire a new approach to worship. The music in it is consciously changed to fit the current style of music. The more formal dress codes are relaxed so that visitors can "come as they are." This service is given titles, such as "progressive" or "contemporary."

Although there are some obvious advantages to this separation, there is a subtle direction change involved. The assumption is that the church cannot be flexible enough for all to worship in the same style of service. It is likewise assumed that neither style preference can be moderated so that both can meet somewhere in the middle. By changing to two styles, we have recognized that the differences are irreconcilable and hardened into concrete.

Surely no one is so traditional that they must sing only songs written by songwriters who have been dead for years. We would hope that no one is so caught up in "what we have always done" that they would refuse to sing new songs, or to sing a song projected onto a screen.

On the other hand, we cannot conceive anyone being so committed to an immediate change agenda that they refuse to sing the old classic hymns. How can anyone contend that songs sung out of a book are inherently inferior to those written too recently to be in a book?

Would not a blend of these two styles be desirable? As long as we don't practice a kind of "in your face" attitude, surely all things are possible. With a little Christian forbearance, all of us ought to be able to worship together in a service which uses anything biblical and reverent toward God. To do otherwise seems to encourage a divisive attitude.

In conclusion, we need to realize that all things we have been discussing are important to the Lord's church, but they are not the core of what will make our worship better. Changing the worship rituals and altering the style of music will never solve our worship problems. Better central planning of the worship and better performers will never touch the problem of spiritual worship. Whatever we change to make things "fresh" will, with time, become stale and drift into being just a new traditional form.

True worship arises from the heart and is dependent on the spiritual preparation of the worshipper. It was David who said, "Thy word have I hid in my heart that I might not sin against you" (Psalm 119:11). Psalm 24:3,4 describes the picture of a true worshipper as someone who has "clean hands and a pure heart." Psalm 100 sketches a picture of the worshipper as someone who "makes a joyful noise to the Lord...comes into his presence with singing...... enters his gates with thanksgiving and his courts with praise" (vs. 1,2,4). David says the secret to approaching God is being prepared for worship. Until we tap into that secret, we will not solve the riddle of lifeless worship. We can work our way around the problem by hiring good performers, but the ultimate answer is better spiritual preparation by each worshipper.

A blind lady in a retirement home once told me the story of a little girl who laughed at an inappropriate time during a class. When the teacher asked her for an explanation, the little girl said, "Teacher, I guess I just smiled so big that my smile busted!" Each one of us needs to come to the worship assembly of the church so full of love for God's awesomeness and reverence for His word that we are quite literally bursting with the desire to praise Him. When each one of us enters worship with that kind of preparation, then and only then will our worship become what He wants it to be.

God wants a praise team, but he wants one so big that every worshipper is on it!

Questions

1. In your opinion, why does so much controversy tend to swirl around public worship versus private devotional worship?
2. If we had to give up either worshipping in "spirit" or worshipping in "truth," which do you think it would be best to give up?
3. What is inherently wrong with making our worship a "perform-ance" versus a "participation?"
4. If worshippers can just listen to the prayer leaders and say "Amen," why couldn't they just listen to someone else sing for for them, and then say "Amen?"
5. Since a praise team of trained singers can do a better job of singing than the average worshipper, why not just let them do all the singing instead of just part of it?
6. If the apostle Paul's instructions about women keeping silent in worship does not mean that they should not take public leadership, what do you suppose it might mean?

7. History tells us the church did not use instrumental music in its worship for at least 600 to 1,000 years. What is the significance of that fact?
8. In your opinion, is having two worship services of differing worship styles going to bring worshippers inside each congregation closer together or put them further apart? Can you explain why you think your answer is true?
9. If you could divide responsibility for worship effectiveness between the individual worshippers and the planners/performers in worship, what do you think the percentage would be?
10. What could you personally do to make public worship better where you worship?

6. A Changing World, An Unchanging God

Allan McNicol

Those who have been around in churches of Christ for some time are conversant with the cry of alarm sounded by some preachers, *"Brethren, we are drifting!"* There is something soothing about things staying exactly the same, particularly in religion, where the verities which we hold are supposed to be eternal. In a world where personal and communal security is increasingly at risk, it is good to know that some things never change.

And yet, as the pre-Socratic philosopher Heraclitus noted by his action in standing in the current of the river, change is an essential factor in the very nature of things. The same water that touched the body of Heraclitus would never pass by that very spot again. To paraphrase the old hymn, *"Change and decay in all around I see."*

How can the church hold to the eternal verities in a world where the pace of change never slows but seems to be in a constant state of acceleration? After giving our lives to the building of a local church is there any assurance that what we labored to build will be around in a recognizable form in the next generation? Will the churches of Christ, as we have known them in the last half of the twentieth century, be a recognizable entity, let alone a dynamic force in the next century? It is fears like these that fuel the widespread *dis-ease*, widely shared by thoughtful brethren, that indeed we are drifting.

84

The Issue of Identity at Home

Put in another mode, what we are discussing here is a question of identity. The rapid pace of cultural changes in American society has overtaken the churches of Christ. As with so many of the institutions in our society such as government, higher education, the media, and big business, the churches, including the churches of Christ, have suffered a certain erosion in the intensity of their power to attract and maintain the strong allegiance of their membership.

A fact that generally has not been appreciated by church leaders in the Restoration Movement is that the widespread disaffection of the sixties generation with organized religion, experienced among the Methodists, Presbyterians, and Episcopalians, has also had a strong impact upon us. Over and over again we hear people of this generation say, "Brand loyalty means nothing to me." Many people who have this sentiment remain relatively active and observant in the large churches of the South-West and Mid-South because these assemblies have multiple staffs and extensive services that are attractive because they meet needs; but as soon as such folk move to the West or the North-East they look for new church homes that provide similar services. Almost certainly these are not found in a Restorationist church because such churches do not have the membership to support these services. Thus, in large numbers, such people go elsewhere and abandon our heritage.

Such a state of affairs has tended to produce a series of responses spanning the extremes of the spectrum. Some would see that this apparent decline in the level of allegiance to the centrality of the Restoration plea is a sign that the plea, as traditionally understood, is no longer valid. In this context change is welcomed as an agent that is breaking up the moribund structure of the institutional church out of which, it is hoped, that some totally new reality may emerge. Change is encouraged for the sake of change. Thus, such gestures as removing the local congregation from historical confessional ties (becoming generic evangelical by calling oneself Oak Ridge Church rather than Oak Ridge Church of Christ, or sending a preacher to a convention of evangelicals rather than the church-related college lectureship) are strongly encouraged and welcomed. It is argued that only when we shed

85

ourselves of the confining baggage of the institutional "Church of Christ," especially in our large urban areas, will we have the credibility to carry out evangelism on a sustained basis - especially among those to whom brand name is no longer relevant. In other words, to be a non-denominational Christian is to reform or even abandon the Restoration Tradition.

On the other hand, of course, there are those at the other end of the spectrum who would retreat into a world where the forms of the church of the first part of the twentieth century are frozen in time. Resistance to change in such small matters as the maintenance of a particular translation of the Bible, or a particular form of hymnody, is set up almost as a test of fellowship. At least in these churches a particular confessional identity is maintained. But to keep change at a minimum a terrible price has to be paid. Such fellowships are not much different than the Amish and other similar Mennonites. They set up acceptance of a particular culture (often the American rural south) as a pre-condition to acceptance of the gospel. It is very clear to this writer that such churches are no more successful than the Amish in their rate of evangelism. Indeed, such congregations are suffering a steady pace of attrition and are having great difficulty in passing the faith on to their children who view their ultra-conservatism as too confining. Such congregations will continue to operate at the margins of both the brotherhood and society.

What we must do is eschew these extreme responses to the current situation in the brotherhood and develop a more viable doctrine of change. We must ask some hard questions about how we can maintain our integrity as a theological tradition and, at the same time, become once again a vibrant growing fellowship. We must find a way to accommodate gradual change. In today's highly charged cultural environment that will not be an easy task.

The Issue of Identity Overseas

Paradoxically, while these developments have been taking place in North America, a very different state of affairs has begun to emerge overseas. In the last forty to fifty years the churches of Christ have been engaged in an unprecedented expansion of mission activity throughout the world. To be sure, valid questions may be raised with respect to the quality of preparation and competence of many who were engaged in this enterprise. Nevertheless, despite the incontestable fact that our mission enterprise

86

could have been better planned and executed with less of a human toll taken on the families who were often sent to the field ill-prepared, much of the work has borne considerable fruit. Almost without our knowing it (and it still remains one of the best kept secrets of the religious world) the churches of Christ have become a world-wide fellowship. Each Lord's Day people within our fellowship in over one hundred countries meet to praise the Lord. Probably by about the year 2000 there will be more members of churches of Christ outside of North America than within. In both Africa and Asia (mainly India) there will soon be in excess of a million members.

Already, in some of these places there are strong regional places of influence with their own indigenous leadership and theological training centers. New ideas and methodologies are bound to emanate from and proliferate within these centers. The potential for the emergence of diverse perspectives is almost unlimited. The question must be raised, "If the churches of Christ in North America manifest a certain unclarity about their identity, what will happen when this unclarity, inevitably, is projected in other places of the world?" If we are confused about our ecclesiology in America, how are we going to be of help to the thousands that are obeying the gospel and becoming members of the churches of Christ in such far away places as Eastern Europe, the former Soviet Union, India, and Ghana? Can a fellowship based on strict congregational polity operate on a world-wide basis?

Those among us who embrace change for the sake of change as an antidote to the perceived legalism of the church of earlier generations may well contemplate this reality. To act willingly to promote change for its own sake, as is done in certain progressive quarters today, given the present state of unclarity about our identity, is like pouring gasoline on a fire. What is needed in the contemporary church both in America and overseas is a common vision for an ecclesiology which promotes stability in the midst of change. Amongst all of our diversity world-wide, what holds us together as a fellowship, and how is that connected to the concept of Restoration which has been the raison d'être of our movement over the years? Only when we come to grips with such theological questions as these will we be able to know who we are and what is the legacy we are passing along to the successive generations. Beyond doubt, now is the time for us to take inventory and assess what is our common identity.

We are historically naive if we consider that the capacity to handle change is a peculiar modern concern. There is no question that the people of God who stand at the center of the biblical story had to wrestle with the same problem. Thus, before we discuss at some length how we may articulate appropriately what our identity is today, it may be helpful for contemporary believers to see how our forebearers in biblical times wrestled with this issue. How can our normative story give us some clues as to how we can approach this daunting reality of continuing change with confidence and integrity?

Specifically, the issue of change in the biblical period can be illuminated by understanding the role of God as the One who is characterized by giving and keeping promises. Very early in the biblical story in Genesis 1-12, God makes a series of promises to his creatures. Despite the fact that his people took many detours from his way and encountered terrible vicissitudes, God kept promise by not abandoning them. Throughout the entire history of the people of Israel there remains one constant - God is the one who is faithful to his promises. Divine constancy amid bewildering human unpredictability is the theological prism wherein the Bible treats the issue of change.

Frequently, the people of God today become discouraged and lose heart because the tenor of trends in our culture seems to be in the direction of a thorough repudiation of biblical principles. Many in the church in the face of these cultural factors have become functional atheists and no longer have confidence in the New Testament promises that the God of Jesus Christ will fully and decisively reclaim the world for his sovereignty and purpose. Thus, an examination of several key instances in the Bible of how God has kept his promises, despite all appearances to the contrary, can be a vital source of encouragement.

Central to the biblical theme of God as the One who keeps promise are the several foundational promises made to Abraham. The giving of these promises and the way that they are brought to a fulfillment is a mini-story within the greater biblical story that has much to teach us on the subject with respect to how God can use change for the fulfillment of his divine purpose. We learn, time and time again, that situations arise whereby there seems to be no way in which God's promises can be fulfilled - and yet - a new reality in history comes into focus that assures the continuity of his promise until its eventual fulfillment. On the basis of the understanding that God may be at work in a similar way today, by studying the story, we can have confidence that he will bring to full realization the promises he has made to the church.

The macro-structure of the biblical promises to Abraham ought to be noted. God promised that from his descendants he would create a great nation (Genesis 12:1-3); and from out of these descendants of Abraham he would bring great blessings to all the peoples of the world (Genesis 18:18;22:18). These promises function as a golden thread that weaves together a good portion of the biblical story. Despite the various twists and turns that the story of the people of God (descendants of Abraham) takes after Abraham, the promises remain constant until they are fulfilled with the blessings being made available to all people through the coming of Christ. In Matthew 28:18-20, upon God's vindication of Jesus by his resurrection from the dead, the risen Lord calls for his claim of all authority to be taken to all nations - the very words used in Genesis 18:18; 22:18. In the span of a few short years, the promises given to Abraham, which had been tenaciously held over hundreds of years, were fulfilled. Through the proclamation of the gospel, a great nation of people (the church), the recipient of the blessings, was now in existence throughout the Greco-Roman world. As Paul wrote to the converts in Galatia,

> *For you are all one in Christ Jesus.*
> *And if you are Christ's, then you are*
> *Abraham's offspring, heirs according*
> *to promise (Galatians 3:28-29).*

Israel had undergone many changes since the call of Abraham. It had been both obedient and disobedient to him. But God had remained faithful to his promises. In a totally unexpected way, for the people of the first century (through the death and resurrection of Christ), God had brought his promises to fulfillment.

Indeed, this mode of God fulfilling his purposes in a totally unexpected way is also a feature of the mini-structure of how God kept faithful to his promises to Abraham.

Even before the death of Abraham the promise stood in mortal peril when Abraham was tested with the call to sacrifice his first-born, the son of promise, Isaac, as a sign of God's claim (Genesis 22:1-18). With a wonderful economy of narration the story unfolds, and it appears that the promise would be nullified; but, at the last moment with the provision of the ram caught in the thicket by its horns, Isaac is preserved and the promise is maintained. The account ends with a ringing affirmation of the promise (Genesis 22:15-18).[1]

And so the various descendants of Abraham begin their march across the stage of history. The book of Genesis ends with the amazing story of Joseph, a later descendant of Abraham, who was thrown by his own brothers into a pit to die, and then sold into slavery (Genesis 37:24-28), only to emerge as second to the Pharaoh in Egypt.

And again, after Joseph, there is the equally wondrous story of Moses, the one destined to lead the descendants of Abraham out of slavery, being placed in the most fragile situation of having his cradle set in the Nile only to be rescued by an Egyptian princess.[2] In such unexpected ways God kept his promises.

Retaining our Identity in the Midst of Change

We are now ready to return to the issue which we raised in the opening pages of this chapter. Given the tremendous diversity operative within churches of Christ throughout the world, how can we come to grips with the riddle of our identity? Confusion about who we are propels some to demand nothing short of a repudiation of our Restorationist heritage while others gallantly refuse to admit that any aspect of our ecclesiology ought to change. How can we respond to the challenges of the time and not come apart at the seams?

The critics of Restorationism continue to have a field day pointing out that the churches of Christ have always been a contentious fellowship and have been characterized by a propensity for factionalism and division. Our study of God's keeping promise with another contentious and unpredictable community (the children of Abraham) reminds us that we do not have to be perfect in order for God to use us as the appropriate vehicles for his purposes. Thus, we have grounds to believe that God has not given up on us. Nevertheless, it is highly questionable whether the churches of Christ can remain for long a viable fellowship without having a certain common understanding of the constants that constitute their special identity. In these concluding pages we wish to venture a brief sketch of what that identity consists and how a fresh re-appropriation of our Restorationist heritage can provide us with the resources to maintain the constants within the current period of turbulence.

The issue of change poses certain problems to the concept of Restorationism. By definition, Restorationists tend to look for an ideal or perfect model for the church through some process of study of the account of the origins of the Christian Faith in the New Testament. There is a natural tendency to consider this model as timeless and almost eternal. It is often argued that anyone can or should understand this simple changeless pattern; and any movement away from it is likely to represent a decline or falling away. The ideal is always to return to the perfect model.

Thus, within the Restoration Movement there is a certain ambivalence towards change. Change is necessary if it involves a return to the perfect model. But change signifies apostasy if it involves a "falling away" or retreat from the ideal.

If there is broad agreement within the brotherhood with respect to the nature of the ideal model for the church, this under-standing of the dynamics of change is manageable. This seemed to be the case in the nineteenth and first half of the twentieth centuries. For such diverse reasons as the growth of churches of Christ beyond a homogeneous rural South, the influence of biblical criticism, and the secularism of the wider culture, this state of affairs no longer exists. In this context change becomes a much more problematic proposition; as we have already noted, for some it is embraced, almost like a mantra, as the necessary pre-requisite for reform while, for others, it is the mark of unfaithfulness. Thus, our understanding of Restorationism must be clarified.

While the scriptures are normative for our faith and practice, generally most of us have come to realize the truth of the dictum, "we cannot go home again." As a result of the passing of the years we cannot repristinate the customs and social structures of the first century church; women do not wear head coverings in the assembly, and we do not give counsel to men as to how they should keep their slaves in subjection. In the course of time, fundamental changes in the nature of our social existence do take place. There are major impediments and limits on what we can restore from the past. We must be prepared to nuance what we mean when we claim to be a Restorationist or restitutionist fellowship.

Here an observation of John Howard Yoder can be helpful.[3] Yoder has argued that Restorationists have tended to overestimate their ability to dig out of the pages of the New Testament a perfect homogeneous model for the church, down to the last detail.

Actually, even in the first century, there was a tremendous amount of innovation and change going on within the church (viz. the missionary activities of Paul). What is necessary for the believing community today, which accepts the normativity of the scriptures, is to determine what were the grounds and warrants that were used to justify these changes both in the biblical period and in later centuries.[4] Have the basic constants that were manifested in the church in the apostolic period been undermined by the emergence of other trends and patterns for doing things? Whether we like it or not, change takes place. What is important is how we assess this change. Yoder argues that rather than assess change and development by some abstract blueprint, it is fruitful to consider that the gospel is eternal and that from the beginning there were certain fields of constancy within basic Christian doctrines which from time to time were subject to subversion by alien perspectives?[5] It is the duty of the church to ask that when change takes place, is it in keeping with the constants of the gospel or is it being pushed by some other alien perspective?[6] This proposal is congruent with Restorationist principles but still allows for a greater degree of flexibility and change as the church lives in history and as it awaits the consummation.

The Issue of Fellowship

We have suggested that change is inevitable, and that the only real issue is how it should be assessed. We have also argued that the appropriate way to assess change is to determine whether development in the life of the church remains faithful to the basic constants of the gospel found in the scriptures. For Restorationists this has proven to be a sensitive area because it has involved the issue of fellowship. The issue has usually been framed in how much diversity in doctrine and practice can be tolerated within a fellowship before principled people are called to separate and withdraw. In this connection, certain brethren invoking 2 John 9-11 have tended to define the constants for their faith and practice by means of a checklist approach. If the demands of this checklist, which they intuit from their peculiar philosophical framework, are not met, they have been prepared to cause fractures within the brotherhood.[7]

Over the past decade, the author of this article has advocated in his writings a more functional approach to fellowship that takes into consideration a realistic understanding of the dynamics of change.[8] The thrust of this approach centers in an attempt to visit again certain areas of the faith in order to determine more precisely what was the intent of Jesus in bringing into being a new fellowship in Israel, upon what grounds was that fellowship maintained in the early church, and in terms of the development of ecumenical Christianity, what is the distinct emphasis of the Restoration Movement in this area?

The intent of these reflections has been to underscore the proposition that Restorationism, properly conceived, is no anachronism but, on the contrary, can make a viable statement to the religious world. To conclude these reflections on the subject of change, I will again emphasize the chief points of my position.

Jesus' Creation of a New Fellowship

Central to the ministry of Jesus was the conviction that a dramatic new era (the coming dynamic kingdom of God) was about to burst forth in Israel. He was absolutely convinced that God was bringing vital renewal and saw himself as the ambassador on behalf of this reality. He appointed the twelve as the vanguard of this new era of the restored Israel; and since this era would be inclusive of all Israel, during regular meals with the twelve, those on the edges of Israelite society were invited to dine with the teacher as a foretaste of the coming blessed time (Matthew 11:19; Luke 15:1-32). Central to the Christian understanding of fellowship was Jesus' action of grace and forgiveness shown to the marginalized at these meals. The Gospels leave us in no doubt that Jesus' activities at the table were seen as metaphors for the actions of a loving God who was in the process of decisively reclaiming for himself the whole creation. It is noticeable that it was the enemies of Jesus who argued that God cared only for a certain elect group of special people who wore special badges of religiosity. It is suggestive to ponder who may be their analogues today. Believers must not forget that it is in the initiative of the heart of a loving God who suffers with his creation and seeks to restore his relationship with it, that the true sense of identity for the Christian community is found; and in turn, this forms the basis for *koinonia* or fellowship.

Thus it was no accident that Jesus found himself at the table with the twelve in the last hours before his death. He explains to them that representatively he must suffer the fate of his people in order to save them from destruction. He offered the bread and the cup to them so that in an anticipatory sense they would receive the benefits of his death which inaugurated the new covenant. (Matthew 26: 26-29 and parr.) At this meal the concept of fellowship had been deepened. Jesus had set the stage for the future time after his death. All who later would come into fellowship with him would come to his table; and there, upon pledging to continue his obedient life in the world, they would receive his benefits.

Maintained in Fellowship

At the heart of the early Christian gatherings in the churches scattered throughout the eastern part of the Roman Empire, were the meetings around the table. There the story (gospel) was told, and there the rites of entry (baptism) into the community and fellowship with the risen Lord (Lord's Supper) were practiced. It was in the continuity of the proclamation of the gospel in word and rite that the early church spread from its origin in a basic Jewish setting into Gentile areas. There were many changes in the Christian movement ranging from different modes of presentation of the word to the emergence of a variety of organizational structures. But one central reality remained - the proclamation of the means of salvation (Christ) and the reception of that salvation in baptism and the table. These were the constants in the time of rapid changes and developments in the first century. Anything that pertained to the means of salvation or its reception needed to be guarded carefully; in other areas there was considerable room for diversity. Restorationists who look to this era as normative may well find here the essential clue to handle change.

The Legitimacy of our Fellowship Today

By the second century the church had become very concerned that as development took place it maintain the truth of its apostolic witness and fellowship. By codifying a certain set of writings used in worship and teaching in the second century church, Christianity forever established the principle that all subsequent developments must be submitted to the control of scripture (i.e. the Canon of the Old and New Testament). In due time ecumenical Christianity of the later centuries developed the marks of apostolicity, oneness, catholicity, and holiness as the marks of a true fellowship.

Since that time various communions have interpreted those marks in their own particular ways. For example, in the Roman

Catholic Church, to be in apostolic fellowship is to accept the authority of the bishop of Rome and the teaching from the magisterium of the Catholic Church which, it is argued, has continuity from the time of the apostles.

Churches of Christ can also accept these four basic marks as expressions of a legitimate fellowship. However, they would interpret them in a very different way. They presume there is one faith, and it is taught in the churches throughout the world (one and catholic). But they understand that to be apostolic is to preach the same means of salvation taught by the apostles (the gospel of Christ) and mode of reception of it (baptism and the Lord's Supper). Finally, to be holy is to manifest holiness not in the sense imputed by the headship of Christ, as in Catholicism or much of Protestantism, but as it is lived out in a way of life which manifests in the present the divine holiness in a peculiar lifestyle separate from the world.

If we perceive the marks of the church in this way, we will be able to maintain in common our traditional identity and, at the same time, have something worthwhile to say to the wider world of ecumenical Christianity. We will have our feet grounded in the apostolic gospel but still have the flexibility to accommodate change. These are the constants we are to maintain within diversity. This is the course we must steer between the shackles of legalism and the pull of every fad and change that comes along the way.

Conclusion

In this chapter we have addressed the problems that rapid cultural change poses to a Restorationist fellowship such as the churches of Christ. Besides acknowledging the obvious that change is a fundamental reality of life, we have explored the different attitudes in the church toward change. Change can be regarded negatively if it leads the church away from the constants of the gospel. It has been regarded as a positive if it involves admission of error and promotes a commitment to come into fuller union with Christ.

In a climate where change in and of itself is invoked as a universal answer to a perceived malaise in the church, there is a great need for general agreement on the criteria needed to assess the nature of that change. Otherwise our fellowship will be in chaos. The biblical teaching of a God who keeps promise enables us to have hope that we will not be overwhelmed by current issues and that a framework will be found to solve these problems. In the

meanwhile, while leaders in the church should welcome constructive suggestions for change, we should remember that the final
reality is not change but the truth of the gospel.

Questions

1. Do you see the witness of churches of Christ having a decreased or increased impact in your community?
2. To what extent is cultural change in the wider society having an impact on the church?
3. Do you think that the churches of Christ have lost the sixties generation?
4. What is fueling the desire of those in the church who agree that we must have change?
5. Can a congregation that sets as deliberate policy not to change from the tradition grow in members?
6. Do you think that the rapid growth of the church overseas will have an impact on the life of your local church?
7. How does the category of promise give us a handle on the biblical teaching about change?
8. Give examples of how God has kept promise in the Bible.
9. Is there anything unusual about how God's promises were fulfilled in the Bible?
10. In your judgment, were the changes that occurred among the people of God in the biblical period positive or negative in scope?
11. Within the Restoration Movement, when is change considered a positive factor and when a negative factor?
12. How do you determine the constants that the church cannot surrender as it exists in time?
13. Why is the issue of fellowship a difficult issue for the churches of Christ?
14. How would you summarize the author's position on the fellowship issue?
15. Despite certain misgivings about change, what is there to be confident about concerning the church as it enters the next century?

7. *Church Growth: Nightmare or Dream?*

Don Vinzant

Prologue

Do you know a story like this?

Michael Scott, dynamic young pulpit minister, at Lakeview North Church of Christ, wanted the congregation to be more exciting and felt that God put that yearning in his heart. Not that Lakeview North was all bad. His wife, Meredith, and his two elementary school daughters were happy there. Two other ministers were on staff. Local evangelism needed more ministerial participation, but the foreign missions program was making progress in Latin America and Eastern Europe. With six hundred members and nine elders, this fifty-year old congregation had seen an increase in Sunday School attendance, membership roll, offerings and building facilities over the years. Lakeview North, an Edge City on the northern suburban fringe of a large southwestern city, had profited population-wise at the expense of troubled, older neighborhoods of a large neighbor city to the south. In recent years the congregation was enjoying transfer growth as well.

Michael was looking for something to make his church livelier, bigger and not so traditional. He was as restless as several of his contemporary preacher friends. They had begun to hear of Church Growth principles, . . . of Carl George and the Megachurch,[1] ....of Bill Hybels and Willow Creek Community Church,[2].... of Rick Warren and Saddleback Valley Community Church.[3] Michael and his preacher buddies were impressed. They began to order tapes, attend seminars and seemed to be competing to make their churches more like what they were hearing about.

The approach was to re-package the church to appeal to the seventy six million members of the Baby Boomer generation, born from 1946-1964.[4] Preaching-style, image, worship - - everything - - needed to be changed to appeal to the Boomers.

Since the Boomer-targeted marketing strategy had brought stunning results in Southern California and in the evangelical neighborhood around Wheaton and South Barrington, Illinois,[5] Michael pushed hard for change, . . . very hard, indeed. At first, the elders went along because they liked Michael and believed in him and Meredith and were crazy about their little girls. But, then some of the more mature members began to resist the changes. They preferred songs with more melody. They liked easy-to-read song books rather than overhead projections. The music purists thought that worship was now resembling fireside devotionals at a children's camp session. Further, the scriptural preaching content was greatly diminished and the time given to stories increased. (One woman, on her way out, said, "Preacher, you need a sermon to go with your story.") Seeing that Michael would not relent in pushing change, some members left to find a more familiar worship format. Suddenly, it seemed that Lakeview North was dying from change.[6]

Michael asked himself, "Is there more involved in Church Growth than I have heard?" He began re-examining what was happening at Lakeview North. Had his attitude been right toward his brethren? He asked himself, "Have I been disrespecting my own heritage?" A conservative academic at college lectureship said that some in the church were becoming "xenocentric." What did he mean? Michael looked up the word. It means "turning against your own people and valuing that which is foreign and alien to your own culture." Maybe some of the members who had warned him against micro-mimicking the huge denominational churches were right: . . . maybe the answer was not to scuttle everything you had been doing.

Was there a way for Michael to position his congregation for the future without crash-landing it or burying it in bankruptcy? Was there a way to go forward without losing so many solid members? Was Church Growth more complex than he had thought? Given what he had been saying, was there an honorable way for him to remain a minister in churches of Christ? Should he follow those preacher-friends who push to drop Christ's name from the church and replace it with "Community?" Would he end up starting one more of those little chapel groups in a rented building?

Or, would he go into secular work and give up preaching the gospel?

The above is a lightly-fictionalized account of what is already happening in some congregations. The part of the story that does not ring true, I am sadly afraid, is the part about Michael stopping to reconsider church growth principles before it was too late for him and for Lakeview North.

This chapter intends to present a balanced view of church growth. It hopes to show a way a church can prepare for the future without dying from change.

I Believe in Church Growth[7]

Those are my feelings as well as the title of a useful book by Eddie Gibbs. *Church Growth* capital letters refers here to the Church Growth Movement: its leaders, authors, its major unique insights, its books and institutions, especially Donald McGavran and his influence since 1955. In small letters "church growth" refers to what gifted church planters/builders have done since Pentecost.

It is only fair that I let you know my own feelings about Church Growth. I believe in it. I have endeavored to practice these principles for many years. I have been a minister in the "mainline" churches of Christ since 1957. The rapid church growth in the book of Acts, and in some contemporary congregations of my acquaintance has appealed to me greatly. Throughout my life's work, I have been a part of some seventeen congregations including having helped plant several congregations in Brazil as a part of the Sao Paulo Mission Team for twelve years (1961-1973). It is my privilege now to preach at the nine-hundred member Edmond Church of Christ and to teach graduate level courses in "Church Growth 5563" at Oklahoma Christian where I have been teaching since 1989.

My earliest involvement with the Church Growth Movement came when I first learned of Donald McGavran in 1961 from fellow missionary, Robert L. Humphries, Jr. who had written a masters' thesis[8] at ACU including insights from Roland Allen and Dr. McGavran. McGavran's early work, *Bridges of God*, grew out of his thirty years of work in India as a Disciples' missionary, educator, and hospital administrator. Church Growth interest was inspired by Methodist missionary J. Waskom Pickett.[9] These men cut through the fog of promotional literature to ask whether and how churches grew or declined. McGavran argued that major resources for missions ought to be deployed among the most receptive "peoples." He observed that "peoples" (families, class, tribes, etc.) shared their faith along natural webs or friend/family networks. The gospel moves easiest when converts do not have to cross cultural, linguistic, social, racial, or ethnic barriers. After completing decades of missionary work in India, McGavran created a Church Growth Institute, first in Eugene, Oregon, then moved it to Fuller Seminary in Pasadena, California. He invited experienced missionaries to study with him and then share their findings about growth in their chosen fields.

In 1965, the Church Growth research studies from Brazil (where the Sao Paulo Mission Team was working) had begun to emerge. *New Patterns of Church Growth in Brazil*[10] was written by William Read, a Presbyterian missionary. Read's observations into demographics in Sao Paulo suburbs were insightful and helpful.

I am honored to have been able to work with the Sao Paulo team where we practiced the best mission strategy we knew to win that world-class city. I have attempted, for nearly thirty years, to stay current with Church Growth research.[11]

In the early 1970's in the United States, Dr. Elmer Towns began publicizing bus ministries, then fueling dramatic attendance statistics at Independent Baptist churches. Other kinds of churches also launched bus ministries. His books on fast-growing churches first came to my attention through Joe Barnett, then minister at Broadway Church of Christ in Lubbock, Texas. I met Dr. Towns and suggested how mutually beneficial it would be for him and the Fuller Church Growth people to be in contact. This could assist his domestic research and enlarge the Church Growth thought at Fuller which then worked in foreign missions. Dr. Towns later went to Fuller and received his second doctorate there. Church Growth began to receive the cross-pollination of insights from overseas, as well as from the United States.

The respected foundational writers in Church Growth have always argued that more is involved than amassing statistics.

Understanding Church Growth

In 1970, Dr. McGavran published his epochal *Understanding Church Growth*.[12] While his emphasis, at that time, was still toward foreign missions, practical applications to North American churches could be deduced.

He explained the importance of excellent and accurate records. Records on a mission field would show the age, sex, ethnic group, family network, social caste, date of conversion, method of outreach utilized, length of time from contact to conversion, etc. Good records of the follow-up or nurturing of each new convert also became important. Eventually, analysis can reveal lessons that influence further work to make it more fruitful.[13] Nonexistent, incomplete or haphazard records grievously handicap those who would attempt to evaluate a specific work or method of outreach. Yet, with all this, the respected writers in Church Growth have always argued that more is involved than merely amassing statistics.

McGavran explained that a church can grow in three ways (biological, conversion, transfer in), and it can decline in three ways (biological, reversion, transfer out). This is illustrated in chart 1. While this information may seem quite basic, it must be admitted that some church leaders in the United States seem not to note the difference between growth by transfer of membership and conversion growth ("swelling" vs. evangelism). McGavran shows a genuine concern for nurturing those who are converted.[14] Never was he interested only in numerical (quantitative) growth.

Chart 1

HOW CHURCHES GROW AND DECLINE

Plus	Minus
BIOLOGICAL	BIOLOGICAL
CONVERSION	REVERSION
TRANSFER IN	TRANSFER OUT

Later, it remained for one of McGavran's disciples, Peter Wagner, to address more fully the application of Church Growth analysis to the North American church scene. Wagner listed "Seven Vital Signs of a Healthy Church."[15] These essential signs can be paraphrased as follows:

1. A minister who is a possibility thinker and whose dynamic leadership has been used to catalyze the entire church into action for growth.
2. A well-mobilized membership which has discovered, has developed, and is using all the spiritual gifts for growth.

3. A church big enough to provide the range of services that meet the needs and expectations of its members.
4. The proper balance of the dynamic relationship between celebration, congregation, and cell.
5. A membership drawn primarily from one homogenous unit.
6. Evangelistic methods that are proved to make disciples.
7. Priorities arranged in biblical order.

Wagner also, candidly listed eight church diseases[16] which can blight the life and growth of a congregation:

1. Ethnikitis - If congregation's membership roll is out of sync with those who live in its neighborhood.
2. Old Age - If the neighborhood is dying out through people moving away and government or industrial complexes appropriating near-by land.
3. People Blindness - If membership is unable to see those around them who are prospects for conversion to Christ.
4. Hyper-cooperativism - If churches become so absorbed in working jointly in projects that they forget to work at evangelism.
5. Koinonitis - Church so interested in fellowshipping itself that it ignores the unchurched.
6. Sociological Strangulation - Facilities too crowded to allow more people to be brought in.
7. Arrested Spiritual Development - A church which is so immature spiritually that it can neither reach out nor maintain any growth that might come its way.
8. St. John's Syndrome - A church, like the one in Ephesus in Revelation 3, which quits practicing love, and indeed, forgets its first love.

These listings by Wagner from earlier books can be quite helpful as diagnostic starting points. One of the most thorough definitions of Church Growth as we are using the term is by Ebbie Smith in 1984.[17]

Balance: A Tried and Tested Formula for Church Growth[18]

Using the title from Dr. Ira North's insightful book, I would propose that healthy and balanced church growth involves four undergirding pillars; the **first** of which is holistic, well grounded growth.

First pillar: Holistic Growth

Holistic growth will involve four kinds of growth: quantitative, qualitative, organic and radiating.

1. *Quantitative Growth.* The book of Acts records numerous statements of quantifiable growth (2:41; 4:4; 6:1; 9:31, etc.). Some, however, have erroneously concluded that those interested in church growth only "count noses and nickels" to see how many people were there and how much they put in the offering. Authentic church growth cannot be solely preoccupied with numbers, for many non-Christian groups also grow quickly.

2. *Qualitative Growth.* Is each individual Christian growing in grace and knowledge? (II Peter 3:18) Are Christian virtues being added? Is the fruit of the Spirit evident in the lives of those who have been enumerated in a statistical chart? Without genuine Christ-mirroring conduct disciples never are the salt of the earth and light of the world.

3. *Organic Growth.* The church is called to be the body of Christ. As such it is united and expected to "....in all things grow up into him who is the Head, that is Christ. From him the whole body joined and held together by every supporting ligament, grows and builds itself up in love, as each part does its work" (Ephesians 4:15-16). This is every-member involvement and teamwork ministry.

4. **Radiating Growth.** Jesus taught, just prior to his ascension, that the word was to be preached in expanding, concentric circles of outreach (Acts 1:8). We cannot be satisfied with mere engorgement of local statistics - - certainly not for bragging purposes. We were reached by Jesus in order to reach out to others - - near and far.

Second Pillar: Recognize God

A **second pillar** is to recognize God as the enabling force in all four areas of growth. Paul shows plainly that the people involved are like laborers on a farm, and that "God made it grow" (I Corinthians 3:5, 7). As long as the glory and recognition are given to God, not men, we are on safe footing. When men are overly lifted up and praised and God is not given the glory, catastrophe follows (Acts 12:23). The recognition of God as the ultimate source of growth keeps church growth healthy.

Third Pillar: Love For The Brotherhood

A **third underlying pillar** is love for the brotherhood. This command by Peter (I Peter 2:17) seems to be sometimes forgotten in zeal to focus on a local church. A congregation can even grow at the expense of neighboring churches. Some of this may occur inevitably as one church is active and another languishing, but we must, as did Paul, have concern for all the churches (II Corinthians 11:28).

Fourth Pillar: Compassion

The **fourth pillar** of healthy church growth is compassion for the least of our own brethren. Some, in a commendable zeal to win those outside God's family, may hurt those already inside the family.   In an effort to avoid <u>ethnocentricity</u> (preoccupation for one's own kind), some may rush in <u>xenocentricity</u> (infatuation for those different and disrespect for one's own kind).

Holistic church growth will have all these undergirding pillars strong and symmetrical.

Donald McGavran said we need "church growth eyes." When that is united with a "church growth heart and head" we can have all systems up and going. Then, healthy church growth can result as God gives the growth.

God Wants It To Grow[19]

Dewayne Davenport, a minister for churches, chose that title for his early book, highly commended by McGavran. In the book Davenport, as have many others, cites benefits and advantages of Church Growth. Reading through Davenport and several recent works in the body of Church Growth literature, one can find at least nine benefits accruing to churches today from the Church Growth Movement:

1. It has served to call foreign missions first, and then North American churches back to the very purpose of our Lord, who is not willing that any should perish, but that all should come to salvation (II Peter 3:9). The Lord wants to find the lost, not merely to seek them. Church Growth reminds Christians, "It is not enough to carry on a perfunctory going through the motions evangelism - not enough to entertain a vague hope that just the presence of Christians or a passionless proclamation is enough." There must be a verdict theology.[20]   A harvest is out there to be reaped. Lost ones are to be "found, folded and fed." Church Growth asks, "How many are being added to Christ's church and how are they being won and from where?" This is not to satisfy purposeless curiosity; it is to make existing and future efforts wiser and more fruitful.

2. Church Growth has helped sharpen and refine the ways whereby helpful information and statistics can be gleaned, utilized

and shared. This moves the church away from satisfaction with imprecise impressions: "Who knows whether the church is growing or not?" When Church Growth insights are employed, there is solid data which can be compared with other factors in the life of that church or contrasted with other churches of comparable circumstances. This is neither to blame nor to exalt any individual or congregation, but to determine whether more souls could be won if more fruitful approaches were followed.

3. Church Growth has created a more optimistic climate for foreign missions and for North American churches by making known the bountiful harvest some are having as they attempt to bring people to Christ. Missionaries and ministers in non-growing circumstances can be motivated to greater hope for winning the winnable, even as others are doing. Church Growth reporting opens the windows to more information than had previously been available.

4. Church Growth studies show that there are identifiable times, circumstances, places and people-groups that offer ripe and receptive opportunities for a great ingathering of souls.

5. W. R. Shenk,[21] shows that the "re-reading" of church history underscoring the growth theme has released new energy which motivates a desire for a more productive harvest today.

6. Another unique benefit from Church Growth has been its utilization of the social sciences, statistical research and analysis to assist the church. The whole science of demographics makes available the newest trends.

7. Church Growth has utilized McGavran's and Pickett's[22] insight that the gospel spreads along webs and networks of family, clans, friendships, etc. This observation came to be called the "Homogeneous Unit Principle," that "people attract like people most fruitfully."

8. Church Growth honestly looks at statistics in every setting, regardless of how painful this might be. For example, McGavran in *Effective Evangelism*[23] points out that on a Labor Day Sunday in Southern California, newspapers reported that over two and a half million people frolicked on the beaches while less than half a million were in church that day.

9. Church Growth distinguishes between missionaries'/ministers' "promotional writing" of their prayers and dreams, and what has been the precise, documentable result. This process of "reality accounting" is indispensable in answering the question, "Where and how ought we to deploy our resources to reap the richest harvest for Christ?"

This partial list of benefits and advantages could become a longer list, but these serve to highlight values coming from Church Growth.

As if to remind one of the old adage, "There are two sides to every story," there have also been some serious criticisms leveled against Church Growth.

Church Growth Under Fire[24]

This book by Wayne Zunkel, deals with some of the arguments against the uncritical application of Church Growth.

A wide search through the literature examining Church Growth finds several criticisms being raised:

1. Church Growth is one dimensional. It looks only at quantitative growth. But the point should be faithfulness to God, not numerical growth. A big church is not necessarily, <u>ipso facto</u>, a good church.

2. Church Growth relies too much on social sciences. It is more sociology than theology. Attempting to use the social sciences, it has ended up being captured by them. Os Guiness has written about this danger in three books, *Sounding Out the Idols of Church Growth,*[25] *No God But God: Breaking With the Idols of Our Age,*[26] and *Dining With the Devil.*[27] The risk is that when one begins to ride the tiger of modernity's viewpoints, high technology, etc., one will end up swallowed by the tiger's value system and world view.

3. Church Growth does not rely, as it should on God, His Spirit and His Sovereignty. A harsh point is made in an article, "Church Growth's Two Faces," when Craig Parro cites and then critiques a statement by current Church Growth celebrity, George Barna. Barna wrote, "If a church studies its market, devises intelligent plans, and implements them faithfully, it should see an increase in the number of visitors, new members and people who accept Christ as their Savior." Parro then observes, "God is not even part of this equation!"[28] It is all too easy for churches to give lip service to prayer while, in fact, trusting in technique.

4. Church Growth over-accommodates to the spirit of the age. It contorts itself to the current culture; specifically, to the Baby Boomers. (Please see Jim Baird's enlightening chapter in this book.) Asking what and how people feel, what they think they need and what they want this week may clarify immediate feelings, needs and desires, but what about the stringent demands of the

106

cost of discipleship? What of God's eternal word and its eternally-relevant message? Is the Lord's only concern with "felt needs" and not real needs? In his introduction to Robert Wenz's hard-hitting book, *No Room for God*,[29] Michael Horton says that in the churches we seem unaware of how much relativism and subjectivism has influenced us. Horton continues, "Doctrine is replaced with 'feel-good' or 'do-good' sermons; A God-ward focus is replaced with human-ward or even self-centered orientation. We seem to believe that coming to church is a matter of picking up a few suggestions to make our lives happier and more successful. Yes, the cross is still a stumbling block. We would rather be consumers than disciples."[30] Instead of the broad, penetrating, thematic sermons we need, we are offered alliterative mini-messages which tease, twist and torture a scripture paragraph until it renders up a tiny lesson on "How to Handle...." some micro-concern of the week.

5. Church Growth relies upon the "Homogenous Unit Principle" which is an immature viewpoint. God can make two peoples one in Christ (Ephesians 2:12-22). The HUP could lead to such abominations as apartheid and racial segregation.[31] Any plan which surrounds one with only one's own kind is not a mature Christian approach.

6. Church Growth utilizes the "targeting" principle which ignores the broad-sowing of the seed (Luke 8:1-11). God can do things with people who look unpromising as candidates for salvation. Targeting one generation or personality can be offensive to Christians who find the approach to be sub-Christian.

7. Church Growth attempts to apply principles which are not transferable to different contexts. Mindless mimicry of what "sizzles" in one place is apt to "fizzle" in a different setting. Something reported to work well with upscale, sophisticated Northern or West Coast yuppies, may not be well received by mature Christians in the Southwest. (One suspects that often the entire story has not been very well told of what "worked" somewhere else. Instead of reaching the unchurched, some modern churches seem to be pulling away members from less "exciting" congregations).

8. Church Growth has fostered some unhealthy competition between congregations. Some of this started back in "bus ministry" days with overlapping routes. This competitive attitude lent itself to isolation. It is a bad spirit which says, "My congregation is the best and it is going to be the biggest." Disdainful ignoring of other congregations of like precious faith is in evidence.

107

Such a spirit is contrary to I Peter 2:17, the "forgotten command," which says, "Love the brotherhood."

These eight criticisms of what passes for "Church Growth" today do not exhaust the backlash comments of those who have seen what was called "Church Growth" and were horrified and frightened.

The most correct course for congregations to pursue will be one that is true to the New Testament, which is the church's guide book. Period. Of course, an effective evangelism knows the contemporary world and brings forth from its treasure house those things which most profoundly engage the truth-seeker. In Athens, Paul was philosophical (Acts 17); in Antioch of Pisidia (Acts 13), he was strong on the Old Testament to a Jewish synagogue audience; and at Lystra (Acts 14), he talked to uneducated pagans of God's goodness seen in nature. It is biblical to teach and preach God's message in a way eternal and contemporary!

It remains a mere academic exercise to do an historical overview and assemble a list of benefits and criticisms of Church Growth. However, when one gets into the skin of Michael Scott and the Lakeview North congregation, theoretical considerations lose out to the practical ministry concern: "How can this congregation in this place grow as we believe God wants it to?"

Some preachers so desperately crave growth that, in their search for something to copy-cat, they have been drawn to models that are inappropriate. This inappropriateness comes in part from the vast difference between the context, ambiance and circumstances in Greater Chicagoland or Southern California on the one hand and the South and Southwest, where many of these preachers are located, on the other hand. Some of the Bible Belt preachers so hungry for greater numbers seem also to have been influenced by the cable TV broadcasts of large charismatic churches. The frightening thought is that the "holy laugh," "holy dance," and healing-lines now seen in some high-profile churches may soon be proposed by our own growth-hungry brethren.

Already some of the terms used by churches of other faiths have been highly touted by some of our brethren; e. g., the substitution of "praise" for "worship." "Praise" for the charismatic is a technical term for the state that is the prelude to ecstasy and tongue speaking. Obviously, when our brethren use some tools and terms, they intend no such thing as intended by those they are copying. Furthermore, a term stolen from others is not objectionable just because it is used as a hidden agenda by them. A more thoughtful evaluation of others' terminology could make us sound clearer and appear less pathetic in our haste to copy others.

Eventually, the question ought to be raised, where can we find some kind of model which would be Christ-honoring and free from the disadvantages of unfortunately loaded meaning or charismatic spill-over?

In the book of Acts, itself, there can be found more than one great model of a church which, when analyzed, offers up several great traits of a growing church. One great model is Antioch of Syria.

The Antioch Effect[32]

Recently, Ken Hemphill's book by the above title was published by Broadman and Holman. Hemphill allows the church in Antioch of Syria (Acts 11:19-30; 13:1-3), to furnish the "...title, outline and much of (the) content" for his book. Hemphill observes, "The solution will not be found in methods, models or marketing strategies . . . they simply are not the primary issue."[33]

He further commiserates with the preacher who goes off to a seminar or workshop somewhere and comes home to "plug in" the "surefire, microwaveable guaranteed-to-grow-your-church strategy only to stare helplessly as . . . people balked and the program fizzled rather than sizzled."[34]

Therefore, Hemphill turns from much-heralded churches of the 1990's to Antioch as the model church and correctly credits the church at Antioch as being, ". . . at the center of much of the mission activity recorded in the book of Acts."[35]

Hemphill is merely one in a long line of writers and preachers to use the church in Antioch as a model for a healthy, vibrant church. Many writers in churches of Christ have done the same long before Hemphill. His particular sketch has the virtue of being a contemporary discussion written against the backdrop of recent fever-pitch interest in Church Growth. Hemphill writes in a series which includes other similar contemporary efforts.[36]

Hemphill's book will supply the growth components with some insights from Rainer and some of my own, as well.

The first characteristic is Supernatural Power. When Barnabas first went to Antioch, he found a congregation established by those fleeing the persecution arising at Stephen's death. The book mentions three proofs of God's power: (1) "the hand of the Lord was with them" (Acts 11:1); (2) "evidence of the grace of God" (11:23); and (3) "The disciples were called Christians first at Antioch" (11:26).[37] Since it is God who gives growth (I Corinthians 3:6), the divine element in Church Growth dare not remain unacknowledged.

The second characteristic is Christ-Exalting Worship.
While our brethren would heartily concur with Hemphill's terminology in his title, we would diverge from some of his explanations. Remarkable, however, are the cautions given by both Hemphill and Rainer on forcing rapid change in worship. The element of corporate worship is precious to church members and those who rail against what they see as dryness in "traditional worship" will find admonition in these books, each written in 1994.

Hemphill sees the church at Antioch spending time in prayer and fasting (Acts 13:2)[38] Yet, worship is more than the front door for a seeker-sensitive program. He rather finds worship to be the " . . . well spring of most elements of church growth." He properly notes that if worship has a target, that target is God. He does not deny that for some seeking the Lord, the worship provides an opportunity to reach the sinner. He does not shy away from the need to confront these with a call to deep commitment and contends that this will turn them on rather than turning them away. He further questions the wisdom of continually courting someone to be a consumer, rather than calling for commitment. In Rainer's book, he mentioned one of his "dear friends," James Emery White, who wrote *Opening the Front Door: Worship and Church Growth.*[39] Rainer advises, however, that, "The traditional church, . . . cannot apply these principles in the same way as a nontraditional church."[40] Rainer also states what some of us in churches of Christ can agree with, from sad experiences of observation, "Massive and sudden change. . . can divide and demoralize a traditional church. Remember, church members who hold tenaciously to the old paradigms are not 'wrong' while you are right. They are children of God loved no less by the Father than those who prefer a different style."[41]

While the Willow Creek model makes much of using the Lord's Day morning assembly as a seeker-service, good arguments can be made for respecting that time when the communion is observed (Acts 20:7), as a time for worship and upbuilding, and then allowing evangelism to flow out as response to having worshiped God.[42] No one should deny that there will be the visitor to the Lord's Day assembly who will find himself/herself attracted to Christ through the worship (I Corinthians 14:24-25); it is a stretch to say that is the primary thrust of a believers' worship hour. Of course, members of the body are enriched by a vibrant and meaningful worship hour and there will be some seekers who will also be attracted by that.

The third element cited by Hemphill as part of the Antioch Effect Is God-Connecting Prayer.[43] That the Antioch church was prayerful is amply documented and that Hemphill spends considerable time declaring prayer's significance for church growth today must be acknowledged. Having attended one of Hemphill's seminars, I am able to state that the emphasis he feels ought to be given to God's role in Church Growth is quite impressive. Perhaps half or more of the seminar was given to the role of God's part, worship and prayer.

The fourth element noted is Servant Leadership.[44] When the preacher develops a Chief Executive Officer attitude and starts ordering people around in the congregation, one can expect there to be a negative reaction to such leadership. In the Antioch church, two of the most talented servant-leaders, Barnabas and Paul, were willing to go into mission work. Sky-high expense accounts, upper-scale living arrangements and six-figures salaries may not be sinful; but to many humble members, they do not model servant leadership. When preachers quit spending so much time tinkering with change in the Sunday worship hour[45] and more time in people's homes teaching the lost and serving the sick and afflicted, the local church can expect to grown again.

The fifth trait cited by Hemphill is Kingdom Family Relationships. As Hemphill comes to the close of his discussion of this characteristic, he says, "For many new Christians the church is the lap that provides warmth, protection, comfort and healing. It is a safe haven and a center for healing those wounded in battle. We can't get caught up in the 'growth-at-any-cost' mind set and fail to provide a safe haven for the members of the family. Your church ought to be place where God's people feel safe and protected, cherished and nourished, secure and loved, healed and challenged. . . It is high time we begin to behave like God's forever family."

Hemphill lists as the sixth characteristic for a highly-effective church God-Sized-Vision. Hemphill cites Robert Dale's emphasis upon an appropriate vision or dream, "A healthy dream is a necessary foundation for a healthy organization. Nothing less than a Kingdom dream will turn a church toward healthy and aggressive ministry." Hemphill emphasizes, ". . . a growth vision will come from God and be founded in His word. It is obedience to this God-given vision that gives the church restraint and provides direction." The vision comes from God through His word, ". . . is centered in the Great Commission, flows through the core values of the community, addresses community needs, and can be accomplished through the full employment of the supernatural resources (Hemphill does not mean showy charismatic displays - DV) given by the exalted Lord."

Hemphill's seventh characteristic of Antioch and of healthy-growing churches today is Passion for the Lost. This is Hemphill's longest chapter of the book. He suggests that among Southern Baptists, his own denomination, 5,771 churches reported that in a recent year, they had no baptisms - that being 16% of the churches in the denomination. He reminds his readers that the Great Commission is not a suggestion, but is to be obeyed in "faithfully fulfilling the totality of the Great Commission." Hemphill gives a balanced vigorous examination to the "seeker service." He urges, "do not allow seeker terminology to dull the commitment to outreach" The seeker mind-set might delude us into thinking that sinful, fallen humanity is seeking God. We cannot swap a "come-see" strategy for a "go-tell" one and be faithful to the Great Commission.

He urges an evangelistic approach which would recognize the degree of readiness to the gospel of any given individual. Hemphill points out that between 76 to 89% of people first attend a church because of an invitation of a friend or family member. A passion for people without Christ is indispensable for the church that wants to grow.

The eighth characteristic observed by Hemphill is Maturation of Believers. The church at Antioch came full circle - founded by those who came from elsewhere because of persecution, the Antioch church itself within a few years was sending out missionaries (Acts 8:1-4; 11:19-30; 13:1-4) The maturation process is one constantly before the eyes of the greatest human missionary of all time, the apostle Paul. He stated his goal, "We proclaim him, admonishing and teaching everyone with all wisdom, so that we may present everyone perfect in Christ. To this end I labor, struggling with all his energy, which so powerfully works in me" (Colossians 1: 28-29). A synonym for "perfect" in this setting would be "mature or full-grown." The soul-winning Christian has a responsibility to bring baby-Christians to maturity. Several steps are involved. To mention just two of them: one crucial step is indoctrination in the faith of Jesus Christ; another is deep, unswerving commitment to Christ.

The indoctrination will never be accomplished by mere "touchy-feely" classes, songs and sermons. It requires assisting the newborn convert to be able to eat and benefit from the meat of the word (Hebrews 5:11-6:3). Hemphill remarks, "For example, the Methodist church, after a period of rapid growth, began to decline because they drifted from historic teachings and practices and grew lax about their demands for distinctive behavioral standards

112

that had once been their hallmark." Little imagination is required to see the application for churches of Christ in the 1990's.

Hemphill comments on the dangers of heightened consumer mentality and the consequent lowering of commitment. Preachers have heard, ". . . conference leaders states that Boomers are unwilling to make deep commitments. Some have responded by lessening the demands of church membership and have marketed for Boomers by promising services and playing down expectations. The results of such a marketing strategy are predictable - - lessened demands results in lessened commitment . . . When it appeared that Boomers were returning to church in the 1980's, new evidence suggests that their attendance is actually dropping. Of greater concern is the emergence of a consumer mentality toward religion."

These characteristics of the Antioch church map out today's growth-hungry leaders in a pathway which is not easy, but it is reliable. It will neither lead to quicksand nor off the cliff.

These characteristics are enough to begin with. Above all, we must remember that "Unless the Lord builds the house, its builders labor in vain. Unless the Lord watches over the city, the watchmen stand guard in vain" (Psalm 127: 1).

May God help us in churches of Christ to leave our ruts, to distinguish between faith and human tradition and to take the transferable concepts from a biblical model like Antioch and apply them today, scrpturally and rigorously.

We will find that growth is like happiness. It comes best when you go about doing what you are supposed to do. Growth, like happiness, then will come naturally and as a by-product. We cannot force the hand of God. There are no shortcuts to the fullness of God's purpose for His church. When we do our part, diligently and faithfully, growth can be a dream come true.

Questions

1. List some of the principles governing church growth found in Acts, chapters one through eight.
2. What are the lessons that may be learned about church growth from the church at Antioch?
3. How do accurate records help in determining whether the church is growing or not?
4. In what three ways may a church grow?

5. Based on a study of the seven churches of Asia (Revelation chapters 2 & 3), what are the vital signs of a healthy church?
6. What are some of the benefits or pluses of the current Church Growth movement?
7. Are there any negative aspects of the current emphasis by the Church Growth movement? If so, what, and why?
8. What part, if any, does knowledge of contemporary culture contribute to the growth of the church?
9. What cautions should be exercised, if any, in adopting procedures used by other churches as models in church growth in the local congregation?
10. Would you agree or disagree with the statement that "worship is the well spring of church growth?" Give a reason for your answer.
11. Will the promotion of small group or house church meetings in the local church produce a positive impact on church growth?
12. How do you determine whether a church is growing or dying?

8. *Human Opinion vs. Divine Doctrine*

Howard Norton

Introduction

One of our greatest difficulties as Christians is living in the world without becoming like the world. We must make certain accommodations to the world without sacrificing the truth of the gospel or giving up our identity as citizens of heaven. Performing on this tightwire between heaven and earth is never easy for the man or woman of God.

To add to this complex situation, we as Christians are not always adept at distinguishing between the world (human culture) which we are not supposed to imitate, and God's revealed will (divine culture) which we are supposed to model for the people around us. Our human tendency is to equate that which our culture believes with that which God wants us to believe and practice. God, however, calls us to see clearly the difference between human and divine ideas and follow the divine. It is no easy task.

Missionaries and others who have lived in cultures other than their own have the advantage here. Even as travelers are more likely to notice the unique characteristics of a new land than are the natives who live there, so Christians outside the familiar sights of the home church seem more capable of distinguishing what is biblical from what is purely cultural. The new culture is so obviously different from our own that what is cultural stands apart from what is biblical much like the ghost in a horror movie stands apart from the body it has just left. Although this phenomenon is much easier to behold when we are outside our own culture than when we are at home in familiar surroundings, God expects us, wherever we are, to make the effort to discover through the study of his word and careful observation the difference between what is cultural and what is biblical.

One of the most difficult struggles of thoughtful missionaries is determining how to accommodate to culture without compromising the biblical message. The challenge for all Christians is the same: How do we accommodate to our culture enough to be effective and, at the same time, not adapt to such an extent that accommodation becomes sinful? This chapter seeks to show that when issues are matters of human opinion or culture, there is room for change; but when issues involve divine doctrine, we have no right to change what God has written in his word. At the conclusion of the chapter, some suggestions are provided to help the reader determine the difference between human opinion or culture and divine doctrine.

Paul Teaches Accommodation

Paul the apostle, the greatest missionary in the history of the church, teaches that accommodation to culture is both permissible and necessary. Perhaps his greatest statement about accommodation in order to reach the lost is in I Corinthians 9:19-23 where he says,

> Though I am free and belong to no man, I make myself a slave to everyone, to win as many as possible. To the Jews I became like a Jew, to win the Jews. To those under the law I became like one under the law. . . so as to win those under the law. To those not having the law I became like one not having the law . . ., so as to win those not having the law. To the weak I became weak, to win the weak. I have become all things to all men so that by all possible means I might save some. I do all this for the sake of the gospel, that I may share its blessings.

These five verses are a small part of a three-chapter discussion of Christian liberty and what Christians can and cannot do about eating meat sacrificed to idols. I Corinthians 8-10 teaches that some circumstances permit eating meat offered to idols and others prohibit it. The constant principle is that Christians can never eat meat offered to an idol as an act of worship. If Christians are invited to eat meat in an idolater's home and they

116

can view it as a mere meal, Paul says, *"Eat whatever is put before you without raising questions of conscience"* (I Corinthians 10:27).

In other words, Christians should accommodate themselves to the meal set before them. Certain circumstances can change what Christians should do, however, and Paul spells out the exceptions. Eventually, whether Christians eat the meat offered to an idol or abstain from its use, they must *"do it all for the glory of God,"* taking every precaution not to cause Jews, Greeks, or the church of God to stumble.

Romans 14 is another Pauline passage that deals with accommodation to culture. It is a great chapter on Christian liberty and deals very specifically with such questions as whether Christians should eat meat or only vegetables, whether they should celebrate one day as more important than another, whether they should eat food considered unclean by some, and whether they should drink wine. The chapter deals with a list of things about which no one can say with certainty, *"This is the right thing to do"* or, *"This is the wrong thing to do."* Paul seems to say that when a thing is neither right nor wrong within itself and a person wants to follow a particular path (i. e., accommodate to the culture), he is free to do so. He is only free, however, as long as he participates with a clear personal conscience, and at the same time, does not cause a brother to fall by encouraging that brother to violate his own sense of right and wrong.

If we look carefully at what Paul teaches in Romans 14 and I Corinthians 8 - 10, we must conclude that he believes and teaches, under the inspiration of the Holy Spirit, that Christians can accommodate to the culture in which they live.

Paul Practices Accommodation

In spite of the dangers of accommodation, Paul practiced it in his ministry. One of the clearest cases involves his decision to circumcise Timothy. The son of a Greek father and a Jewish mother, Timothy embraces the Christian faith and is recommended to Paul and Silas by the brothers at Lystra and Iconium. Luke succinctly tells of Paul's desire to accommodate Jews when he writes, *"Paul wanted to take him [Timothy] along on the journey, so he circumcised him because of the Jews who lived in that area, for they all knew that his father was a Greek"* (Acts 16:3). By circumcising Timothy, Paul lives up to his own teaching that he is willing to *"become all things to all men."* A young man of both Greek and Jewish parentage would be seriously handicapped in his effort to preach to Jews if it were not clear that he respected his Jewish heritage enough to be circumcised.

Another example of Paul's practice of adapting to culture is found in Acts 21:17-26. Paul and his traveling companions are in Jerusalem, having just completed the third missionary journey. After Paul *"reported in detail what God had done among the Gentiles through his ministry,"* James and the other apostles tell Paul that many of the Jewish brethren have heard that he has taught Jews of the Dispersion to reject the teachings of Moses, and not to circumcise their children or follow the religious customs of the Jewish people.

To counter this false propaganda circulating about Paul, James and the apostles recommend that Paul follow their advice as contained in the following words:

> There are four men with us who have made a vow. Take these men, join in their purification rites and pay their expenses, so that they can have their heads shaved. Then everybody will know these is no truth in these reports about you, but that you yourself are living in obedience to the law" (Acts 21: 24).

What does Paul do? He apparently follows their counsel to the letter. Why? He acts like a Jew in order to reach Jews more effectively for Christ. Numerous commentators believe that Paul goes entirely too far with this accommodation. If he does, Luke gives no hint that he crossed the line into sinful compromise. Paul possesses a strong conscience and is more than willing to adapt as far as truth will allow him in order to proclaim Christ.

Still another example of accommodation can be seen when Paul refuses to accept financial support from the Corinthian church (I Corinthians 9:11-18) but accepts it without hesitation from other churches (II Corinthians 11:7-12; Philippians 4:14-19). For some reason, Paul feels strongly that accepting money from the Corinthians will hinder his effectiveness as a preacher of the word even though he affirms he has the right to such support. He does not show that same hesitation when other churches are involved. These situations exhibit Paul's ability to read cultural situations and determine the best way to deal with them. Accommodation in and of itself does not imply sinful compromise; and when accommodation without sinful compromise furthers the spread of the gospel, Paul willingly adjusted his methods to the circumstances.

Paul Stands Against Accommodation

We make a serious mistake, however, to assume that Paul always willingly accommodates. There are times when any accommodation flies in the face of revealed truth. Here Paul draws the line.

He will not, for example, allow any hint of accommodation when the gospel itself is at stake. Paul clearly states this to the Galatians when he writes,

> But even if we or an angel from heaven should preach a gospel other than the one we preached to you, let him be eternally condemned! As we have already said, so now I say again: If anybody is preaching to you a gospel other than what you accepted, let him be eternally condemned" (Galatians 1:8-9).

The gospel itself must not be changed. The message is non-negotiable. No accommodation to human opinion or culture is permitted.

Paul also insists that no one has the right to bind his man-made laws on others. Three passages show how strongly Paul resists those who seek to force their own human views on other people as if their human views had divine validity.

First, Galatians 2:1-5 shows the apostle's refusal to accommodate to Jews who insist that Titus, a Greek, should be circumcised. In Titus' case, the issue is not that he should be circumcised in order to work more effectively among Jews, but, evidently, that he should be circumcised in order to be saved.

Second, the issue of circumcision is thoroughly discussed in Acts 15 when Paul and Barnabas visit the Jerusalem church. Certain Jewish brothers had been teaching the Gentiles saying, *"Unless you are circumcised, according to the custom taught by Moses, you cannot be saved"* (Acts 15:1). Even during their meeting with the leaders of the Jerusalem church, Luke says, *"Some of the believers who belonged to the party of the Pharisees stood up and said, The Gentiles must be circumcised and required to obey the law of Moses"* (Acts 15:5). Paul and the leaders in Jerusalem all draw the line by steadfastly refusing to require a type of accommodation that changes the central message of Jesus' gospel from one of salvation by grace through faith to one of salvation based on keeping the Old Testament laws.

Third, Paul urges the Colossians not to accommodate to the instructions of people who seek to enslave them through the teaching of human philosophy. He says, *"See to it that no one takes you captive through hollow and deceptive philosophy, which depends on human tradition and the basic principles of this world rather than on Christ"* (Colossians 2:8). He urges non-accommodation to *"deceptive philosophy"* when he adds, *"Such regulations indeed have an appearance of wisdom, with their self-imposed worship, their false humility and their harsh treatment of the body, but they lack any value in restraining sensual indulgence."* (Colossians 2:23). The apostolic message is that there are times when accommodation violates the will of God because it requires conduct that repudiates the gospel of Jesus Christ.

In summary, accommodation to culture is not a new phenomenon, and neither is the temptation to carry it too far. Some accommodation is right, and some of it is wrong. As Christians we have as our goal to accommodate to culture without compromising divine truth. This, though, may be easier said than done.

Current Controversy Abounds

Much of Christendom is in controversy today concerning what changes can and cannot be made by churches in order to adapt to modern culture. Not surprisingly, some of these issues have surfaced in churches of Christ all across America. Churches of Christ across the United States and even in foreign countries are suffering a great deal of stress today because of controversy over change. Some of our members demand change, and others adamantly say the church should remain exactly as it is. I am thankful for people who have taken a strong stand against accommodation that contradicts the scriptures, but I am appalled at those on both sides of certain issues that willingly divide their congregations over concepts based purely on human opinion.

Let me list some issues that, in my judgment, are clearly in the realm of human opinion and can be settled more than one way without violating biblical teaching. Here are some controversial issues of our day: (1) whether the church must meet once or twice for worship on Sunday; (2) whether or not there must be a Sunday night service at the building; (3) whether or not the order of worship in the public assembly may be changed; (4) whether or not there is a prescribed position for prayer; and (5) whether one can or cannot raise his or her hands when praying.

Going further with this thought, there are competing human opinions concerning: (6) whether to have Sunday School in the morning or at night; (7) whether we can sing a song, read a scripture aloud, or whether we must remain absolutely silent during the Lord's Supper; (8) whether or not we should spend more time in observing the Lord's Supper or less; (9) whether or not those serving the table and leading public worship must be dressed in coat and tie; (10) whether or not it is acceptable to applaud within the assembly; and (11) whether people can or cannot eat a meal in the church building.

There is a clash of human opinions at time concerning: (12) whether or not the church can occasionally have singing done by a special group during the worship hour; (13) whether songs should be traditional or contemporary; (14) whether songs should be read from the hymnal or from an overhead screen; and (15) whether singing should be in unison or in four-part harmony.

Continuing the list of topics involving human opinions, there are debates concerning: (16) whether or not every sermon or church service must include the plan of salvation and include an exhortation to be baptized; (17) whether there must always be the singing of an invitation song; (18) whether or not church services must begin and end precisely on time; (19) whether or not we should have gospel meetings and whether they should last an entire week, three days, or one day; (20) whether or not it is acceptable to change a church service at the building to a time when the entire congregation breaks up into small groups in church members' homes; and (22) whether or not a certain version of the Bible must be used by the preacher in the pulpit.

Every one of the above issues must be decided on the basis of human judgment. These issues depend on culture and not on a "thus saith the Lord." What is so tragic about the above list of topics - topics that can be decided either way without violating the Scriptures - is that there are people on both sides of these issues who are dogmatic. Some people are willing to divide churches and create hard feelings that will last a life time rather than compromise their opinions in order *"to keep the unity of the Spirit in the bond of peace"* (Ephesians 4:3).

121

Some Accommodation Is Sinful

Let me quickly add that some in our brotherhood are expressing a willingness to accommodate to culture in ways that are sinful because their accommodation sacrifices the teachings of Scripture. Here are some areas that are non-negotiable because of what the Bible teaches concerning them: (1) the saving message of Jesus Christ, Galatians 1:6-9; (2) certain great biblical doctrines outlined in Ephesians 4:1-6; (3) the Lord's Supper, I Corinthians 11:17ff; (4) basic morality, I Corinthians 6:9-11, Ephesians 5:1-17, and Galatians 5:19-21; and (5) the exclusive use of a cappella music in the public assembly, Ephesians 5:19 and Colossians 3:16.

Other items under discussion today that violate New Testament teaching are as follows: (6) the concept that elders have no authority in the church or that the evangelist is the person with the final word in church leadership; (7) the theory that church growth is the ultimate test of a congregation and that whatever methods will produce such growth are permissible even if they disrespect both the spirit and letter of the New Testament; (8) the use of women to lead the public assembly in preaching, praying, reading the Scriptures, congregational singing, and the celebration of the Lord's Supper; (9) the willingness to give up biblical teaching on the need for baptism by immersion for the forgiveness of sins; and finally, (10) the willingness to accept as a brother every person who claims to be a Christian, regardless of whether or not that person has obeyed God's clearly stated plan of salvation.

The path that some of our preachers and teachers are taking is frightening beyond description. They seem more anxious to adapt to culture than to adhere to the word of God. At the very moment when mainline denominational people are looking for a church that still respects the Bible, standing firmly for its teachings in spite of what a pagan culture demands, some of our own leaders and their followers have chosen to imitate the denominations' tired, bankrupt practices. I fear that some of our leaders sell out to culture because of an inordinate desire to free churches of Christ from embarrassments that stem from being out of step with American society. We all would do well to remember the adage, *"He who marries the culture of this generation will be a widower in the next."* When accommodation to culture sacrifices biblical principles, it is sin.

Guidelines To Help Us

Human culture is the *"world"* in which Christians must live without becoming contaminated by its false values. While the evil aspects of our culture threaten us, we cannot escape the fact that Christianity must exist within culture and, to some extent, accommodate to it. We, as Christians, must be flexible and willing to adapt to culture *except* when divine principles are involved. Perhaps the following guidelines will help us accommodate without compromising our souls or the truth of the gospel.

First, Christians can adapt to culture only in those areas in which Jesus Christ has given us freedom to make choices. Our task, then, when our beliefs and modern culture clash is to discover whether our beliefs deal with issues that are human or divine. We can only know this through a prayerful study of God's word, the Bible. Before we even consider adapting to culture, we must seek to know whether God has, or has not, spoken to the issue concerning us. In order words, we must find an answer to the question, *"Is this a biblical issue?"*

Second, if God has spoken on the subject, we must determine through careful study what the Bible says about it. Whatever the Bible authorizes on the subject is the conclusion Christians want to reach. In short, the Bible authorizes on the basis of direct commands, necessary inferences or principles (See F. LaGard Smith, *The Cultural Church*, 1992), and approved apostolic examples. Our challenge as Christians is to follow whatever the Bible teaches us on a subject regardless of what the culture urges us to do.

John R. W. Stott wrote in *Christian Counter-Culture* (1978) that God is calling his people to be different from the world in which they live. He says,

> Indeed, if the church realistically accepted his standards and values. . . and lived by them, it would be the alternative society he always intended it to be, and would offer to the world an authentic Christian counter-culture.

When Christians so accommodate to the world that the church loses its identity, the body of Christ ceases to be the light of the world and the salt of the earth.

Third, if God's word does not speak to a particular issue through direct command, necessary inference (principle) or approved apostolic example, or if His word makes it clear that a particular matter can be resolved in more than one way depending on the circumstances, we have no right to bind personal opinions on others. We have always referred to these issues as matters of expediency, and they must be settled on the basis of God's teaching, brotherly love and common sense.

Even in matters of expediency, God provides important instruction. First, we must not violate our own conscience by the choices we make. To involve ourselves in a practice which injures our own conscience is a sin. Second, we must not provoke others to violate their conscience. We should seek their good rather than our own so as not to *cause anyone to stumble, whether Jews, Greeks or the church of God"* (I Corinthians 10:32). Third, we should not condemn a brother who makes a choice in the realm of opinion that is different from our own. Fourth, the Bible says that when we are accommodating to culture, we should *"make every effort to do what leads to peace and mutual edification"* (Romans 14:19). Fifth, everything we do to adapt to culture must be done for the glory of God.

These God-given principles that regulate matters of expediency are vitally important. A proper respect for them will reduce tension that exists in congregations polarizing over issues that are purely matters of opinion.

Conclusion

Living in the world without becoming like the world is not an easy mission to accomplish because the world, or human culture, is so perverse. In spite of its perversity, it is where we and our contemporaries live. Although our associates form their values primarily on the basis of what the culture teaches, Christian values must be based on the divine principles that God has revealed through Jesus Christ in his written word. We dare not compromise them. What we can do, however, is find areas of human culture that are neutral zones, and use them as vehicles for reaching out to our generation with the gospel of Jesus Christ. This is accommodation without compromise. This is the proper blending of human opinion and divine doctrine.

Questions

1. How would you define culture?
2. Give examples where culture affects the church.
3. Give examples where you can accommodate culture without compromising.
4. Could a Christian in the first century eat meat offered to an idol?
5. When did Paul accommodate culture?
6. When did Paul oppose accommodation?
7. How do you distinguish between matters of opinion and matters of faith?
8. How do we distinguish between being stubborn and being true to God's word?
9. On matters of opinion how far should we go to keep the unity of the church?
10. List changes in the church that trouble you. Now using the principles you have learned, are these things matters of opinion or matters of unchangeable doctrine?

9. *The Mystery of Baptism -*
A Personal Odyssey

Prentice A. Meador, Jr.

I'll never forget it! The moment is etched in my memory as though it happened last night. It didn't happen last night. It happened on a Thursday night, April 23, 1948. I was sitting toward the back of the Hillsboro church building in Nashville, Tennessee, trying to listen to the sermon by N. B. Hardeman. I say *"trying"* because I had already decided I was going to be baptized that night.

About a year earlier, I had raised the subject of my baptism with my parents. I noticed that they almost tried to talk me out of it as they asked me several questions. They seemed to think that I ought to wait. But now I had decided that I wanted to be baptized and no one was going to talk me out of it.

So I sat there nervously waiting until Hardeman finished his sermon. I guess most ten year old boys are nervous in church. I sure was. I had been thinking about it all week while listening to the white-haired N. B. Hardeman speak in this special series of meetings.

At about 8:30 P. M., Hardeman concluded his message with an invitation to become a Christian. As the audience stood, Leslie Self began the invitation song *"Almost Persuaded."* My hands grew cold. The thought of walking down a long church aisle in front of hundreds of adults scared me to death. It *"almost persuaded"* me not to do it. But in the middle of the first stanza, I heard the words *"seems now some soul to say, 'go, spirit, go thy way'. . .".* When I heard the word *"go,"* I went. As I walked quickly down the green carpeted aisle to the front, I looked up into the warm smiling face of B. C. Goodpasture, our preacher. He asked me to fill in a *"response card,"* though he probably knew why I had come to the front.

Before a hushed audience, I confessed that I believed that *"Jesus is the Christ, the Son of the living God."* We then made our way back to the dressing room where I put on a white shirt and pants for the baptism. Brother Goodpasture led me down into the comfortable water and said, *"Upon your confession and for the remission of your sins, I now baptize you in the name of the Father, the Son and the Holy Spirit."* He then very carefully immersed me backwards into the water just like he was burying me. As he raised me from the water, I felt a sense of relief, joy, and great satisfaction.

Following my baptism, lots of adults came and hugged me as they welcomed me into the Hillsboro church family. I especially remember the pride and love which Mom and Dad expressed to me that night on our way home. For a ten-year old boy who had done a bunch of things wrong, I now felt I had done something right.

Baptism My Defining Moment

Even though I didn't thoroughly understand all of the things that happened at my baptism on that Thursday night, I knew that it was a pivotal point in my life. A defining moment. It was the outward expression of my inward faith. It became my true *"birthday."* A time to celebrate. A moment to remember. The beginning of a journey. A signal that something was happening in my life - new and different. My prayers became a little more personal. The Bible was not just a rule book, but a road map. *"Church"* was not just something you go to, but a group to which I belonged. As G. R. Beasley-Murray writes, *"to be baptized . . . is to undergo a drastic experience"* (*Baptism in The New Testament,* p. 142).

On that Thursday, I really didn't realize that baptism is so frequently mentioned in the New Testament. I didn't know, for instance, that in the 269 chapters of the New Testament, *"baptism,"* appears more than 100 times. I did know that God wanted me to be baptized, that it was necessary for me to become a Christian, and that everything would look different after that "night."

It would be a little later in my life that I would begin to ask, *"What really happened at my baptism?"* As I began to read through the New Testament I made a surprising discovery: **the** most profound statements on *"baptism"* are really addressed to those of us who have already been baptized. I had earlier thought that most of the Bible teaching on *"baptism"* surely was directed to those who had never been baptized. But apparently God wants us to continue to look back at this defining moment in our spiritual journey. He wants us to savor it, to appreciate it, to understand it, and to be strengthened by it. No wonder everyone in the Bible who becomes a Christian with obedient faith is baptized! It's truly life's defining moment.

My Forgiveness of Sin and Guilt

The first *"wrong"* thing that I remember doing was stealing Eddie Derryberry's water gun. I hid it under a hedge outside my bedroom window. I thought no one saw me. That night, my conscience began to really hurt me. I knew I'd done something wrong, because Mom and Dad had already taught me that stealing was wrong. As Mom put me to bed, she asked that question that mothers seem to know exactly when to ask, *"Is there anything you want to tell me?"*

"Where did that come from?" I thought. Did she know? Had she seen me? What would she do to me if she had seen me? In a matter of moments I was in tears. Somehow, just telling her gave me relief.

The next day we went to Eddie's house where I returned his water gun, told him and his mother what I had done, and promised to never do it again. Guilt can be humiliating. Add to this all the other things I had said and done which were not right and I knew that God was not pleased with me.

So, one of the things that I most appreciated about my baptism on that Thursday night was the forgiveness of my sins. When my guilt was gone, I felt even greater relief than I had felt when I confessed to my mother. I didn't know that baptism had its roots in the Old Testament Jewish ceremony of purification, the washing of body and of clothes in order to be spiritually clean. So David cries out to God, *"Wash me"* (Psalm 51:2).

On numerous occasions, I had heard brother Goodpasture preach, *"Repent and be baptized, every one of you, in the name of Jesus Christ so that your sins may be forgiven"* (Acts 2:38a). Or *"And now what are you waiting for? Get up, be baptized and wash your sins away, calling on His name"* (Acts 22:16). While I did understand that my sins were forgiven on that Thursday night during my baptism, I did not understand *"how"* that happened. (I

128

wonder if the early Christians had difficulty understanding that.) It was really much later that I began to see that the blood of Jesus Christ had been operative on that Thursday night in my baptism. The Hebrews writer frames it this way:

> How much more, then, will the blood of Christ, who
> through the eternal Spirit offered himself unblemished
> to God, cleanse our conscience from acts that lead
> to death, so that we may serve the living God!
> (Hebrews 9:14)

I certainly wanted a clean conscience. So, I was impressed to read Peter's words: *"and this water symbolizes baptism that now saves you also---not the removal of dirt from the body but the pledge of a good conscience toward God. It saves you by the resurrection of Jesus Christ who has gone into Heaven and is at God's right hand"* (I Peter 3:21-22). In some mysterious and unseen sense, the precious blood of Jesus Christ had cleansed my soul of all my sins and all my guilt while being baptized on that Thursday evening. *"But you were washed, you were sanctified, you were justified in the name of the Lord Jesus Christ and by the Spirit of our God"* (I Corinthians 6:11). I still don't understand it, but I am so grateful for it!

Much later in my life, while studying church history, I encountered second century writers who spoke of baptism as the moment in which one's sins were forgiven:

> The tower which you see building is myself, the church. . ..
> hear then why the tower is built upon the waters. It is
> because your life has been, and will be, saved through
> water. For the ower was founded on the word of the
> Almighty and glorious name, and it is kept together by
> the invisible power of the Lord.
> *(The Shepherd of Hermas, Vision III:3)*

These early writers on baptism confirm the writers of the New Testament---God longs for a new me. He sees in me divine possibilities that come from a *"new"* relationship with God. No wonder all Christians in the Bible experienced baptism! No wonder immersion was never an option! This new beginning was essential to their salvation and mine.

On that Thursday evening, I really didn't understand that baptism reenacts a birth (John 3) and the death, burial and resurrection of Jesus (Romans 6). I just knew that in some way my life was intersecting the life of Jesus and he was changing me forever by forgiving me of my guilt.

God Fills Me With His Spirit

"Now that the remedy of sin has been provided, all that remains is receiving it---not having every related question answered" (C. S. Lewis, *Stress Fractures,* p. 181). Lewis put his finger right on the point for me. I certainly did not have *"every related question answered."* In fact, I didn't understand how God came and lived with me at my baptism.

I had heard verses in Goodpasture's sermons and in Bible classes, like *"Repent and be baptized, everyone of you, in the name of Jesus Christ so that your sins may be forgiven. And you will receive the gift of the Holy Spirit"* (Acts 2:38). Or *"For we were all baptized by one Spirit into one body"* (I Corinthians 12:13). No wonder G. R. Beasley-Murray quotes a British minister who says, *"Baptism, in its New Testament context, is always a baptism of the Spirit"* (*Baptism in the New Testament, p. 277*)

As a ten-year old, I was really puzzled by Jesus' conversation with Nicodemus. I just didn't understand it. It was much later that I discovered the key principle in this night time conversation: *"Flesh gives birth to flesh, but the Spirit gives birth to spirit"* (John 3: 6). It is in the new birth that God's Holy Spirit regenerates my spirit, bringing new life into me. So, baptism is the occasion where God's Holy Spirit comes and lives in me as a new person. On that Thursday evening, I had been born of the water and the Spirit. As Helen Young puts it, *"To become a Christian is to be changed in such a radical way that it is like being reborn!"* (*21st Century Christian,* February, 1993, p. 10). Paul said it best, *"If anyone is in Christ, he is a new creation; the old has gone, the new has come!"* (II Corinthians 5:17). On that Thursday evening, God began to live in me.

A New Relationship With God's People

At age ten, I loved team sports. I spent hours each day playing basketball, football, and baseball. The idea of being on a *team* really appealed to me. So my dad used *team sports* to explain that at my baptism, I became a part of a great *"team of God's people."* That was his way of helping me to understand these words: *"And the Lord added to their number daily those who were being saved"* (Acts 2:47). Or *"For we were all baptized by one Spirit into one body"* (I Corinthians 12:13).

Dad also used the analogy of our *family* to explain to me that at my baptism God placed me in *His* family. I had one sister, Linda, who was five years younger than I. But now, he explained, I had lots of *brothers and sisters* because I had been born into God's great family. To a ten year old who liked team sports and who loved his family, this was a most reassuring idea of support. Baptism is not a private affair, a solo flight, an individual matter where one *"pulls himself up by his own boot straps."* John Wilson reminds us that our baptism places us in God's group and that we are now in relationship with other Christians.

It is good that most baptisms take place at public meetings of the congregation, or at least in the presence of many friends. The presence of these other people should help remind a new Christian that becoming one with Christ involves becoming one with all those who are themselves already one with Christ. "You are the body of Christ." Paul reminds us "and each one of you is a part of it." An isolated Christian can no more continue to thrive and grow than an isolated eye, ear, or heart, or liver. (*21st Century Christian*, February, 1993, p. 16).

On that Thursday night I proudly became a part of the group. I still am! Yes, I have heard all the arguments about how the church is political, racist, hypocritical, judgmental, and motivated out of self-interest. And, while I would never condone the sins of my brothers and sisters, I will defend them. They are my family! I am a part of them and they are a part of me. Over the years, I have learned not to waste my time reading or listening to hurtful accusations directed toward my spiritual family. I have learned that even though we have different opinions, back-grounds, viewpoints and experiences, my baptism continues to remind me that we still form one family.

Jesus In Control

On the night of my baptism, I felt so aware of my sins and my guilt that one thing stood out as appealing about Jesus---his offer to save me. Of course, if you are stealing water guns and doing other bad things, you really need a Savior.

Sometime later, I understood that at my baptism I also took Jesus to be my *"Lord."* When I turned my life over to Jesus, I had decided that he would rule my life. As Paul wrote,

> That if you confess with your mouth, "Jesus is Lord," and believe in your heart that God raised him from the dead, you will be saved. For it is with your heart that you believe and are justified and it is with your mouth that you confess and are saved. . . Everyone who calls on the name of the Lord will be saved (Romans 10:9-10,12).

Even though Jesus took me *"just as I am,"* he didn't leave me that way. He wants to change me daily into a person more nearly like himself. In order to be transformed, I have to decide that Jesus will rule my life. In my baptism, I surrendered to a new authority. I pledged a new loyalty. I learned a new freedom---a freedom that comes by placing my life under his control. This is the very point Royce Money makes when he writes, *"It is precisely in the act of obedient baptism that I meet Christ in my life. My life intersects with his, and I am changed forever. It is a most intimate form of identification, this being 'with Christ.'"* (20th Century Christian, February, 1993, p. 19).

But letting Jesus run my life was proven most difficult. There have been many times that I wanted to run my own life. But each time that I take back control, each time I *do as I please,* I really mess things up. I've just about figured out that Jesus wants me to return daily to my baptism, marking not only the end of an old life, but the beginning of a new life. Of course, he doesn't want me to be rebaptized every day. Rather, He longs for me to realize that I can't run my own life. So, when I was immersed into Jesus Christ on a Thursday night, he took charge of my life. Since then, I have learned that everything in the Christian life must be decided based upon his Lordship. Every step must be under his control. He covers us like our clothes: *"You are all sons of God through faith in Christ Jesus, for all of you who were united with Christ in baptism have been clothed with Christ"* (Galatians 3:26-27). Jesus is Lord! What does that mean?

* I am not in control.
* Fate is not in control.
* Evil is not in control.
* Things are not in control.
* Death is not in control.

Each time I baptize someone or see someone baptized, I remember my own baptism. At that moment, God redirected my whole life. I no longer live as I please, but I daily try to let Christ rule me. Tough? Yes! But God has a way of reshaping forgiven sinners into people who look more and more like Jesus. That's who I want to look like.

A life of Discipleship

I don't guess any Christian fully realizes the journey he begins at his baptism. I know I didn't. You just can't predict the pot holes, ruts, hills, rocks, and ditches that are along the road of discipleship. One of my professors once gave me the advice, *"Don't look at the entire journey; just look at the next few feet."* Good idea! Life's road will wind through ups and downs, unexpected, sharp curves, and *falling rocks.* Baptism is the beginning of the journey, not the destination.

However, the beginning of the journey is very crucial. That's what Mom and Dad taught me on that Thursday night. I would now wear a new name----*"Christian."* They taught me that as I began to walk down life's road, I would walk in the Christian lifestyle. Having accepted God's grace, I would no longer live in fear. John writes, *"There is no fear in love. But perfect love drives out fear, because fear has to do with punishment"* (I John 4:18).

Over the years, I have learned that God wants me to continually look back into the waters of baptism to remember who I am. I am forgiven. And he wants me to continually remember my baptism so that I will <u>feel</u> forgiven. He wants me to act forgiven. He wants me to praise him in worship. He wants me to bring my most intimate thoughts and needs to him in prayer. He wants me to claim his promises. He wants me to give myself in total commitment and ultimate loyalty. He wants me to never forget my baptism because that's where the journey started. He wants me to find his presence and support within his family, the church, and in his comforter and counselor, the Holy Spirit.

Imitating Jesus' Death, Burial and Resurrection

Many years after my baptism, I stood beside the foundation of a newly discovered church building that dates from the second century near the city of Corinth. Not only have archaeologists discovered that the church could accommodate hundreds of

Christians, but that the architecture tells us something about early Christian faith and practice. I stared at a huge baptistery in this ancient church building, larger than I would see in any modern church building. Nothing ambiguous here! The stones of the second century speak loudly to our modern moment---early Christians believed in and practiced baptism by immersion. About the time Christians were being baptized in that ancient church building near Corinth, a second century Christian wrote these words: ". . . we indeed descend into the water full of sins and defilement, but come up, bearing fruit in our heart, having the fear of God, and trust in Jesus in our spirit." (Epistle of Barnabas, 130 A. D.).

During my junior year in high school, I heard our new pulpit minister, Batsell Barrett Baxter, deliver a sermon entitled "Scriptural Baptism" on February 27, 1955, at the Hillsboro church building. Baxter presented the following requirements for Biblical baptism:

> Requirement #1 - A human administrator
> Requirement #2 - The use of water
> Requirement #3 - The use of much water
> Requirement #4 - A going down into, a coming up out of
> Requirement #5 - Likeness of a birth
> Requirement #6 - Likeness of a burial
> Requirement #7 - Likeness of a resurrection

In making a strong case for immersion, Baxter concluded his message with these words,

> In keeping with our desire to follow God's pattern as closely as we can, we urge you to be baptized in the way that you can be sure of, by immersion. As a mature person, old enough to believe, give yourself to the Lord and be buried with him in baptism. He will then raise you to walk in newness of life. What we have said in this message is not designed as a criticism of anybody. It is designed as a statement of the Lord's truth for the good of all of us.

I later heard John McRay of Wheaton University state that departures in baptism occurred in the second century only in the mode, not in the purpose. (Baptism and Conversion: A Biblical Examination, Southwest Missouri State University). In another sermon on baptism, I heard Baxter refer to this departure.

The earliest mention of sprinkling is in *the Didache,* published about the middle of the second century. This work is an uninspired work and therefore does not carry the authority of the Holy Spirit . . . "clinical baptism" was practiced after the middle of the second century only in cases of emergency. It was not until the council of Ravenna, in 1311, under the jurisdiction of Pope Clement V, that sprinkling was substituted for immersion as the official doctrine of the Roman Catholic Church. It is interesting to know that there are Roman Catholic churches in Europe today, which boast full size baptisteries *(Baptism---What? Who? Why?,* October 20, 1957, at the Hillsboro Church of Christ, Nashville, Tennessee).

I have often been struck with the following paragraph from the *Catholic Encyclopedia* which accurately states the case for baptism as immersion.

The most a ncient form usually employed was unquestionably immersion. This is not only evident from the writings of the Fathers and the early rituals of both the Latin and Oriental churches, but it can also be gathered from the Epistles of St. Paul who speaks of baptism as a bath (Ephesians 5:26; Romans 6:4; Titus 3:5). In the Latin church, immersion seems to have prevailed until the 12th Century. After that time it is found in some places even as late as the 16th Century. Infusion and aspersion, however, were growing common in the 13th Century and gradually prevailed in the Western church. The Oriental churches have retained immersion, though not always in the sense of plunging the candidate's entire body below water. *(Catholic Encyclopedia,* "Baptism," Volume 2, pp. 261-262).

Baptism was clearly a positive experience for early New Testament Christians. It was a hinge on which a person's life turned, a powerful moment of change. No wonder nobody in the New Testament ever asked the question, *"Do I have to be baptized to be in Christ?"*

Just like these early New Testament Christians, my baptism marked my entrance into the Christian life. No wonder it is not a hazy memory, a vague, oblong blur. It is clearly recorded on the tape of my memory and I find myself replaying that tape over and over. I continue to be amazed at the profound, spiritual implications of what took place on that Thursday night. All I brought was a willing heart and a guilty soul. He did the rest. And there is no doubt in my mind that he was the real actor in that moment. In fact, when my religious friends argue that baptism is a work I now say "Yes, baptism is definitely a work. . . but not my work." Faith is my work. Coming to God is my work. But the real accomplishment is not my performance but his. And, interestingly enough, this is precisely how Paul put it:

> In him <u>you were</u> also circumcised, in the putting off of the sinful nature, <u>not</u> with a circumcision <u>done by the hands of men but</u> with the circumcision <u>done by Christ</u>, having <u>been buried</u> with him in baptism and <u>raised</u> with him throug h your faith in the power of God, who raised him from the dead. When you were dead in your sins and in the uncircumcision of your sinful nature, <u>God made you alive</u> with Christ. <u>He forgave us all our sins</u>, having canceled the written code, with its regulations, that was against us and that stood opposed to us, <u>he took it away</u>, nailing it to the cross. And having disarmed the powers and authorities, he made a public spectacle of them, triumphing over them by the cross (Colossians 2:11-15).

Every mention of my part in baptism is passive. It is done to me, not by me. And God is clearly the major player, the surgeon performing spiritual surgery, cutting off my *sinful nature,* bringing life and forgiveness.

Personal Reflections

Why address the issue of *"baptism"* in the anecdotal form? Why not approach it theoretically, formally? Why frame a discussion of baptism from a *"back then"* to a *"here and now"* perspective?

After four decades of pulpit ministry, I have discovered that baptism means much more than a formal teaching or a doctrinal topic. Frankly, I have come to see that much more transpired that

Thursday night than I understood. This doesn't mean, however, that baptism isn't an issue of doctrine, much discussed within churches of Christ and without.

While preaching for the last forty years, I have been involved in more discussions on the subject of *baptism* than any other religious topic. People outside churches of Christ have asked questions concerning the mode, purpose, relationship to personal salvation, necessity, and validity of baptism. Even today, there are those within churches of Christ who question the necessity and importance of baptism in an effort to be tolerant and broadminded. Some would move baptism away from the dead center of one's life and out to the periphery so that it ceases to be important. Because *baptism* continues to be such a *"hot"* topic, I want to share some personal reflections drawn from my own story.

My baptism was Jesus-driven and Christ-focused.

Neither a sectarian ritual nor a High-Church sacrament, baptism was not designed to achieve personal merit before God. Only Jesus "earned" anything before God. He alone achieved merit on the cross. This is why my baptism was Jesus-driven. Through baptism, my life intersected with his. It was when I was finally with him --- *"crucified with him," "buried with him," "with him . . . in his death"* and *"with him in his resurrection"* (Romans 6:4-6). Neither was my baptism camouflaged legalism. My personal faith in Jesus Christ brought me to my baptism. Christ achieved my salvation on the cross and I simply accepted what he offered me. As I obeyed Christ in my baptism, I learned the crucial lesson that everyone must learn about salvation --- salvation does not result from what I do, but from what Christ did on the cross for me. My baptism showed me that while I can't earn salvation, I can receive God's precious grace. In fact, my baptism took me back to the cross of Jesus. That's where the story of my salvation really started!

My baptism by immersion signified my death to sinful living and my new life in Christ.

Do you not know that all of us who have been baptized into Christ Jesus were baptized into his death? Therefore, we have been buried with him by baptism into death, *so* that, just as Christ was raised from the dead

137

by the glory of the father, we too might walk in <u>newness of life</u> (Romans 6: 3-4).

My baptism ended the reign of my old sinful self and began my new life under the reign of Jesus. In my baptism, God performed an act of *"circumcision"* that marked me as his child (Colossians 2: 11-12). Since my baptism closed out the reign of my old sinful self and brought me under the lordship of Jesus, it defined my future existence and my identity. It answered the major question: ***"Who Am I?"*** My baptism let me know that I had made the right choice at the crossroads of my young life, although God was not finished with me yet.

My baptism also taught me that God is interested in the whole person - the affective <u>and</u> the cognitive together.

Baptism, for me, was not simply an emotional high. It was that, but it was much more. Over the years, I have returned to my baptism in order to plumb its depths---to focus and re-focus on what really happened to me at my conversion. This intellectual journey has affected my commitment, my persistence, and my connections to the community of faith, the church. Apparently, many begin the journey but don't complete it. This problem exists not only within churches of Christ but other religious groups as well. The Sunday School Board of the Southern Baptist Convention has found that 49.3% of their members are inactive (Lewis Wingo, *Inactive Church Member Survey* the Sunday School Board of the Southern Baptist Convention, July 1985, p. 5). In the churches of Christ, we're having to convert at least two in order to keep one. In exploring the connection between emotion and cognition, Dave Malone has recently shown that retention is a major problem within churches of Christ because of certain patterns of disengagement. *Assessing Patterns of Disengagement and Re-entry in Two Local Congregations of churches of Christ,* Doctor of Ministry Thesis, Abilene Christian University, May 1992). In short, New Testament baptism involves my will, my mind, and my heart. We must help young people today connect baptism to their whole life, if we expect them to finish the Christian journey.

Furthermore, a believer's baptism versus infant baptism reveals the importance of decision, willpower, a complete commitment, and an intellectual understanding.

Early Christians taught the innocence of infants. The <u>Apology of Aristides</u> makes this very point:

> And when a child has been born to one of them, they give thanks to God; and if moreover it happened to die in childhood, they give thanks to God the more, as for one who has passed through the world without sins." ("Baptism," *The Encyclopedia of Religion and Ethics*, p. 392.)

None of the baptism accounts in the New Testament mention infants. The movement from adult baptism to infant baptism begins to take place in the third century.

> Among the many variations accompanying the history of baptism, the most important was the transition from adult to infant baptism. That the prevailing custom in the early church is admitted. Evidence that a change was taking place is abundant in the third century. This change is one of the most significant that has passed over the history of the church. (Alexander Allen, *Christian Institutions,* pp. 406-407).

God clearly wants me to understand my sinfulness, my dependence upon his grace, and my need for Jesus Christ. Infants do not possess this intellectual and affective process.

My baptism, like no other physical event in my life, imprinted upon my soul life's basic spiritual truth: **I must die to live**.

> He saved us through the washing of rebirth and renewal by the Holy Spirit, whom he poured out on us generously through Jesus Christ, our Savior, so that, having been justified by his grace, we might become heirs having the hope of eternal life (Titus 3: 5-7).

All nature illustrates this truth. The old must die for the new to live. It is a lesson that God never wants me to forget. My baptism is a visible, tangible reminder of my need to daily die in order to experience renewal, forgiveness, regeneration.

We should never isolate baptism from the whole life.

For instance, my mother and dad played a critical role in my early faith formation before and after baptism. We had lots of conversations and discussions about my baptism prior to that Thursday night. After my baptism, they continued to reinforce its meaning. Shortly after my baptism, my sister did something to me and I did it back to her. My mom said, *"You're supposed to act differently. You've been baptized."* That was the same idea Mom and Dad had in mind when they reminded me as a teenager, *"Don't forget who you are."* In addition to Mom and Dad, I had teachers like Irene Foy, Arlie Gibson and Clarence Buffington who continued to reinterpret and affirm the meaning of my baptism to me. They and others made me the beneficiary of their affirmation, instruction and assistance. I also remember godly elders of the Hillsboro church who in my teen years helped me connect my baptism to my future. Several of them suggested that I might consider ministry as a career. Mack Craig and Batsell Barrett Baxter affirmed that choice and assisted me in my own faith formation. I paint this scene in my own personal odyssey because in the 1990's latch-key children must rely on peers and TV for their faith formation during the crises of puberty and preparing to leave the nest. In other words, one of the reasons we are losing young people who have already been baptized is that they are not the beneficiaries of another generation's instruction and affirmation. They have become *"spiritual"* latch-key children too. During the critical preteen and teen years, latch-key children may not connect their baptism with the whole of their life. If their baptism is not constantly redefined, extended to everyday life, we will lose them. It is a problem that we must address within churches of Christ.

"Baptism" will likely continue to be a controversial topic, especially outside churches of Christ. Recently, an ecumenical group in Connecticut sought to find unity among diverse baptisms by

> promoting a new Ecumenical Baptismal Certificate that it developed with the support of Protestant, orthodox and Roman Catholic churches. While the baptismal rites may differ, the evidence that it took place will be uniform, symbolizing the notion that all are baptized into one broader Christian community." **(The New York Times**, February 8, 1992).

While the group may be successful in selling many baptismal certificates, the fact remains that New Testament baptism places a new Christian into a special relationship with Christ and with all others who have been so converted. To treat all baptisms as the same, regardless of mode, regardless of purpose, regardless of age, regardless of belief, is to play fast and free with one of the most significant doctrines in all of the Bible.

Finally, my baptism changed my life forever.

It is the one moment of my life that I can be absolutely certain about. No doubt! No gray area! No ambiguities! No uncertainties! Imagine what it was like to walk with the group who followed Moses to the Red Sea. You watch as the sea opens. You make the long march through. And then, on the other side, you stand in fearful amazement as the mighty waters close behind you. Imagine that you are standing there, with the spray on your face, and the sound still ringing in your ears. Would you wonder if anything had really happened to you? You would be overcome and overwhelmed with the experience. But you wouldn't wonder if it had really happened. Paul calls the Red Sea story a baptism (I Corinthians 10: 1-2), and like that ancient baptism at the Red Sea, my baptism was concrete and real. I do not wonder if anything really happened to me. As I continue to study his word and to serve him in ministry, I am profoundly aware that I will constantly appreciate what happened to me on a Thursday night, April 23, 1948. At that moment---at that precise moment in my life---he cleansed me, changed me, accepted me. He brought me through the Sea . .. to freedom!

No wonder he wants me to remember my baptism.

Questions

1. In what sense is baptism a *"defining moment?"*
2. What is the purpose of the anecdotal form of presentation in this chapter?
3. If you have been baptized, what is your story?
4. Why do we continually need to revisit our baptism?
5. Why does the Scripture encourage us to live as we were baptized?
6. Mention three or four things that happen at our baptism.
7. Even though we may be baptizing our young people, why do so many of them leave the church?

8. In what sense do we want Jesus to be our Savior, but not our Lord?
9. Mention two or three of the figures of speech in the Bible that describe baptism.
10. How and when did religion begin to change New Testament baptism?
11. Why do early Christians never ask this question? *"Do I have to be baptized to be in Christ?"*
12. What does our baptism teach us?

10. Gospel vs. Epistle, Jesus vs. The Church

A Misplaced Debate

Michael Weed

Within the array of voices presently defending and criticizing the beliefs and practices of churches of Christ, a thesis is emerging that we must recover the place and purpose of the Gospels in the life of the church. One of our errors, some suggest, has been in anchoring our efforts to restore early Christianity solely in the Acts and Epistles rather than in the Gospels. This argument occasionally leaves the impression that the Gospels and Epistles stand in some tension, even competition. Thus the impression may be left that Christians must choose between Gospel and Epistle, or that one is clearly of less value than the other.[1]

Borrowing a now famous phrase from James Gustafson, this whole conversation is rapidly becoming a "misplaced debate." Clichés and slogans--conservative or progressive--are inadequate tools for serious analysis and discernment. The hour is late and the stakes are high: we need to be able to speak openly and honestly about important issues facing God's people. The following comments are directed toward clarifying the issues and promoting constructive conversation.

It appears that there are at least six interrelated but separable reasons or motivations behind the present call for churches of Christ to return to or to "recover" the Gospels.

First, there is a desire on the part of some to recover something of the informality and intimacy of the early house churches. This movement has largely concentrated on reconstructing, if not romanticizing, the life in the Pauline churches.[2] Recent efforts, however, have been made to reconstruct a prototype for a different form of discipleship and "church" based on the simple life of the earliest followers of Jesus in Palestine.[3] The nature of the Christian community envisioned here is basically familial, small, and informal. While this approach is obviously not a recipe for large churches, modifications of it have been adapted to suit more ambitious visions of the church, e.g., so-called "fellowship groups" within larger churches.

Second, a recovery of the Gospels is important because Jesus brings strong words of judgment against many of the religious practices of Judaism in his time. He can be quoted as opposing tradition, ritual, hypocrisy; for some, he is even portrayed as the exemplar of change par excellence. A select reading of the Gospels provides a number of Jesus' statements which may be used by would-be renovators to denounce traditions (with notable exceptions) and rituals which have over the years developed among Christians.[4]

Third, some appear to find in Jesus a freedom from structure--order and tradition--a freedom which is necessary to evolve into large generic Protestant evangelical communities. A return to the Gospels and supposed informal camaraderie of Jesus' first followers is necessary to extricate ourselves from restrictive beliefs and practices which are thought to obstruct and inhibit evangelism in the modern era.

Fourth, there is a concern to recover the social-ethical passion of the great prophets of Israel as they are drawn to a focal point in the person and teaching of Jesus. Jesus announced the inbreaking of the long-awaited Kingdom, or Reign of God. He brought "good news to the captives," to the poor and the outcast. Only a recovery of the social-ethics announced in the Gospels will enable the church to break out of its self-entrapment as a "life-style enclave" meeting in the suburbs and hamlets of white middle-class America.

Fifth, one occasionally hears commitment to Jesus played off against loyalty to the church as a rhetorical device enabling the speaker to legitimate criticisms of the church in the name of a "higher allegiance" or "greater good."

Finally, there is a concern to correct views and practices that have appeared in the Restoration Movement which may be interpreted to distort the recovery of early Christianity and biblical faith. For example, there is a concern to correct a hyper-dispensationalism which on occasion has characterized Restoration theology.

While the first of these impulses seems somewhat at odds with the second and third, clearly all may interrelate in complex fashion. Before turning more directly to these approaches, however, a brief historical overview may offer some perspective from which to do so.

Historical Perspectives

Reassessment and criticism of the existing church in the name of faithfulness to the essence of the Christian faith, while varying in specifics, has been constant throughout the history of Christianity. An argument may be made that much of the New Testament itself reflects this basic characteristic. Certainly the New Testament writings are, in the first instance, written to different Christian groups, both criticizing them and encouraging them to hold fast to that which they have received. Unquestionably, Christians remain in debt to courageous reformers who down through the ages have pointed out distortions and corruption and called for renewal in the church.

A less prominent note within the history of the Christian movement has been one with considerable parallels to the above but also with significant differences. From very early in the history of the church there have been critics who, in the name of Jesus or Christianity, not only denounced corruptions of the church, but also set themselves in opposition to the church itself. That is, there have been critics and movements for whom the very concept of the church is rejected.

Early on, Christianity struggled with those such as the Gnostics who found the church either unnecessary or actually a hindrance to the attainment of individual maturity, wisdom, and true spirituality. Later, the rise of monasticism carried within its self-understanding a tension not only between true spirituality and the distractions of life in the world but also between deep spirituality and everyday life in the church. Unquestionably, groups such as the fourteeneth-century Brethren of the Common Life greatly diminished the role of the church in the life of the truly spiritual believer and promoted versions of Christian mysticism.

In the nineteenth century, liberal Protestant thinkers variously turned to the Gospels for an understanding of early Christianity. They played Jesus off against the apostle Paul and later developments of the church reflected in the New Testament itself. Jesus was said to be the founder of Christianity, while Paul (and others) founded the Christian cult; Jesus preached the kingdom, and Paul (and others) established the church. In this construction both Jesus and Paul were caricatured. Jesus was portrayed as calling individuals into relationship with a loving Father and entrance into a universal but invisible brotherhood. Jesus founded no church or organization. Adolf Harnack, for example, in his classic statement of Protestant liberal theology *What is Christianity?* (1900) could state that "Jesus never had anyone but the individual in mind."[5] For Harnack, Jesus did not in any sense intend a church--Roman Catholic or Protestant. In fact, the emergence of the church was a falling away from the "pure inwardness of the gospel."[6] For Harnack, Ernst Troeltsch and others, the church represents a distinct loss of the almost entirely ethical message of Jesus.[7] With the appearance of the church, one sees the emergence of ecclesiastical power, hierarchy, institutionalism, dogma, rigid orthodoxy, and sacramentalism.

In a sense, Harnack *et al*, represent the extreme of setting the Gospels in opposition to the Epistles, Jesus in opposition to the developing church.[8] This whole movement has been thoroughly discredited by biblical scholars. As Albert Schweitzer and others pointed out, the Liberal portrait of Jesus was an artificial reconstruction more indebted to nineteenth-century philosophical and methodological presuppositions than to historical fact. In turn, these presuppositions were driven by concerns other than scholarly objectivity.

Fortunately, it is no longer possible to contend that the church is merely an invention of Paul or other early Christian missionaries with no fundamental connection with the intentions of the historical Jesus. The Liberal argument, however, remains instructive. It cautions us against too readily accepting efforts to recover or reconstruct a "Jesus" (or any history, for that matter) cut conveniently to fit contemporary concerns.

It is now recognized by biblical scholars that Jesus, the Gospels, and the church are inextricably interrelated. Clearly, many of Jesus' own actions and teachings presume and anticipate the emergence of the community founded by his life and teachings (e.g., the calling of twelve disciples, the new covenant, etc.).[9] The Gospels simply cannot be used to reconstruct an early "churchless Christianity"--whether that of Protestant Liberalism, Protestant evangelicalism, or some other version.

Further, the Gospels themselves are produced years after the writing of the first epistles. They are written both in and for the life of the early church. That is, the Gospels are not merely apostolic memoirs preserving interesting historical information about Jesus. While the Gospels record the life of Jesus, they do so with a constant eye toward presenting the founding events of the Christian church (e.g., the last supper, the cross, resurrection) in a way that illuminates the present circumstances of the life of the church in the world. Importantly, the one whom the Gospels portray is not simply a revered but now departed teacher; nor is he presented merely as the founder of a new religious movement. Rather, the Jesus of the Gospels is understood in the Gospels as the now-reigning, resurrected Lord of the church.[10]

In summary, it is now clear that not only the Epistles but also the Gospels presuppose the existence of a faith-community or church. Both the Epistles and the Gospels envision a church to which an authoritative body of teaching (even "tradition") has been entrusted. From this teaching, the community draws its life and orders its affairs; it lives in a manner congruent with the word and as a visible realization of it.

Not surprisingly, both Gospels and Epistles envision and presuppose a community which makes rigorous demands upon those who would break with the old age, enter its ranks, accept its discipline, and become part of the "new age." Both Gospels and Epistles reflect a church ordered and organized in a fashion to provide instruction to new members, to give encouragement and exhortation to all members, and faithfully to pass the word on to coming generations. Gospels and Epistles reflect a community organized to meet opposition from outsiders and deal with problems emerging within its own ranks (e. g., lapses into sin and the presence of false teachers). Quite simply, concern for church order is implicit and explicit in both Gospels and Epistles.

As previously indicated, the "return to the Gospels" impulse in churches of Christ is driven by a number of concerns. It does appear that the first three of these concerns, to the extent we have accurately understood their intent, find little justification or warrant in the Gospels. Quite simply, concerns to recover informality and intimacy, repudiate tradition and ritual, and recover an undefined and undemanding simple pre-ecclesiastical Protestant Christianity cannot be based on the Gospels.

The Gospels reflect a community that makes rigorous demands on its members. Moreover, its corporate life is organized, even hierarchical, in part drawing on practices of the Jewish synagogue and the Hellenistic household.[11] To be certain, these sources are reconfigured as they are brought into conjunction with the founding events of the church (e.g., footwashing, the sacrificial Shepherd, ultimately, the cross). Still, while the early church was in many ways familial, this is not to say that it was in any modern sense "informal," egalitarian, or without structure and organization from the outset.[12]

Further, Jesus' invective against tradition, ritual, and religious hypocrisy cannot simply be taken to discredit all ritual, tradition, or tiresome practices found in the contemporary church. Although Jesus clearly opposes human traditions and rituals which distort and obscure the meaning of true faithfulness to God (Mark 7:9f), he does not oppose all traditional practices (e.g., fasting and almsgiving), and he himself initiated new traditions among his disciples. While the Lord's Supper and the Lord's Prayer clearly designate "religious practice" narrowly defined, Jesus may also be seen to initiate disciplinary practices which become ecclesiastical traditions (e.g., Matthew. 18:15-17). Moreover as the church exists under the charge to pass on the faith, it inevitably develops practices or "secondary traditions" for accomplishing its task.

The desire to recover the social and ethical passion of Jesus and the prophets is certainly commendable. As a reaction to forms of apolitical pious individualism, this approach is understandable. It does, however, involve distortions of Jesus, the Gospels, the church, and Christian political responsibility.

Jesus does not present a social theory, nor does he offer strategies for political action. The kingdom of God is brought by the Father; it is not the result of human effort, nor is it a human achievement. Failure to recognize this fact occasions countless abuses. Inevitably, it requires reading some contemporary political theory (e.g., socialism or Marxism) back into the Gospels. Further, it invariably sanctions political maneuverings within the church and tempts Christians with the various seductions of modern politics. Finally, it promotes self-righteous and utopian pretensions within the broader political arena.

While Christians must (as circumstances permit) seek to make proximate gains in establishing a just and compassionate society, this cannot and must not be equated with establishing the Kingdom of God. The role of the church in the broader political arena is not that of social engineer. Rather, the proper role of the church vis-a-vis the social and political institutions of the world is that of critic--roughly the role of Israel's prophets.[13]

The fifth concern, namely, claiming a greater loyalty to Jesus than to any particular expression of the church, should be viewed with considerable suspicion. Years ago, I was surprised to find that the seminary which I was attending was very reluctant to accept students describing themselves simply as "Christian" or "ecumenical." A professor explained to me that while the seminary accepted students from all denominations, they had had bad experiences with students claiming allegiance to Jesus and perhaps membership in an amorphous "world church." These students, it was explained, invariably "slept in" on Sunday, perhaps attended a vespers somewhere, but displayed no loyalty to any tangible expression of the Body of Christ.

Those who separate and juxtapose loyalty to Jesus and loyalty to the church, or who distinguish between loyalty to the invisible church and commitment to its visible manifestations, subtly undermine Christian loyalty and commitment in the name of their artificial "greater good."[14] Although these distinctions may be rhetorically effective and attractive to a kind of Christian sophisticate, they are biblically and theologically indefensible.

The Gospels and the Restoration Movement

It is perhaps only the last motive listed at the outset of these comments which appears to have the greatest plausibility--even promise. That is, a return to the Gospels may serve to correct certain tendencies which have appeared within the Restoration Movement which distort both early Christian faith and practice, and which contradict the best intentions of the Restoration Movement itself.

Nearly thirty years ago this writer was a young minister teaching an older adult Bible class. Our topic was the Gospel of Matthew. An elderly member, visibly annoyed at the announced topic, informed us that the Gospels were only "icing on the cake" and "not really necessary for salvation." We would, he told us, do a lot better studying Acts. The logic was clear----and familiar: the church began on Pentecost. The Gospels were interesting and informational but largely irrelevant to the practical matters of being a Christian or organizing a church.

Whether this view represents the best of Restoration thinkers or not, it does capture a widespread and at one time prevalent attitude. The effects of this orientation are devastating. It probably lies behind the frequent lament that we "have restored the letter but not the spirit of the early church." Until this nettle is firmly grasped, we will continue struggling to restore the form of the church while bemoaning our failure to restore its substance. The church requires both Epistles and Gospels. Attempts to understand, much less to live, the Christian faith on the basis of either without the other of necessity produces attenuated, incomplete, and anemic versions of Christianity.

Although the effects of this attitude are far-reaching, one particularly illustrates the depth and breadth of the problem. Put succinctly and graphically, we have separated and perhaps severed the Great Commission from the Great Commandment. [15] It is not merely that we have failed to give equal attention to both. Rather, we have failed to note the integral and inescapable relationship between the two. We have tended somehow to envision the Love Command as adjunct, incidental, or ancillary to the Great Commission.

The Gospel of John makes it inescapably clear that the Love Command is integral to mission and evangelism. It is through obedience and embodiment of the Love Command that "all men will know that you are my disciples" (13:35). Likewise, two times Jesus petitions the Father for the unity of all the disciples "so that the world may believe" (17:21,23). It is the agapic unity of the church, brought and sustained by the Holy Spirit or Paraclete (14:18-23), that reflects the very nature of the relationship between the Father and the Son ("as we are one," 17:11,21,22; cf. 5:19-24). It is in this fashion that the God whose covenant love becomes incarnate in Jesus continues to address his estranged creation.

Conclusion

We should not be forced to choose between the Gospels and the Epistles. Both are Christian scripture. The choice is not between a vaporous, ill-defined and every-changing "Jesus movement" or a sterile preoccupation with minute and petty requirements. Both of these alternatives are equally disastrous.

More important, we must realize that the Gospels themselves envision an obedient and disciplined community and that the Epistles everywhere indicate that the church is rooted in and reflective of the fullest incarnation of God's character and intention--covenant love.

Questions

1. What are some of the commonly given reasons behind the emphasis which call for a return emphasis on the Gospels?
2. What were the early Christians urged to do regarding the truth they had received?
3. With what group that found the church unnecessary to the achievement of wisdom and true spirituality did the early Christian struggle?
4. How do the Gospels, Acts and the Epistles relate to one another?
5. When (in the relationship to the Epistles) and why were the Gospels written?
6. What events do the Gospels relate that point to specific things in the church?
7. What is clearly presupposed in both the Gospels and the Epistles?
8. What is the ultimate result of failing to recognize that Jesus did not come to present a social theory or offer strategies for political action?
9. Do the New Testament scriptures suggest that it is not possible to loyalty to both Jesus and the church?
10. Would a greater emphasis on the Gospels serve to correct any distortions of faith and practice today? If so, what?

11. *The Ministry of the Holy Spirit Among Us*

Jimmy Jividen

What does the Holy Spirit do? God works in the world in sustaining His laws of creation. Christ works in the world in His church. But what is the ministry of the Holy Spirit?

This has been a recurring issue among churches of Christ. It was the belief that the Holy Spirit was still working miracles and giving new revelation that caused Sidney Rigdon to break with the nineteenth century restoration movement and unite with Mormonism. It was Robert Cave's sermon in Saint Louis on December 6, 1889 denying inspiration of Scripture that brought a theological division in the restoration movement which resulted in the Disciples of Christ.

On one hand, most leaders in the church have rejected the Calvinistic doctrine of the miraculous internal prompting of the Holy Spirit that was so prominent in the conversion experiences at camp meetings on the American frontier. On the other hand, most leaders in the church have rejected the doctrine of Deism, which entirely divorced the activity of God from the affairs of men. At some times and in some places some leaders of some churches have been in sympathy with both of these extremes, but the extremes have not been the norm. Most recently, discussion of the ministry of the Holy Spirit has centered around the *Word Only*[1] operation of the Holy Spirit and the *Charismatic*[2] workings of the Holy Spirit in the world.

The understanding that the Holy Spirit works only through the Word of God became popular among churches of Christ in the first part of the twentieth century in reaction to the false claims of Pentecostal miracles and Calvinistic conversion experiences. Debaters who rightly refuted experiential religion by showing what the Holy Spirit does not do neglected to affirm what the Holy Spirit does do.[3]

Some historians suggest that the "Word Only" view was the norm among churches of Christ until very recent times. A check of the written documents does not support this view. Books published about the Holy Spirit by leaders of the church most often affirm His personal indwelling and activity in the world. In 1892, J. W. McGarvey published his *New Commentary on Acts of Apostles* in which the personal indwelling of the Holy Spirit is affirmed. Other books on the Holy Spirit by Ashley S. Johnson, H. Leo Boles and J. D. Thomas affirm the same. I published a series of articles in the *Firm Foundation* in 1960 showing the personal indwelling and the present work of the Holy Spirit. It is presumptuous to suggest that a depersonalized view of the indwelling Holy Spirit was the church's standard view.

Several problems exist if one understands that the Holy Spirit works only through the word of God. The first and greatest problem rests in the interpretation of relevant texts. The scriptures clearly teach that the Holy Spirit dwells in a Christian: Peter stated on the Day of Pentecost, "Repent and let each of you be baptized in the name of Jesus Christ for the remission of your sins; and you shall receive the gift of the Holy Spirit" (Acts 2: 38). Although the text does not say how the Holy Spirit dwells in a Christian, the scriptures state that in fact He does. God dwells in a Christian (Philippians 2:12). Christ dwells in a Christian (Colossians 1:27). There should be no problem in affirming the scriptural teaching that the Holy Spirit dwells in a Christian.

The second problem centers around the nature of the Holy Spirit. The Holy Spirit is Divinity. He is personal, as is God the Father and God the Son. He can be grieved, lied to, and resisted (Ephesians 4:30; Acts 5:3; 7:51). He speaks, guides, and teaches (I Timothy 4:1; John 16:13; 14:26).

The "depersonalization" of the Holy Spirit was to be found in the language of those who held to the Calvinistic doctrine of the "direct operation of God on the heart of the sinner." This doctrine purported that the word of God was not sufficient to convict the sinner and produce faith unto salvation. The sinner had to wait for

God to work on his heart in a "better-felt-than-told" way before he could be saved. This "work of grace" was an emotional experience and was rightly identified by the neuter pronoun, "it". Instead of the Holy Spirit being personal Deity, He becomes a neuter force. The Holy Spirit must not be depersonalized into an emotional feeling. He is a person with whom we can have a relationship, not an emotional, ecstatic experience. The Holy Spirit must not be made into a magical genie who can be manipulated by the secret formula held in the hands of the magic worker. The Holy Spirit is God and is not under the control of men.

Some who refuted experiential religion also depersonalized the Holy Spirit. They rightly rejected emotional experiences as being the work of the Holy Spirit, affirming instead the orderly, consistent work of the Holy Spirit as revealed in Scriptures. Some went so far as to say that the Holy Spirit worked only in and through the word of God. In reaction to this view, some critics claimed that members of the church believed that the Holy Spirit was to be found between the leather covers of the King James version of the Bible. This minority reactionary view of the Holy Spirit was not the norm. Instead of an erroneous view of the Holy Spirit being taught in the majority of churches, it appears that during this period Christians received little teaching on the Holy Spirit at all.

The Holy Spirit is not to be considered some impersonal force of a mechanical universe that has always existed. Such a view of ultimate reality might fit into the fantasy of "Star Wars" fiction, which dramatized the conflict between the forces of good and evil, but it does not describe the God portrayed in Scriptures. The work of the Holy Spirit cannot be described by the benediction, "May the force be with you."

The third problem with this view is that it fails to take seriously certain activities of the Holy Spirit which are independent of the word of God. The question is not whether or not the Holy Spirit works through the word of God. Certainly He does. He inspired the word of God. Through it faith is produced and by it God's will is known. There is no problem in saying that the Holy Spirit works through the word of God. The problem comes when the little word *only* is added.

Many of the things which the Holy Spirit does are also done by the word of God. Scripture affirms that both the word of God and the Holy Spirit dwell in the Christian, give comfort and sanctify (Romans 8:11; Colossians 3:16; Acts 9:31; Romans 15:4; II Thessalonians 2:13; John 17:17).

Certainly there are ways the Holy Spirit and the word of God can be related, but the language of the text does not show them to be identical. If the Holy Spirit wanted to show that, He had adequate language to express it. Two phrases in Hebrews 6:4-5, "have been made partakers of the Holy Spirit" and "have tasted the good word of God," show the Holy Spirit and the word of God to be different. Paul's description of the Christian's armor shows a similar distinction between the Holy Spirit and the word of God. "The sword of the Spirit is the word of God" (Ephesians 6:17). Just as a sword is different from the soldier, the word of God is different from the Holy Spirit.

The Holy Spirit is the worker, and the word of God is His work. They must not be confused. The word of God is only one of the works of the Holy Spirit. The word of God cannot be separated from the Holy Spirit, but the work of the Holy Spirit can be separated from the word of God. It should be noted, however, that all we know about the work of the Holy Spirit is revealed in the word of God.

The scriptures affirm that the Holy Spirit helps the Christian beyond what He does in the word of God. When we do not know how to pray as we should, He helps with "groanings too deep for words" (Romans 8:26). When we are tempted, we have the help of God (Holy Spirit included) so we will not be tempted beyond what we can bear (I Corinthians 10:13). When God (Holy Spirit included) works providentially, we know He causes all things to work together for good (Romans 8:28). When Paul wrote his doxology to the Ephesians, he spoke of the Holy Spirit: The Holy Spirit ". . . is able to do exceeding abundantly beyond all that we ask or think . . . ." (Ephesians 3:20).

Charismatic Understanding

The *Charismatic* understanding of the Holy Spirit has had more serious consequences among churches of Christ than the *Word Only* understanding because it deals with religious authority. Espousing the *Word Only* understanding of the Holy Spirit centers on how the Holy Spirit works in the world--directly or through the medium of the word of God. Espousing the Charismatic understanding of the Holy Spirit centers upon whether or not God still works miracles, causes people to speak in tongues, and gives new revelation. It challenges the sufficiency of the scriptures as the authority for the faith and practice of the church. It allows for latter day revelations and a subjective, individualistic view of truth.

To a Charismatic, reason and logic are not as important as "how you feel." If one were to accept that God still breaks His laws in nature to work a miracle, it is a short step to accepting that God breaks His laws in scriptures.

Charismatic religion had historically been associated with the Pentecostal and Holiness churches. It broke into the mainstream denominations in the early sixties. Rector Bennet of the Saint Mark Episcopal Church in Van Nuys, California, experienced "speaking in tongues" in the mid 1960's. He, along with other denominational leaders of different backgrounds, organized the Full Gospel Business Men Fellowship International which spread the "Charismatic Revival" throughout both Catholic and Protestant denominations. In 1970, they claimed to have between two and three million adherents in the United States alone. The methodology of these Charismatics was not to form a new church, but to work from within the existing religious groups to change their teachings and practices.

Churches of Christ had already weathered similar challenges to their faith. First, before 1850, there were the Mormons under the leadership of the apostate Sidney Rigdon. Second, after 1900, there were the "Pentecostals" who claimed "speaking with tongues" was a part of New Testament Christianity that must be restored.

The Charismatic revival of the sixties was different from these former challenges in two ways. First, the extreme teaching by some church leaders who affirmed that the Holy Spirit worked only through the word of God left a vacuum of understanding on how the Holy Spirit works in the world. This allowed a reaction from the opposite extreme. Second, a number of influential leaders in churches of Christ espoused the Charismatic revival. Perhaps the most influential was Pat Boone. His book, The *New Song*, openly advocated "speaking in tongues" and was critical of churches of Christ. There were few churches, either in the United States or overseas, who did not have to deal with this doctrine.

Although a few churches and a number of preachers espoused the Charismatic teachings and ceased to be associated with churches of Christ, the apostasy was not great in number or influence. Three reasons might be suggested for why the Charismatic movement did not have as great a following in the church as in other religious organizations. First, the church had already dealt with similar teachings of the Pentecostals and the Mormons and had seen the consequences of espousing such a doctrine. Second, the strong reliance upon scripture as the only religious authority for faith and practice caused a clear rejection of religious authority based on experiential feelings. Third, Christian leaders boldly challenged and refuted the Charismatic doctrines and practices.

Some positive consequences came from confronting the Charismatic movement. First, it forced a restudy of the Holy Spirit, miracles, and spiritual gifts. We saw more speaking and writing on these subjects in the late sixties and seventies than in all the previous generations. Second, the Charismatic movement exposed the weakness of the cold, rationalistic, duty-worship ritual practiced in some churches and forced a rethinking of the nature and purpose of worship. Not only was the irrational, experiential excitement of the Charismatics false worship, but so also were the dull, mindless, "word only" rituals of the other extreme. Third, the Charismatic movement showed the joy of sharing one's faith. To the Charismatics, arguments were not as strong as testimony and what the Bible says was not as important as "how one feels." In spite of the theological and logical errors of this position, one cannot deny the importance of feelings and testimony in the Christian life. Confronting the Charismatics, I believe, has caused members of the church to be more open and joyful in expressing their faith.

In spite of its appeal, the Charismatic movement was rejected by the church because of some fundamental errors in its teachings.[4] First, the claim that the contemporary ecstatic utterances are the same as "speaking in tongues" in the New Testament is completely without basis. The New Testament tongues were the languages of men (Acts 2:4-8). Ecstatic utterances experienced by Charismatics today can be found in different world religions that are completely foreign to Christianity. They are the common psychological phenomenon of automatic speech.

Second, the New Testament tongues were signs to confirm the message as being from God (Mark 16:17). If "tongues" exist today, then so does new revelation. If there is new revelation, then the scriptures are incomplete. Tongues and new revelation go together.

Third, the scriptures show that miracles have ceased. When the epistles speak of "signs" being performed in the latter times, they are called false wonders by false teachers (I Timothy 4:1-2; II Thessalonians 2:7-12). Even Jesus predicted such: "For false Christs and false prophets will arise and will show great signs and wonders, so as to mislead, if possible even the elect" (Matthew 24:24). The Gospels and Acts speak of many miracles. The early epistles speak of miraculous gifts, but the later epistles speak of none. Paul predicted the passing of spiritual gifts (I Corinthians 13:8). The purpose of miracles was to confirm the word as it was being revealed (Mark 16:20). So when the word was confirmed, the need for miracles ceased.

Fourth, there is no evidence that contemporary miracles happen. The New Testament miracles were such that even the enemies of the church could not deny them (Acts 4:14-16). Contemporary claims of miracles are delusions and deceit without real evidence. Testimonies of deluded or deceitful witnesses do not constitute proof. If you believe this kind of witness, then "Elvis is alive and well." A lot of confusion exists about the meaning of the term, "miracle." Sometimes it is used colloquially to mean nothing more than that which is "out of the ordinary" or paranormal. This is not the way the New Testament uses the term. A New Testament miracle is an event contrary to the laws of nature, which is used by God to show His approval of a man and/or His message. Contemporary miraculous claims do not fit this definition.

Fifth, the Holy Spirit is not an emotional experience. Perhaps nothing has caused confusion in understanding the Holy Spirit more than identifying Him with an emotional or psychological experience. Emotional feelings of awe, fear and love are common among all humans. Religious experiences of "conversion," "terror" and "joy" are common in all religions. While there is nothing wrong with experiences, they become wrong when identified as a miracle from God.

The claims of miracles, speaking in tongues, visions, and new revelation from Divinity are a part of most world religions. If these claims are to be accepted in one religion, how can they be rejected in others? Both are supported by the same kind of evidence. How can two people who believe and practice contradictory doctrines both be getting their guidance from the Holy Spirit? One or both of these persons must be deceived. If one claims that the Holy Spirit has revealed some doctrine or practice, the other cannot deny it without denying his own claim of the Holy Spirit. A person cannot rely on "how he feels" for his religious convictions. This practice would make "every man do what seems right in his own eyes" and make his own feelings his religious authority.

Perhaps the most serious negative influence of the Charismatic movement in the church is the way some view the scriptures. Instead of accepting them as the absolute, objective, unchanging word of God, they view them as time bound, culturally tainted, and relative. The "words of men" in the scriptures become, to them, the word of God when they are experientially related to their contemporary situation. This may be some of the background to what is being called "the new hermeneutic."

Present Work of the Holy Spirit

In spite of the tendency of some to depersonalize the Holy Spirit into a force and others to emotionalize the Holy Spirit into an experience, He still works in the church and Christians today.

The Holy Spirit is God. While we might not be able to describe the Trinity in Aristotelian thought patterns, we know that the Father, Son, and also the Holy Spirit are equally God. The scriptures affirm it. In the account of Ananias and Sapphira's dishonest giving in Acts 5:3-4, Luke recorded that Ananias lied "to the Holy Spirit," and that he lied "to God."

The Holy Spirit is personal. He is not a neuter thing or an impersonal force. Jesus uses the masculine personal pronoun in referring to the Holy Spirit: When *pneuma* stands alone or is the antecedent of the pronoun as in Romans 8:26, the neuter form is used. When *parcaletos* is the antecedent, then the masculine pronoun is used. "But the Helper, the Holy Spirit, whom the Father will send in My name, *He* will teach you all things" (John 14:26).

The Holy Spirit dwells in the church. The church was planned by God and purchased with the blood of Jesus, but the Holy Spirit dwells in it today. Paul said we "are being built together into a dwelling of God in the Spirit" (Ephesians 2:22). Paul warns those who would divide the church into parties of the consequences of defiling the temple of God in which the Holy Spirit dwells: "Do you not know that you are a temple of God, and that the Spirit of God dwells in you?" (I Corinthians 3:16).

The Holy Spirit dwells in every Christian. We receive Him at baptism just as we receive the forgiveness of sins (Acts 2:38). Receiving the Holy Spirit is not a miraculous event any more than receiving the forgiveness of sins is a miraculous event. Both are real and according to God's promises. Both give reason for rejoicing. Neither gives the receiver supernatural powers. Just as the Holy Spirit dwelling in the church makes her holy, the Holy Spirit dwelling in the Christian identifies him as a child of God. The Holy Spirit is the "tie that binds" us to one another and to God. Paul wrote: "And because you are sons, God has sent forth the Spirit of His Son into our hearts, crying, Abba! Father!" (Galatians 4:6).

The Holy Spirit inspires the word of God and works through the word of God in the world. Peter affirms that the scriptures did not come by the will of men, "but men moved by the Holy Spirit spoke from God" (II Peter 1:21). The word of God is holy because it came from the Holy Spirit. He continues to work through the word of God in accomplishing the work of God in the world. It is only through the word of God that one can come to faith (Romans 10:17). It is only through the word of God that one can know the will of God. The Holy Spirit works through the word of God to help the Christian fight the Devil. Our weapon to overcome the Devil is "the sword of the Spirit, which is the word of God" (Ephesians 6:17).

The Holy Spirit helps us in expressing our devotion to God. Human language is limited and cannot fully express our inner feelings of devotion or anguish of spirit. We want to praise God more than words can express. We want to petition God with greater intensity than language can convey. Does God know our feelings? Can He understand our desires? Paul answers such a question clearly and affirms the help of the Holy Spirit in our prayers: "And in the same way the Spirit also helps our weaknesses, for we do not know how to pray as we should, but the Spirit Himself intercedes for us with groanings too deep for words" (Romans 8:26).

Other activities of the Holy Spirit in the world are affirmed in the New Testament. He helps us have "blessed assurance" that we abide in God and God abides in us: "By this we know that we abide in Him and He in us, because He has given us of His Spirit" (I John 4:13). He helps in "putting to death the deeds of the body" (Romans 8: 13). He helps us bear the "fruit of the Spirit:" love, joy, peace, patience, kindness, goodness, faithfulness, gentleness and self-control (Galatians 5:22-23). Every time we see these attributes in a Christian, we can know that the Holy Spirit is working in him.

Just as we do not know all of the workings of God in the world, we do not know all of the workings of the Holy Spirit. He is God, and He still works in the world. We must not set limits on God beyond what is revealed. God has limited Himself in both creation and revelation. The laws of God which He spoke into existence at the beginning give us orderliness in the world. God can do what He wants to do, but He limits Himself to follow His laws of creation. The truth of God which He spoke into existence in revelation gives us His will and His promises. God can do what He wants to do, but He limits Himself in following His laws of revelation.

In describing the ministry of the Holy Spirit among us, we must avoid two things. First, we must not claim for the Holy Spirit that which is not according to His will in scripture or is contrary to

God's laws in nature. Second, we must not put a limit on what He does when that limit is not given in scripture. We do not know all of the activities of God: "For who has known the mind of the Lord, that we should instruct Him?" (I Corinthians 2:16).

We cannot set limits on the activity of the Holy Spirit except as He Himself has revealed in the scriptures or in nature. He still works in the world in sustaining nature, in keeping the promises He has made to give us help and in bringing about the providential plans of God. Paul wrote that the Holy Spirit "is able to do exceeding abundantly beyond all that we ask or think" (Ephesians 3:20). We cannot know how He helps in not allowing us "to be tempted beyond what [we] are able" (I Corinthians 10:13). We cannot know how He helps in causing "all things to work together for good" (Romans 8:28). We cannot know how He helps in answering our prayers. He is God.

Conclusions

The ministry of the Holy Spirit among us is affirmed in scriptures. Jesus has not left us "orphans" in the world. He sent the Holy Spirit, the promised Helper. The Holy Spirit inspired scripture and still works through scripture. The Holy Spirit dwells in the church and still makes it holy. The Holy Spirit dwells in Christians and helps us in ways far beyond what we ask or think.

In affirming the present help of the Holy Spirit, we must not fall under the Charismatic deception that the Holy Spirit is an experiential force that contradicts God's will in nature and in scriptures. Such a view depersonalizes the Holy Spirit. In affirming the ministry of the Holy Spirit, we must not fall under the error of Deism, which makes God totally unconcerned with man. If this were the case, prayer would be useless and providence a delusion.

Questions

1. Who is the Holy Spirit?
2. What part did the Holy Spirit play in revealing and confirming the word of God?
3. What part does the Holy Spirit play in conversion of sinners?
4. Is the Holy Spirit the Word of God? (see John 1: 1 & Ephesians 6: 17)

161

5. What does the Holy Spirit do besides guiding men to write the word of God?
6. Discuss the three reasons that the churches of Christ were not greatly affected by the Charismatic movement.
7. Discuss positive consequences that came from confronting the Charismatic doctrines and practices.
8. List and discuss five reasons the Charismatic movement was rejected by the church.
9. Discuss the Holy Spirit dwelling in the church and individual Christians today.
10. Discuss two things that must be avoided in describing the ministry of the Holy Spirit today.

12. Boomergeist: The Spirit of the Age

Jim Baird

"The next war will be between young and old!" So pundits warn of the coming conflict over social security and other entitlements of the elderly. But many of us in the church feel that we have been fighting this war for years. Recent church conflicts have often had a strong young-versus-old feel to them. Something seems to have severed the connection that is supposed to allow a non-disruptive transmission of values and leadership from one generation to the next. Instead, "they" think and talk so differently from "us" that even simple issues can lead to calls for bloody revolution from one generation and ruthless suppression from the other.   Meanwhile, church leaders find themselves shuttling between the generations faster than Palestinian negotiators, simply trying to avoid bloodshed for one more Sunday.

Part of the solution to this intergenerational breakdown must come in greater understanding of the generations themselves. As my title suggests, the spirit of our age is a different spirit from that which held sway thirty years ago, and those of us who reached maturity in the meantime think and talk differently as a result. This chapter is an attempt to analyze two large-scale processes in American culture which have widened the gulf between young and old in our churches.

The first process is secularization. A society is secularized to the extent that religion is shorn of power in the public culture and is increasingly allowed to exist only in private. Secularization is an old process in western civilization, but certain forces have made American culture of the last three decades one of the most intensely secular societies ever. Whether we recognize it or not, the hyper-secularized culture in which we now live alters our own practice of Christianity. What we want out of our churches, what kinds of arguments we take to be convincing, even what we will and will not accept from our leaders; all of these are affected by our hyper-secular environment.

The second process is cultural diversification. While there is still a dominant culture in America, all of us recognize the increasing need to co-exist with other cultures. As we live side by side with people who have different views about the fundamentals of life, our attitudes cannot help but be changed. In the face of wider cultural diversity, Christians tend toward different views about the nature of the absolutes in Christianity and the relation of our community to others.

Obviously, not all the effects of these two processes are bad, just as not all are good. The important thing is that they are real, and they lead to real differences of viewpoint between the generations. By understanding them more fully, we may help bridge the chasm which has opened in so many of our congregations. And we may be able to identify strategies which will help churches survive and even flourish in the changed environment these processes are helping to create.

Hyper-secularization

The claim that American culture is hyper-secular certainly sounds odd at a time when pollsters are telling us that at least nine out of ten Americans believe in God.[1] But being secular is not the same as being irreligious. The crucial measure of secularization is the extent to which religion is denied an overt role in the *public* life of the culture. A secularized society is classically one in which religious institutions are denied overt political power, refused direct support from the government and removed from control over higher education. Secularization increases as religious standards become less and less important for the setting of public policy, as religion enters less and less into our public discussions and as the role of religion is de-emphasized in all the public paths by which our culture is disseminated and passed on to the next generation. By this standard American culture in the last thirty years has been secularized on a massive scale, for all its private religiousity.[2]

The roots of the drive for secularization in western civilization are legion, and most have been operating at varying levels for centuries. So what is special about the last three decades in America? I would argue for two crucial differences. One of these, quite obviously, has been the success of challenges to public religion based on the anti-establishment clause of the First Amendment to the Constitution. The other, less obviously, is television.

In 1962, the Supreme Court effectively removed school-sponsored prayer from our public educational system.[3] My own feelings about this are still quite mixed. I remember school days which opened with a ritualistic recitation of the "Lord's Prayer," but I cannot remember the experience being a particularly edifying one. I had a six-year old's suspicion that it was all an elaborate plot to trick me into some kind of false doctrine. I knew that we believed that the kingdom had come on Pentecost, so I scrupulously altered the wording to "Thy kingdom grow." In addition, I always tried to insert a quick "In Jesus' name," just to be on the safe side. So I did not grieve much when the morning prayer was quietly dropped in our school system. But looking back, I have to admit that for sheer symbolism, the suppression of school prayer by the highest legal authority in our land because it conflicted with the document which was the guarantee of our liberties, ranks as the watershed in the secularization of American culture. We Christians have felt a little like aliens in our own country ever since.

But symbolism aside, we should consider the overall cultural effect of increased secularization of education and culture in the last three decades. As not just prayer, but many other activities that might suggest the promotion of religion were challenged and removed from school, how were those who were being educated affected? It is in school that most of us find out those things our society thinks are important enough for us to learn. For that reason, silence about a subject in public schools is hardly neutral. Students understandably feel that whatever is not presented in schools is not, apparently, worth knowing. This gives the bite to Stephen Carter's recent complaint, "One problem with the public school curriculum....is that the concern to avoid even a hint of forbidden *endorsement* of religion has led to a climate in which teachers are loath to *mention* religion."[4] For many students raised in such a climate, the conclusion is obvious. Religion is hardly mentioned in school, therefore religion is largely irrelevant to what they perceive as "real" life.[5] In this so-called "real" life, the original framers of our government were influenced by Rousseu and Voltaire, but not, apparently by Moses and Jesus. In "real" life, those who fought to end slavery were moved by the utilitarianism of Jeremy Bentham, but not the Sermon on the Mount of Christ. In "real" life, it is forgotten that America's major universities started as ministerial training schools, and the fact that most hospitals, orphanages and charitable missions were built by religious people is passed over in silence. Religion had no significant influence on the development of art, music, theater and literature in "real" life, nor were the Copernican and Newtonian revolutions carried out by scientists who professed Christian faith. Why should we blame students for learning the lesson that public education, by its silence, proclaims so loudly? Religion may have significance in private life, but in "real" life, religion simply does not count.

If this segregation of religion from "real" life is insinuated by our system of public education, it is beamed straight into our brains by network television. Most of us are unaware of the powerful effect, but it is real nevertheless, and was particularly potent before the multiple channels provided by cable, when the Big Three networks were the only providers of national television programming. The reason for this was simple enough. We have probably all complained about the "lowest common denominator" quality of most network television, driven by the need to appeal to the widest possible number of viewers from all regions of the United States. This same need made it unprofitable for the networks, during their heyday, to create programming which depicted religion the way most Americans experienced it. Americans will, apparently, sit through hours of laugh-track comedy and implausible action, and seem to be moved to turn off the set only when irritated. Since religion has always been a touchy subject in America, and since the positive depiction of any actual religion runs the risk of irritating those viewers who belong to competing faiths, it has almost always been safer to avoid showing any religion in a positive light, except when safely confined to the past. On the other hand, religions or religious actions which are universally deplored by the viewing public will irritate few and titillate many. Thus religious hypocrisy, scandal and fraud make television that is both popular and safe. Add to this the observation at least as old as Plato that, dramatically speaking, evil is a lot more interesting than good, and it is not hard to see why positive depictions of religion were so scarce during the heyday of network television and are now usually confined to only those few channels dedicated to the religious market.

Imagine for a moment what theories alien sociologists would form about our culture if they were judging us simply by the television programming we have been sending them at the speed of light over the last thirty years. They would certainly know a lot about handguns and ways to wreck cars. Thanks to laugh-tracks, they would probably have elaborate (and wildly incorrect) theories about what we think is funny. And they might well conclude that *the* fundamental decision of every American's life, the decision that ultimately decides social, sexual and economic success, is what mixture of caramel-colored, gas-laden sugar water to drink. But whatever conclusions they reached, it is certain that they would not conclude from television that nine out of ten of us believe in God, eight out of ten of us pray regularly, seven out of ten of us are church members, and six out of ten of us claim that religion is very important in our lives. Our culture as shown on television for the past thirty years simply does not include religion.

Meanwhile, television has achieved a dominance in our lives that no other art form has ever approached. We are told that someone who makes it to age eighteen in America will have watched close to 19,000 hours of television.[6] That is 6,000 more hours that he will have spent in school, and even if his parents are very religious, it is 15,000 hours more than he will have spent in church. So why should his conclusions be any different from our hypothetical alien sociologists? His natural assumption will be that religion is just irrelevant to the culture at large. Even if his own family carries on a high level of religious activity, he is tempted to think of that as "odd" and somehow out of step with the world. Religion as he experiences it is never on television and television is by far the single biggest avenue by which the public world communicates with him. Why not conclude that religion may be important as a private matter, but it has no role to play in the public world?

It is this *sequestering* of religion by public education and television that has created the effect I call "hyper-secularization." Religion is shoved into a contemplative little corner, talking its special talk, walking its special walk. Meanwhile, the rest of life goes blistering past with a whole different vocabulary and a very different set of rules. A Christian who wants to get along in the larger culture must master its rules, even if he manages to avoid letting the rules master him. Of course, Christians of every age face the challenge of being in the world but not of the world. However, because of the sheer amount of television and public education they experience, Christians who have been raised in our hyper-secularized society face a uniquely powerful suggestion that religion is out of step with reality.

There are a number of ways this hyper-secularization of the environment in which Babyboomers came to maturity can create problems between the generations. For instance, *The Worldly Church* by Leonard Allen, Richard Hughes and Michael Weed, gives an outstanding analysis of the tendency within the last thirty years to judge the activities of the churches by what are essentially secular standards.[7] They argue that church activities or teachings are more likely to be judged 'good' if they meet some here and now need---they prevent divorce or heal the victims of abuse or recruit more members---while they are more likely to be seen as 'irrelevant' if they promote merely spiritual goods---holiness, purity, obedience, truth, joy, peace and love. I believe Allen, Hughes and Weed have sounded a needed warning, and I recommend their work.

A more fundamental effect of hyper-secularization can be seen as a fundamental change in the people we are trying to reach. There was a time when most of the people we tried to talk to about Christianity already had a highly developed loyalty to some brand of Protestant Christianity. That meant that they had already submitted in large measure to many of the moral teachings of Christianity and that they had a strong desire to follow the Bible. Given this great pool of Bible-believing, basically moral people, we had the luxury of focusing our message almost exclusively on purity of faith and practice. Others had done the work of convincing people of the Lordship of Christ and the authority of scripture. Ours was by and large a ministry of teaching the way of the Lord more perfectly. Our literature, our evangelistic methods, our educational systems and even our forms of worship were shaped to serve this end.

But in the meantime, our environment was changing. Now public education and television bring secularization into the most religious of homes. Now the very fundamentals of Christianity are live issues even for dedicated church members. And even in the deepest depths of the Bible Belt, we now face a variety of non-Christian religions and a lot of just plain pagans to boot. It is no longer enough to know just how to win an argument with a Baptist. Our people now need to have something to say to Buddhists and Ba'hais, too.

In this new environment, many of our traditional doctrinal selling points have become secondary. I do not mean that correct doctrine and practice are unimportant. They are and always will be essential. I am simply pointing out what we all instinctively know, that it is foolish to argue about correct modes of church government with someone who is not even sure he is going to follow Jesus. We must face up to the challenge of converting people to the Lordship of Christ. Then and only then will we have reason to continue on to the full counsel of God.

But as we face this challenge, things change. The tracts, songs and sermons which were designed for an environment in which pure doctrine was our main selling point often seem to miss the mark now. Instead, our struggle is to create basic faith in a world in which religion is treated as an irrelevance. We work to help our people rise above the secular morality and worldview which is beamed into their homes up to five hours every night. Our forms of worship and our styles of communication are now being shaped primarily by these new struggles. I am convinced that many of the conflicts which are now arising in our churches are fueled at least partially by the unease that these gradual changes create. Disputes are triggered by specific issues, some of which seem so trivial that it's hard for church leaders to believe they are real (until the contribution starts to drop). But often the root of the difficulty is not a substantial disagreement about doctrine, but simply a difference in emphasis. In particular, I think that a lot (though not all) of what has been said about the distinction between the "core" gospel and other doctrine really boils down to an attempt to articulate the shift in emphasis brought about by the modern need to deliver our message to a increasingly secular world.

This in turn suggests a couple of ways of reducing the intergenerational tension at this point. First, we will all be helped by understanding the massive change that has taken place in our culture. Once we realize some of the ways that our forms of religion were shaped by an environment that no longer exists, it will take some of the sting out of our adjustments to the new, hyper-secular situation. Second, we can remove a lot of worry about the future of the church by re-affirming the importance of correct faith and practice in Christianity. Even though the issues of doctrinal purity that used to be so prominent in our movement are now often eclipsed by the more fundamental issues of faith and morality, we should not fall into the simple-minded assumption that doctrinal purity no longer matters. When people are brought into Christ and when they submit to His will in their lives, they must still learn how to worship, how to organize, and so forth. There is simply no other guide for these matters than the New Testament. So this is not time for us to give up doctrinal purity, and we can avoid a lot of misunderstandings simply by making that clear.

A third effect of hyper-secularization that often shows up in intergenerational conflicts is the fact that explicitly religious claims are judged "guilty until proven innocent," while for secular beliefs the converse is true. To take a case in point, the Bible clearly teaches that homosexual actions are sinful. Meanwhile the secular culture is pushing with increasing momentum the view that homosexual actions are simply the natural results of an innate characteristic of no more moral significance than skin color, and no more worthy of condemnation. Or course, any Christian who wants to defend the biblical position in the public arena will face an enormous amount of resistance. But what is interesting to me is the amount of resistance the biblical view meets in many overtly Christian settings. It often seems that the biblical teachings on this subject are viewed with deep suspicion, so that we continue to hold to the Bible's condemnation of homosexual actions only because the biblical case is so air-tight. Furthermore, we always seem to breath easier if the biblical teaching can be reinforced with some good hard scientific data--the kind of data that secular world deems acceptable. In essence, we are saying that the Bible is wrong until shown to be right. What is the source of this "guilty until proven innocent" view of biblical teaching, if not the insinuations of the larger culture? In effect we are insisting that biblical teachings meet standards of evidence far higher than those we require of the pronouncements of our secular culture. We have brought the stance of the secular culture into our churches.

The complementary effect is that we spend little or no time investigating the credentials of the conflicting secular belief. To see this, we need only ask ourselves how much confidence we would have in the secular dogmas about homosexuality if we held them to the "guilty until proven innocent" standard. Can anyone seriously claim that any of the evidence put forward so far amounts to *proof* that homosexuality is an innate characteristic of no moral significance? Deep down we are all aware that the secular dogmas about homosexuality have far more to do with our particular political situation than with anything we *know* scientifically.

Nor are these observations restricted to homosexuality. There are a host of cases in which we put the Bible on strictest trial because of the unsupported allegations of our hyper-secular culture. It is time for us to realize that we are being duped. All beliefs should be held to the same standards of evidence. When we find ourselves having difficulty accepting some apparent teaching of scripture, we need to spend a little time looking into the source of our doubts. If investigation shows that our doubts stem mainly from the pounding propaganda of our culture, we will be less impressed. After all, it is the testimony of Christ that validates for us the teachings of scripture. We believe that He will bring the whole world into judgment, and that certainly gives His word the right to judge the latest dictates of political correctness.

If we level the playing field in this way, we will find that Christianity is an impressive intellectual competitor. It has confronted and vanquished many powerful world-views in the past and I am convinced that it is more than a match for the mushy, bend-in-the political-wind hodge podge that passes for the thought system of our culture. Indeed, one of the great opportunities the churches have to flourish in the face of the Boomergeist is to capitalize on the emerging intellectual and moral vacuousness of the larger culture. We need to learn to identify those hidden assumptions in the secular view that grants it undeserved acceptance, and we need to expose those assumptions with glee to a world that is just starting to ask "Where did we go wrong?" Most of all, we Christians need to rediscover our pride. After all, we are the true rebels now, the true revolutionaries standing against a corrupt system, outnumbered and despised, but fighting. As our culture collapses and people begin to look for light, God can use our fight to make us shine like a city set on a hill, the entrance into the kingdom that will never pass away.

With that bright vision in mind, let us turn to the second major process which is driving the spirit of this age.

Cultural Diversification

The United States grew as an immigrant society, prospering through the influx of people from all over the world, and enriching itself culturally from their diversity. Nevertheless, the numerical and economic dominance of white, Anglo-Saxon, Protestant culture was a given. Subcultures tended either to dissolve into the dominant culture, or to maintain their identity through various techniques of isolation and group cohesion. Either way, the average American could take assumptions and structures of his culture pretty much for granted. It was the job of minority cultures to become aware of their own systems and that of the dominant culture, and to make whatever adjustments were necessary to live within it.

But more recent times have seen an important change in this pattern. As subcultures have grown in political and economic strength, there has been a decreased willingness to remove themselves so effectively from the public life of the dominant culture. Instead, they have insisted on the right to live and act publicly according to their own cultural norms, without assimilation and without withdrawal into their own communities. In addition, and quite justly, they have demanded the right to be protected from discrimination based on cultural differences. This ongoing process is called cultural diversification. It is sometimes painful, especially to those who used to enjoy the favored status granted them by the dominant culture. But it is certainly a good process in the long run, if for no other reason than that the obvious alternative is to attempt to re-impose white, Anglo-Saxon Protestant dominance, resulting in a nasty nationalism not essentially different from that of the Ku Klux Klan.

Nevertheless, though I claim that cultural diversification is a good process overall, it is not without its negative effects. Of greatest concern is the fact that cultural diversification creates a fertile breeding ground for relativism. By relativism, I mean the view that culture is the ultimate foundation of morality. According to relativism, different cultures simply create different patterns of right and wrong, and there is no absolute standard by which any culture can criticize any other. Actions can be judged right or wrong within the confines of a particular culture, but no actions are right or wrong in themselves. Cultural diversification does not mandate relativism by any means, but the difficult intellectual and moral problems generated by cultural diversification create a climate in which relativism seems to offer a seductively easy set of solutions.

In a monolithic culture, individuals receive an overwhelmingly standardized set of answers about most issues of morality and value. Parents, teachers, neighbors and ministers all speak with one voice. As a result, individuals face life already sure about how they should act as a child or parent, husband or wife. They know what attitudes to take toward different jobs and they have definite beliefs about what balance should be struck between work and family, duty and leisure. They have a clear vision of what actions they should be ashamed of, and what actions are acceptable. Such standardization can of course be very oppressive if the individual thinks the answers given are wrong, but it is a luxury for most, since it saves the time and anxiety that would otherwise have to be spent deciding these fundamental issues.

But the increase of cultural diversity removes this luxury. In a culturally diverse society, we are always running into people who hold views of family, morality or life which are radically different from our own. Worse, they are just as sure of their values as we are of ours. We are constantly forced to judge between these many competing "certainties," and often we have very little time in which to do so. Ideally, we would be able to enter into a thorough dialogue with those who hold conflicting views, gradually increasing our understanding of each other until we found some moral or rational common ground on which to agree. But the practical solution is often to adopt an attitude of "live and let live," in which the holders of opposing moral views do not discuss their way to common ground, but simply agree to try not to bother each other too much. This practical solution has become almost mandatory in the political arena. Given the structure of our society, we simply do not have a cost-effective way to reach quick agreement about the many issues of family, work and morality over which we now have widely different cultural views. Often the best available political solution is for the government to tolerate both positions, with the message that neither can be judged to be in error.

These personal and political decisions to "live and let live" are often the best we can do in the concrete situations in which we find ourselves. Of course, it is psychologically possible to adopt the "live and let live" stance as the purely pragmatic decision that it is, without drifting into the notion that it reflects some deeper truth about the universe. Nevertheless, the repeated exercise of the "live and let live" option does create a relativistic bent of mind. A culture which is constantly saying "neither side can be judged wrong" creates the strong impression that there is simply no such thing as right or wrong. For this reason, those who grew up during the last thirty years of cultural diversification face the strong temptation to adopt the relativistic view in which there is no objective right and wrong, and in which every certainty is called into question.

Once we recognize this tendency toward relativism, we can begin to guard against its effects on our congregations. Relativism views with suspicion every authority by which one person might criticize the actions of another. The characteristic phrase of relativism is "Who am I to say that it is wrong to....?" This kind of environment is naturally hostile to the use of the Bible as an absolute standard by which to judge the faith and practice of Christianity. It cannot immediately remove appeals to scriptural authority, but it tends over time to erode such appeals by laying a heavy burden of proof on anyone who claims to find fault with another group based on the Bible. Instead of asking, "Is this doctrine or practice in accordance with scripture?" we tend more often to ask, "What right have you got to say this doctrine or practice is wrong?" This steady pressure constantly reduces the areas in which we feel that the Bible speaks with enough clarity to allow us to say certain practices or doctrines need to be reformed. We feel the comforting approval of the culture on each issue about which we can say "live and let live." The culture urges us toward the simplistic view that tolerance can solve all of our problems.

Of course, tolerance is built into Christianity, and has not received the emphasis that it should have. Even those with whom we strongly disagree are to be treated with respect, and more than respect, with love. But the idea that tolerance alone is sufficient to solve all of our problems is naive. First of all, tolerance alone is not sufficient to deal with the messy problem of deeply ingrained divisions among those who profess Christ. Whatever words of détente we mouth with other groups, nobody really doubts that on the gritty ground we will still be in conflict and competition with them. The world will still have grounds to scoff at "those Christians who try to convert us when they cannot agree among themselves." Jesus' desire of John 17:20, 21 will still be frustrated.

In fact, the policy of complete tolerance perversely institutionalizes whatever differences exist. If we give up on all attempts to resolve differences by appeal to the jointly accepted authority of scripture, we will be left with nothing more than the emotional strength of our differing traditions. Our appeal for unity can only be to "come and do it our way," which no one from a different tradition has any reason to accept.

This talk of divisions and standards points to a deeper problem with the relativistic tendencies of the Boomergeist. We need to remember that the real root of relativism is despair. It is the loss of hope that people from very different backgrounds can enter into dialogue with some hope of finding rational common ground. Instead the relativist tends to believe that our backgrounds determine our thinking so completely that there simply is no rational common ground.

As this spirit invades religion, it encourages the assumption that there is no real hope for dialogue between people from deeply divergent traditions. In our congregations, this loss of hope undercuts our efforts to let the New Testament serve as a basis for unity. Our restorationism is based on the belief that people can read the Bible alike and come to unity on the basis of it. The spirit of the age increasingly influences us to doubt this.

It must be said that the environment that shapes us religiously affects us to our core, and in ways still far too intricate for reason to unravel completely. We cannot sweep these influences away by any simple act of will, no matter how sincere we may be. The belief that we can attain such complete objectivity about our own deepest beliefs and motives is part of the overconfidence in reason that is the characteristic illusion of the Enlightenment. We can no more recognize all of our prejudices and dismiss them through sincerity than we can jump out of our

174

own skin. Consequently, sincere disagreement over the teachings of scripture are quite possible. Recognizing this will help us to realize that not everyone who disagrees with us is just willfully rejecting the truth.

On the other hand, God *is* real and He *has* chosen to reveal the mystery of Christ to us in scripture. Prejudiced, weak, and fallible as we are, He has set us the task of uncovering that mystery and clinging to it. The massively divergent traditions which drive the current disagreements in Christendom were not erected in one day and it is naive to think that they can be dismantled overnight. But to conclude from the depth of disagreement that the whole project of trying to find common ground is hopeless is the characteristic illusion of our relativistic culture. Just because dialogue is difficult is no reason to conclude that it is worthless. We overcome bits of prejudice all the time, and the willingness to enter into a difficult discussion between passionately held and widely different views is often blessed by God with new understanding and a richer grasp of the truth. The discovery of deeply ingrained disagreement between people is not the end of the discussion, but just where the discussion gets interesting.

For this reason, it seems clear that God has called us to enter vigorously into dialogue with all those who profess Christ. Such dialogue must be carried out with mutual respect and tolerance, but with an urgent desire to tell the truth to the best of our limited ability. We must acknowledge that we are ultimately unable to judge the intricacies of the human heart, and we must thank God that He is able to make those judgments in the abundance of His justice and grace. But if we use the fact of God's ultimate gracious judgment as an excuse to hide the truth, we will not be blameless. If we sincerely believe another who professes Christ is displeasing Him in some belief or actions, can we really convince ourselves that it is love that tells us to keep silent? Won't we know it is really cowardice? If we speak and are wrong, perhaps we will be led to correct our error. If we speak and are right, perhaps the other will be led to correct his error. It is only if we are silent that error seems certain to prevail.

Conclusion

Having surveyed some key elements of the spirit of the age, we should end by reminding ourselves that the spirit of the age is making the age very sick. Secularism and relativism are literally soulless, and no culture can endure them for very long. Sooner or later, our culture will vomit them out, and begin seeking something that can give it back some reason for continuing. It will need a vision of objective truth and moral standards, with purposes that somehow get beyond the trivia of the here and now. I am convinced that when that day comes, Christianity can be there to supply that need, but only if Christianity has not succumbed to secularism and relativism itself. How sadly ironic it would be if, just when the larger culture begins seeking the truths we have clung to for so long, we leave them to embrace the very values that the culture has found so deeply empty.

Questions

1. What is the difference between an irreligious culture and a secular culture?
2. What are some ways in which American culture has become more secular in the last few decades? Are there any ways in which it is becoming less secular?
3. Are you in favor of re-introducing prayer in schools? Why or why not?
4. How might public schools maintain true neutrality toward religion?
5. How will the increasing importance of video rentals and cable alter the secularizing effects of television today more or less secularizing than it was in the heyday of the Big Three networks?
6. Does cultural diversification really promote relativism in the way the author suggests? Can you think of exceptions to his claims? Can you think of examples of the process he describes?
7. What did the author mean when he suggested that relativism is based on a kind of despair? Do you agree or not?
8. Are there areas in which relativism is particularly disturbing to you? Are there areas where relativism is called for? Does scripture ever endorse relativism on any topics?
9. How does a policy of "live and let live" tend to institutionalize religious differences?

13. *Is The Bible Inerrant?*

Edward P. Myers

A story is told about telegraphers in the early days when they did not use punctuation in the process of transcribing a message. It seems that a wealthy lady on vacation in Europe wired her husband asking permission to purchase a very expensive item. The husband wrote back, "No, expense too great." Without punctuation, the message read, "No expense too great." The lady bought the item, to the dismay of both husband and telegraph company. From then on, telegraphers used punctuation -- on all telegraph messages. This story illustrates how strategic and important details may be. Very little things can mean a lot."[1]

History is marked through time by important events. Some of these, by virtue of their nature, have been of such significance they changed the course of human history. One such event which recently occurred in the evangelical world was the dispute over the inerrancy of the Bible.

To affirm biblical inerrancy is to affirm biblical authority. When one speaks of the Bible as inerrant, he is claiming the Bible contains no errors at all -- none in history, geology, botany, geography, astronomy, science, or in any area whatsoever.

Biblical Doctrine and Inerrancy.

After all is said, the question must still be asked, "Does the Bible teach (or claim for itself) inerrancy?" Everett F. Harrison says the Bible "says nothing precisely about inerrancy. This remains a conclusion to which devout minds have come because of the divine character of Scripture."[2]   After discussing the Bible argument, Stephen Davis says, "We can conclude, then, that the Bible teaches that it is inspired, authoritative, and trustworthy. But it neither teaches, implies, nor presupposes that it is inerrant."[3] The only way Davis can make such a statement is to get one to accept his definitions of the words "inspired," "authoritative," "trustworthy," and "inerrancy."

The word "inerrant" derives from the Latin "in" ("not") and "errare" ("to err," "to make a mistake"). Such a word correctly describes the nature of holy scripture. To say the Bible is inerrant is to say it is absolutely true in everything it says. It is totally without error. It may be true that the word "inerrancy" is not found in any passage of Scripture. But, that is no more of a reason to reject the doctrine of inerrancy than to reject the doctrine of the Trinity on the basis that the word "trinity" is not used in scripture. The teaching of the Trinity is biblical, just as is the teaching of inerrancy.

Scripture owes its origin to God. "For prophecy never had its origin in the will of man, but men spoke from God as they were carried along by the Holy Spirit" (II Peter 1:21, NIV). This is the claim of the Bible about itself.

Discussions regarding the authority of the Bible and its inerrancy are many.   Does inspiration equal inerrancy?   Is it possible for a document to be inspired and not inerrant?   Do inspiration and inerrancy stand or fall together? Is it important to accept the Bible as inerrant? Does inerrancy pertain to all parts of the Bible? Or, does this apply to matters of doctrine and not history?

The Importance of Inerrancy

Why is inerrancy so important? Should one be a preacher of the gospel of Jesus Christ and refuse to accept the inerrancy of scripture? How do we account for scribal errors and hold to the doctrine of inerrancy? Does the existence of such errors invalidate the argument for inerrancy? Since we do not have the original autographs, how can we argue for inerrancy?

178

These and other questions like them are a mystery for many people regarding the claim for biblical inerrancy. According to some, to claim biblical inerrancy is to make a claim that is not found in scripture and therefore should be discarded. On the other hand, while the word inerrancy is not used, the concept and claim of inerrancy are found in the Bible. Our concern centers around the question, "Is a belief in inerrancy essential?" What exactly is at stake?

The doctrine of the inerrancy of the Bible is of vital importance. Why? What makes the doctrine of inerrancy of such paramount importance? One way to understand the importance of any doctrine is to see that doctrine in relationship to other doctrines taught in scripture.

First, biblical inerrancy is important because the Bible teaches the perfect character of God. Often in scripture we are told that God cannot lie (Numbers 23:19, I Samuel 15:29; Titus 1:2; Hebrews 6:18). Paul declares (Romans 3:4) that God is true, and His truthfulness cannot be changed by the lack of faith that some have. In His prayer to the Father, Jesus said, "Thy word is truth" (John 17:17). If the scriptures are from God and His character is behind them, then they cannot err.

We believe the Bible to be the infallible word of God because the Bible is God's word and God Himself is infallible. B. B. Warfield wrote, "What scripture says is to be received as the infallible Word of the infallible God, and to assert biblical inerrancy and the infallibility is to confess in (1) the divine origin of the Bible and (2) the truthfulness and trustworthiness of God."[4] If the Bible is the word of God and men wrote it under God's supervision (through His Spirit), then to charge the Bible with error is to charge God with irresponsibility or error. Therefore, the very character of God is at stake.

Second, biblical inerrancy is important to the doctrine of inspiration. Closely connected with the previous thought is that of biblical inspiration. II Peter 1:21 says men who wrote scripture were carried along by the Spirit of God. A Bible that is inspired is a Bible that is inerrant, or biblical inspiration means nothing.

Some claim that the Bible is inspired in the same way any writing might be inspired as written by gifted people. This is an incorrect view of biblical inspiration. This is an effort by some to preserve inspiration without inerrancy. The claim is made that the Bible is inspired in doctrinal areas which concern faith and practice, but in "lesser" matters (e.g., historical and/or scientific matters) it is only inspired but not inerrant. According to this theory, errors in scientific and historical matters are not important for faith and practice. Therefore, it is insignificant if they occur.

One of the most significant passages in the Bible regarding its authoritativeness refutes this theory. The apostle Paul, under supernatural guidance of the Holy Spirit, wrote, "and that from childhood you have known the sacred writings which are able to give you the wisdom that leads to salvation through faith which is in Christ Jesus. All scripture is inspired by God and profitable for teaching, for reproof, for correction, for training in righteousness; that the man of God may be adequate, equipped for every good work" (II Timothy 3:15-17, NASB). A person would be hard pressed to find a fact stated more plainly about the inspiration of sacred writings.

The Bible was not written primarily as a scientific or historical textbook. However, when the Bible speaks in matters related to scientific knowledge and historical knowledge, it is accurate and speaks with as much authority as it does when it speaks about matters of faith and practice. If there are parts of the Bible which are not inerrant, then the question arises, who decides which parts are true and which parts are erroneous? An errant scripture demands the critical judgment of Bible specialists. Therefore, instead of scripture sitting in judgment of men, it would have to be winnowed by man's wisdom to determine how much can be accepted as true and how much rejected as false. Finally, the person who rejects the inerrancy of scripture has to fall back on the inerrancy of his personal judgment and give up the whole idea of a written word from God. There is no other logical ground short of complete skepticism about what the Bible contains. In fact, the doctrine of inspiration is that God inspired his writers of scripture to guard against errors; the very thing some people say the Bible contains.

Third, consider biblical inerrancy in relationship to the testimony of the Bible itself. Scripture testifies to its own infallibility (I Peter 1:10-12; II Peter 1:20-21; II Timothy 3:14-17; John 14:26; 16:12-13; 10:30-39; 17:14-19; 20:30-31). If it is not infallible then it bears false witness and cannot be trusted in any matters on which it speaks. Biblical inerrancy, therefore, is important to the claim of the Bible for itself.

Fourth, biblical inerrancy is essential in relationship to biblical authority. If someone says authority is found in Christ and not in His written word, he would miss a claim of the Bible (cf. John 12:48-50; 20:30-31). How can Christ Himself have any authority if the witness to Him (the Bible) is not infallible? If it is infallible, then it has authority also.

Fifth, what did Jesus believe about the scripture's (Old Testament's) trustworthiness in matters of history and science?

Did He accept modern skepticism that the Hebrew Bible was to be trusted only in matters of religious doctrine?

No! Reading the testimony of scripture as to what Jesus said, we learn that He regarded statements in scripture as historically accurate and reliable. In Matthew 19:5, Jesus quotes Genesis 2:24 about marriage, and clearly believed in the historicity and trustworthiness of the account of Adam and Eve.

In Matthew 24:37-39, Jesus made reference to the flood of Noah's day and affirmed its historical accuracy. To read the words of Jesus demonstrates that He believed in a literal Noah, a literal ark and a literal flood. If not, how could the warning have any significance that Jesus is giving?

Jesus believed that during the forty years in the wilderness, the Israelites were kept alive by the manna God sent down from heaven (cf. John 6:49). He contrasts this with the spiritual bread of life that He offers.

The confirmation of Jesus' belief in Old Testament historical events comes from Matthew 12:40. The Lord compares His burial in a tomb and resurrection from the dead to the literal, historical antitype event of Jonah and the whale. To reject these events, viewed by our Lord as historical happenings, a person would have to claim to have more knowledge than Jesus Himself.

The Bible, which is the word of God, cannot err. If the Bible is the word of God, then to admit error in it is to charge God with error. The only ways to deny inerrancy are (1) to claim God can err or (2) to claim the Bible is not the word of God.

Biblical Inerrancy is an important teaching of scripture. To say the Bible has errors is to allow for the possibility that the Bible is untrustworthy. It also says God is incapable of communicating with man in such a way that man can be sure of what God has said. If the Bible is the written word of God and is untrustworthy, then where does that leave man? It is essential, therefore, to believe that the Bible is the inspired, authoritative, inerrant written word of God.

Inerrancy and Authority

There is no biblical authority without inerrancy. If is not possible for a book to have any clout to tell someone what is right and what is wrong if it cannot be trusted to tell the truth.

Consider a class schedule for a university. When the schedule tells what class will be offered, when and where the class will be taught, if there are errors in the schedule, then it cannot be trusted. If there are errors or misprints, then its authority to tell what is offered is ruined and students can't depend on getting the class they plan on taking. Authority and inerrancy go together; authority and errancy do not. How can any document, especially a document claiming to have come from God, have any authority and yet contain errors? If the Bible is to be our all-sufficient rule for faith and practice, and it has errors in it, then its authority is severely damaged.

Either the Bible has errors in it, or it does not. If it does not contain errors, then it sits in judgment on man and his actions. On the other hand, if the Bible contains errors, then it is man who sits in judgment on the Bible to decide which is an error and which is not. And who decides which is error and which is truth? What is the basis of that judgment? How can such judgment be validated, questioned, or contested if there is no infallible text with which to properly evaluate?

Inerrancy and the Autographs

Our claim for biblical inerrancy is for the autographs and not for the copies that have been handed down generation to generation; and certainly not for the various translations produced throughout any generation. But when this statement is made, someone asks, "How can we claim inerrancy for the autographs since we do not possess any of these autographs?" The answer is, we do not have to possess the exact autographs to have certainty regarding their message. There is a difference between the autograph itself and the text of the autograph. The actual codex --- the physical document penned by the inspired writers in their original words --- is lost. But its text --- the message it contained --- has been faithfully transmitted to the present in the existing copies of scripture used today.

Someone says, "You are hedging on the issue; you can't produce an inerrant autograph, so we should not argue for inerrancy." In response it could be said, "No, I cannot produce an inerrant autograph; but neither can anyone produce an errant autograph." The presupposition that just because we do not possess the autographs that they must contain errors is without foundation. Besides that, in proclaiming the inerrancy of scripture, we are proclaiming the truthfulness of God. If God promised to inspire scripture writers, then it is reasonable to believe they would be without mistakes, unless God could not do what he promised to do. It seems to me that when God planned to use the instruments of fallible men to write His infallible word, he must have known of the possibility of errors creeping in and that is the very reason inspiration was necessary. The possibility of error makes inspiration a necessity.

Inerrancy is not a theory or philosophical concept. It is a logical conclusion of the teaching of scripture. A syllogism can be produced that shows this to be true.

Major Premise:	Every word God speaks is true (inerrant).
Minor Premise:	The Bible is God's word.
Conclusion:	The Bible is true (inerrant).[5]

Many who believe in inerrancy have a list of reasons "why." In conclusion to our study the following list will help in understanding "why" one should accept the doctrine of inerrancy.[6] While the list might not be conclusive for the issue, it does present a strong case when each reason is studied in detail. Biblical inerrancy should be accepted because: (1) the Bible teaches it, (2) Jesus affirmed it, (3) believers in the Bible as God's word throughout history have believed it, and (4) the character of God demands it.[7]

Conclusion

The inerrancy of the Bible is important. The Bible is not just any book. Its communication is from God to man. God communicates to man through scripture. That communication is a matter of life and death. John said, "These things *are written* [italics mine] that you might believe that Jesus is the Christ, the Son of God, and that believing you might have life in his name" (John 20:31). The message God speaks to man is of such importance it would not be given to fallible man in such a way as to allow room for error. Therefore God, through his Spirit, supervised the writing of the message to assure man there would be no error.

Dr. James Boice said it well by quoting John Wesley; "If there be any mistakes in the Bible, there may well be a thousand. If there be one falsehood in that book, it did not come from the God of truth."[8]

Questions

1. Define inerrancy and tell what is affirmed by claiming that the Bible is inerrant.
2. How does biblical inerrancy declare biblical authority?
3. Why is the doctrine of biblical inerrancy vitally important?
4. Since the word "inerrancy" is not found in the Bible what internal evidence suggest the concept that the Bible is the infallible word of God?
5. List some reasons for maintaining faith in the inerrancy of Scripture.
6. What did Jesus believe and teach about Old Testament Scriptures.
7. If the Bible is God's word, what is the charge against God if one claims that the Bible contains error?
8. What are the only ways to deny inerrancy?
9. Is biblical authority possible without inerrancy? Why, or why not?
10. How can inerrancy be claimed when we do not possess the autographs (the original writings) for comparative purposes?

14. Trends In Church Leadership

Flavil R. Yeakley, Jr.

There is a need for a change in the style of church leadership. The authoritarian style of church leadership is wrong. It is not scriptural. It is not practical. It does not work. But in their efforts to flee from Rome, some are going all the way past Jerusalem and ending up in Babylon. Some are going to an opposite extreme that is equally wrong. Instead of changing the style of church leadership, what they are doing is to change the structure of church organization.[1]

That was the situation, as I saw it, in 1979. Nothing that has happened since then has caused me to change my assessment. The truth is still found between opposite extremes. In the past fifteen years, some have taken positions far more radical than those being advocated in the late 1970s, but wisdom is still found in moderation. The principle of Joshua 1:7 still applies: we should be careful to do everything God has commanded and to "not turn from it to the right or to the left."

Recent Trends

Churches of Christ in the United States include 13,000 independent congregations with no formal written creed or central organizational structure to impose conformity. It is not unusual, therefore, that there are many different approaches to church leadership among these congregations. We will look at several of the more important trends in church leadership styles.

Some schools, lectureships, and religious journals can always be counted on to defend the status quo. The messages heard from this segment of the brotherhood defend the absolute authority of the eldership. The only way they see for the faithful ("conservative") minority to impose its will on the unfaithful ("liberal") majority is through the legitimate power vested in the eldership. They insist on lifetime tenure for elders. They do not want elders to delegate any significant decision-making authority to anyone. They do not like surveys, questionnaires, congregational meetings, or other channels of communication that get the members involved in the decision-making process because that sounds too much like democracy. They view the preacher as an employee of the eldership, rather than as an important leader of the congregation.

The Discipling Movement

In recent years, another system has developed that is more extreme. Its leadership style is not just authoritarian; it is totalitarian. The Crossroads Movement became the Boston Movement, and that has now become a cult known as the "International Church of Christ." In 1986, Kip McKean announced the formation of an ecclesiastical hierarchy. McKean now claims apostolic authority. He uses the model of Paul's relationships with Timothy and Titus as a pattern for his authority to disciple the lead evangelists of the pillar churches around the world. They, in turn, control the lead evangelists of churches in big cities, who control the lead evangelists of churches in small cities, and so on through as many levels as may eventually develop.[1]

In order to implement his new system, McKean had to renounce the doctrine of congregational autonomy. That doctrine has been followed by all heirs of the Restoration Movement--until the Disciples of Christ went through "restructure," turning over control of local congregations to a central denominational organization. Churches of Christ and Christian Churches (non-instrumental and instrumental fellowships) still defend the doctrine of congregational autonomy. "Congregational autonomy," as McKean and his followers point out, is not a biblical term. His critics point out, however, that "Trinity" is not a biblical term either, but the doctrine of the Trinity is a biblical doctrine. In the same way, they argue, the doctrine of congregational autonomy is biblical since the New Testament authorizes local congregations but does not authorize any kind of ecclesiastical hierarchy above the level of the local church.

The Discipling Movement led by Kip McKean, in my opinion, is like the "dark side" of the Restoration Movement. They have taken everything bad about the legalism and authoritarianism characteristic of some congregations and they have exaggerated it to a point far worse than anything seen before. Those who defend the traditional authoritarian approach should look carefully at the totalitarian system in this cult because that is the ultimate conclusion of the system they defend.

Opposite Extremes

In 1979, when I wrote *Church Leadership and Organization*, one of my major concerns was that some people wanted to do more than improve the style of church leadership. What they advocated would, in effect, change the structure of church organization. These positions were especially being advocated at the bus ministry workshops that were being held throughout the nation. We were hearing such things as the following. "Elders are role models and father figures who lead by example only, but who have no decision-making role at all." "The preacher in his role as a preacher is not under the oversight of the elders." "Elders do not have the authority to fire a preacher without the consent of a majority of the members." "Decisions in the church should be made by the majority vote of the members." Please note that the objection here is not to majority rule in churches that have no elders. Instead, the objection is to congregations that have elders, but claim that all decisions are made by majority vote of the members--when really it is the preacher who runs the church.

These ideas are still being advocated, but an even more extreme position has emerged in the past fifteen years. The Examiner, a religious journal edited by Charles Holt in Chattanooga, Tennessee, is an example of this extreme. In my opinion, the positions advocated in this journal are, in effect, anti-eldership, anti-treasury, and anti-assembly. The effect of this system would be anarchy. Each Christian would be expected to live a godly life and a few might get together for devotionals in homes from time to time, but congregations as we know them would no longer exist.

187

Problems in the Middle of the Road

A growing number of congregations are making an honest effort to move away from the authoritarian leadership style. The elders in these congregations have delegated everything they can to deacons or others in the congregation. These elders are trying to put more emphasis on their spiritual counseling and teaching role as shepherds. But in some of these congregations, the deacons and others are complaining about a lack of guidance from the eldership. One deacon told me that he was quite willing to take the ball and run with it, but he needed to know what play had been called and he needed to know the game plan. Deacons in many congregations are complaining that when the elders turned over the day-to-day operational management to others, the elders failed to make the right shift in the decision-making they continued doing. They should have shifted the focus of their decision-making to the level of strategic planning. Instead, they kept their focus on operational management. And since they had turned over operational matters to others, these elderships, in effect, became "Veto Boards." What they do now is overrule the operational decisions made by the deacons.

A Dynamic Model

A few elderships are learning to focus on strategic planning. They establish a climate of open communication. They keep the members informed about all major issues being considered and actively seek the input of the members before the elders make their decisions. Furthermore, instead of resolving problems by making decisions, they try to build consensus. They lead by teaching, persuasion, and example rather than by making rules and giving orders. In these congregations, the elders regularly ask the congregation if they want the elders to continue serving. If so, they do. If not, they step aside (not "down") and serve in other ways. These congregations believe that since the Bible is silent on the subject of tenure, the lifetime tenure tradition should not be made into a law.

Once this climate of open communication has been established, the elders get the entire congregation involved in clarifying its mission. They set goals for the congregation as a whole and objectives for each ministry. They measure how fully the aims, goals, and objectives are being achieved. As they get information from this assessment, they revise their aims, goals, and objectives. In this way, the elders focus their decision-making on the most important policy decisions that influence the entire congregation.

When the elders in these congregations delegate decision-making authority, they establish clear guidelines, limits, expected results, a schedule for completion, and a system of accountability. Those who work under their direction have the freedom to use their own initiative in achieving the expected results. They are not required to work just exactly the way the elders would have -- they just have to get the job done within the general guidelines set by the elders. When results are not being achieved, the elders in these congregations do everything they can to motivate, inspire, and encourage--but they are also willing to reprove, rebuke, and correct when needed. They care enough to confront.

Influences on Perceptions

Several factors influence our perceptions of church leadership. The natural human tendency is to assume that what **is** and what **ought to be** are identical. We easily take our traditions and read them back into the Biblical text. Humility should compel us to admit that total objectivity is not possible, but we can be aware of factors that influence our perceptions and correct for them as much as possible. The church's historical context and current generational differences form two important factors influencing our perceptions about church leadership.

Church History

Most religious groups in Christendom regard church organization as an incidental, rather than as an essential element of the Christian experience: a matter of opinion rather than a matter of faith. Those of us who believe that the New Testament presents a normative pattern for the church in all places and for all time are unwilling to alter church organization unless we are fully persuaded that the change brings us closer to the New Testament pattern.

Throughout the history of Christendom, there have been three major approaches to church organization: episcopalian, presbyterian, and congregational. These are not just the names of different denominations. Virtually all religious groups in Christendom have one of these three forms of organization, differing primarily in the location of power. Religious groups with these three systems of church organization give different answers to a key question about the location of power: **"Who has the authority to select or remove leaders in a local church?"**

Churches with an episcopalian form of government say that the bishop is the one with such authority. The word "episcopalian" comes from the Greek word for bishop or overseer. In the New Testament pattern, the overseers were also known as elders and shepherds. In Acts 20:17-28 and 1 Peter 5:1-3, the three terms are used in reference to the very same group of leaders.

Originally, each independent congregation was guided by a plurality of leaders known as elders, overseers, and shepherds. Those leaders were members of the local church they led. Over the next few centuries, however, a different system evolved patterned after the Roman Empire. In this system, a bishop was an officer in an ecclesiastical hierarchy and one bishop ruled a plurality of local churches.

Churches with a presbyterian form of organization say that the authority to select or remove leaders in a local church centers in the eldership. The presbyterian form of church government finds its name in the Greek word for "elder." Denominations using this system differ in the amount of control exercised by the ecclesiastical hierarchy over the local churches, but they all agree that the primary power rests in the eldership of each local church. In this system, the eldership functions as a self-perpetuating board of directors. When new elders are selected, the present eldership selects them. The members may be allowed to raise "scriptural objections" regarding the qualifications of the candidates, but it is the present eldership that decides whether or not to sustain the objection. Decision-making is the primary function of this office in the presbyterian system.

Churches with a congregational form of government say that the authority to select or remove leaders in a local church is centered in that congregation's membership. When elders and deacons are selected, for example, the congregation does the selecting. This pattern follows the model of Acts 6:3, where the apostles told the congregation to select the seven special servants who then administered the program of caring for the widows. David Lipscomb was asked if a congregation had the right to remove an elder who was no longer living a godly life. Lipscomb answered that if the congregation had the right to appoint him in the first place, it most certainly had the right to "dis-appoint" him. In this answer, Lipscomb was following the congregational rather than the presbyterian model. I believe that the New Testament authorizes the congregational system and that the episcopalian and presbyterian systems contradict the New Testament pattern.

In *Discovering Our Roots*, Leonard Allen and Richard Hughes demonstrate how much history influences our perceptions.[2] Churches of Christ in the United States trace historical roots back to a Restoration Movement led by Barton W. Stone, Thomas Campbell, and Alexander Campbell. All three of these leaders were educated as ministers in the Presbyterian Church. In relation to control over local churches by an ecclesiastical hierarchy, they rejected both the episcopalian and presbyterian systems in favor of the congregational system. At the level of the local church, however, they seem to have accepted uncritically the presbyterian model of an eldership as a self-perpetuating board that focused primarily on decision-making. Though this presbyterian model has influenced the thinking of several generations as to what an eldership should be and how it should function, the congregational model remains more biblical.

Generational Differences

The second major factor influencing our perceptions about church leadership is generational differences. Virtually all religious groups in America are experiencing pressure from the younger members to make two important changes. First, the younger members want to replace the authoritarian style of their present leaders with a more open, participative style that gets the members more involved in the decision-making process. Second, these younger members want a more informal, spontaneous, praise-oriented worship style. Churches of Christ are not the only religious groups experiencing these tensions, a fact that supports the conclusion that the differences are more generational than theological.

Popular studies of differences among generational cohorts have typically focused on the "Baby Boomers," those born between 1945 and 1965 when there was a sharp increase in the birth rate. This generation has been compared with the "Pre-Boomers," those born before 1945, and the "Post-Boomers," those born after 1965. One of the major differences researches have noted has been in the attitudes of these three generations toward authority. The general rule, according to these studies, is that **"Pre-Boomers respect authority; Baby Boomers question authority; Post-Boomers ignore authority."**[3] However, Strauss and Howe in their book *Generations* regard this three-part division as over-simplified.[4] They suggest looking both at characteristics of life stages and of different generational cohorts as they pass through these life stages. Both approaches, however, come to the same basic conclusion about the present tensions churches are experiencing over leadership styles. What is happening in the 1990s, is that the first of the Baby Boomers are moving into positions of leadership in government, education, business, industry, and in churches. The generation born before 1945 was much more comfortable with an authoritarian leadership style. That did not make it scriptural, but authoritarian leadership was relatively effective and efficient as long as it was tolerated. The generation born after 1945, however, has been unwilling to tolerate authoritarian leadership, rendering this style of leadership ineffective. In my opinion, it never was God's pattern for His church.

The present tension is especially stressful for elders born before 1945. Many of them became elders when a different social contract existed. A social contract is the unwritten agreement between an organization and its leaders. The old social contract asked elders to spend a few hours each month in decision-making meetings. Now they are being told that they need to spend many hours each week, with most of that time spent in pastoral or administrative work rather than in decision-making meetings. One elder told me that he did not think that it was fair for the church to change the rules on him in the middle of the game.

The Baby Boomers are just now beginning to come into elderships in significant numbers and that is one of the causes of the present tension. The Boomers, because of their numbers, may keep the Post-Boomers out of the eldership until around 2020. But some time around 2020, churches and other institutions will likely experience the same kind of tension being experienced today--the tension caused by one generational cohort replacing another in the positions of leadership.

A likely scenario around 2020. The Baby Boomers will predominate in the eldership, with the Post-Boomers waiting to move into these positions. And the "Millennial Generation," those born around the turn of the millennium, will come to the Baby Boomer elders with a request for a change in the worship style. They might say something similar to the following:

"We've just discovered an old hymnal called <u>Great Songs of the Church</u>. It has some kind of funny shape notes that we don't understand, but the music and the lyrics are great! It has a lot of the classical and traditional Christian hymns. There is music by Bach, Beethoven, Mozart, Handel, and a lot of other great composers. We want to get that book and start singing some of those songs." Then the Baby Boomer elders will say, "Absolutely not! We will keep on singing the devo songs the way we always have!"

Sources of Power

Many of the issues in the current discussions about leadership styles could be resolved, in my opinion, with a better understanding of the sources of power. The classic study in this field was done by French and Raven.[5]   More recently, Yukl and Falbe expanded on this system.[6] In the original analysis, French and Raven outline five sources of social power: (1) **Reward Power:** the ability to control valued organizational resources or rewards. (2) **Coercive Power:** the exercise of control over various punishments or threats. (3) **Legitimate Power:** the authority to control others by virtue of an organizational position. (4) **Referent Power:** influence based on a positive attitude toward the power holder. (5) **Expert Power:** the accepted belief that the individual has valued skill/ability.

Building on this work, Yukel and Falbe identify eight different sources of power in two broad categories: (1)   **Position Power,** which encompasses French and Raven's ideas of legitimate, reward, and coercive power and adds control of information; and **(2) Personal Power,** which includes the ideas of expert and referent power and adds persuasion and personal charisma. By applying these two broad categories of position power and personal power to the various approaches in church leadership, we can both identify distinguishing char- acteristics in these various approaches and see the impact the source of power makes. One of the most important differences among the various approaches to church leadership involves the sources of power. These differences can be used to identify distinguishing features of various approaches to church organization.

In Matthew 20:25-28 and 1 Peter 5:1-3, the New Testament presents an approach to leadership that was a radical departure from the authoritarian leadership style practiced in the Roman Empire. Jesus taught His followers to be servant leaders rather than lords.   The traditional/authoritarian view, following the presbyterian model, is that the difference between servant leaders and lords is a matter of style and attitude. According to this view, both leaders and lords depend primarily on position power (legitimate power, power by virtue of office) and both lead primarily by making decisions and giving orders. The difference, we are told, is that servant leaders exercise authority and make decisions in a gentle manner with a loving concern for people, but lords exercise authority and make decisions in a harsh unloving manner. The problem with this view is that **Jesus is Lord!** And Jesus is more like what this definition calls a "leader" than what it calls a "lord."

The real difference between leaders and lords goes beyond style and attitude. Lords depend primarily on position power, but their authority is <u>not</u> based on the consent of the people. It comes from some higher source. Leaders, on the other hand, have authority that <u>is</u> based on the consent of the people they lead. That is why the episcopalian and presbyterian systems are wrong. Both involve leaders exercising authority without the consent of the members.

Tom Yokum did a word study that included the Greek words for: (1) the positions of a leader, (2) the functions of a leader, and, (3) the responses to leaders. His study notes which words were used, were not used, or were rejected in the New Testament.[7] He concludes that the words for power by virtue of position are specifically rejected for church leaders and the only words that are used with approval are those for personal power.

In many traditional/authoritarian congregations that follow the presbyterian model, the preacher does the pastoral work, the elders are the operational managers, and the deacons are not quite sure what they are supposed to do. One of the main problems in this approach is the fragmentation of the leadership roles as presented in the New Testament According to the traditional/authoritarian view, an eldership is primarily a decision-making body similar to a board of directors. Those who hold this view know that in the New Testament, elders are also called "overseers" and "shepherds." Their view, however, is that elders fulfill their role as overseers by making their decisions in view of the total program of church work that they direct. And they fulfill their role as shepherds by making their decisions with a genuine concern for the flock. But overseeing and shepherding are not things that they do separate and apart from their decision-making work. That traditional view, however, is not supported in the New Testament.

A more biblical view is that the three terms--elder/presbyter, overseer/bishop, and shepherd/pastor--describe three different leadership roles: decision-making, administration, spiritual counseling/teaching. Notice that in the New Testament pattern, the most important policy decisions are made by those in closest touch with the spiritual needs of the individual members because of their work as shepherds--and by those in closest touch with the big picture because of their work as overseers. In many churches today, the full-time church-supported ministers come much closer to fitting that pattern of integrated leadership than do the elders who function only as a decision-making body.

In the New Testament pattern, according to 1 Timothy 5:17-18, some of the elders were preachers who were supported by the church for full-time work. There is no New Testament parallel that I know of to the full-time church-supported ministers who do all of the preaching, most of the pastoral work, and most of the administrative work--but who have no decision-making role.

The role of "the minister" in the church today is very frustrating. They have the personal power because of their Bible knowledge, natural endowments, and visibility in the church. They devote their full time to church work, and they are in positions with tremendous responsibility. Usually, the preacher is best suited to articulate the developing vision. His preaching is vital to this process, but he preaches, as Fred Craddock says, "as one without authority."[9] But all of the position power is held by men who have far less education in these areas and who have trouble finding a few hours a week to function as the decision-making body for the church.

In an effort to solve this problem, some have moved toward a doctrine of evangelistic oversight. The Mutual Edification churches with roots in the ministry of Daniel Sommer teach that doctrine. Many Black churches practice it. The Discipling Movement has taken it to a cultic extreme. But that is not the way to solve the problem. We do not need preachers who lord it over the church any more than we need elders who lord it over the church. What we need are elders and preachers who lead by personal power rather than by position power.

A Summary of Church Leadership Systems

The following discussion will compare and contrast four systems of church leadership: (1) the **totalitarian** system of the Discipling Movement; (2) the **authoritarian** system of elderships that follow the presbyterian model; (3) the **dynamic** system of congregations with servant leadership; and, (4) the **democratic** system of "majority vote" churches. The anti-eldership, anti-treasury, anti-assembly approach discussed earlier is not really a system of church leadership. It is anarchy and for that reason it is not included in the following outline.

What Are the Sources of Power in These Systems?

Totalitarian:	Reward/punishment power, control of information, and a claim of legitimate power for the discipling hierarchy.
Authoritarian:	Legitimate power claimed for the eldership.
Dynamic:	Personal power exercised by the elders and the preacher.
Democratic:	Legitimate power claimed for the membership--but exercised by the preacher who runs the church.

What Are the Primary Expressions of Power in These Systems?

Totalitarian, Authoritarian, and Democratic: Decision-making.
Dynamic: Building consensus, leading by teaching, persuasion, and example.

Where is the Focus in These Systems?

Totalitarian:	Lead evangelist and discipling hierarchy.
Authoritarian:	The eldership.
Dynamic:	The members.
Democratic:	Focus appears to be on the members, but it is really on the preacher who runs the church.

Who Has the Authority To Select or Remove Leaders in These Systems?

Totalitarian:	The lead evangelist.
Authoritarian:	The present eldership.
Dynamic:	The members.
Democratic:	The preacher (in effect), although this authority is claimed for the members.

What Tenure System Is Used for the Elders in These Systems?

Totalitarian:	As long as the lead evangelist wants them to serve.

Authoritarian:	Lifetime tenure.
Dynamic:	Limited tenure with regular review by the congregation.
Democratic:	Lifetime tenure is still typical.

What is the Role of the Preacher in These Systems?

Totalitarian:	Cult leader with absolute power over the congregation.
Authoritarian:	An employee of the eldership.
Dynamic:	A key leader working with the elders.
Democratic:	The preacher runs the church.

Conclusion

Churches need to move away from authoritarian leadership toward the dynamic model, avoiding the extremes of the totalitarian, democratic, and anarchy positions. Churches need elders and preachers who are what Lyle Schaller called "transformational leaders."[10] We do not need politicians who want to know which way the parade is going so they can get out in front and lead it. We need leaders with vision, who instead of imposing their vision on the church will build consensus. We need leaders willing to involve the whole church in clarifying its mission, and leaders able to model the principle that, "Everyone always has his or her say, but no one always has his or her way". When the church raises up transformational leaders, then the result will be that the members will claim ownership of the vision, realizing that it really is their vision, not the vision of the elders or the preacher.

Questions

1. Most organizations have the kind of leadership they want. There is some kind or reward for the members built into every leadership system that the members tolerate. What do you think the reward might be for members in the totalitarian, authoritarian, dynamic, democratic, and anarchy approaches in this chapter?
2. Organizational systems have costs as well as benefits. What

costs do you see for the members in the totalitarian, authoritarian, dynamic, democratic, and anarchy approaches discussed in this chapter?

3. Some people go to school for years to prepare for the ministry of preaching. Why do so few prepare for the ministry of church leadership? What elements of the present system have made people reluctant to prepare for the ministry of church leadership?

4. What could be done to encourage more young men in the church to get the kind of education that would help them prepare for the ministry of church leadership?

5. Why is it important for the decision-making to be done by people who are actively involved in the administrative and pastoral work? What is likely to happen if the decision-making is done by people who function only as decision-makers?

6. What benefits would come from having elders go to the congregation regularly to ask whether or not the members want the elders to continue serving?

7. What disadvantages might there be in a limited tenure system for elders?

8. What are the advantages and disadvantages of a lifetime tenure system for elders?

9. In Acts 6, when the Jerusalem church selected the seven special servants who administered the program of aid to the widows, the congregation was not selecting "deacons at large." They were able to match the men to the job. What are the advantages and disadvantages of selecting deacons (ministry leaders) for specific tasks rather than selecting them "at large?"

15. How To Be Undenominational In A Denominational World

Stafford North

"We are a denomination. Why don't we just admit it?" Such a statement would not have been made in churches of Christ fifty years ago, but today it is being said among us by writers and speakers who believe we cannot and should not seek to be undenominational.

We are hearing several different positions on this matter. (1) The church of Christ is a denomination like other denominations, and we are fooling ourselves to think otherwise. (2) The church today is the product of a 19th century movement and cannot escape the effects of this origin. (3) Members of churches of Christ are leaving for denominations because they see nothing wrong with denominations, and they find something elsewhere they prefer. (4) The church should not be a denomination, but sometimes we act like one. (5) The church should continue to oppose denominationalism and should stand firmly against any encroachment of denominationalism among us.

Obviously, this subject requires a definition of terms. *"To denominate"* means to name, to classify, or to name the sub-units of a class. Thus, we name different units within our paper money, calling the one-dollar bill, the five-dollar bill, and the ten-dollar bill *"denominations"* of bills. Similarly, as Protestant churches began to form during the Reformation Movement, they were eventually considered sub-units of the Christian church at large and, thus, a denomination. The term *"non-denominational"* usually refers to a group not using church or denominational distinctions and which accepts those from any denomination into its fellowship. A non-denominational meeting, then, would be open to those of all denominations. *"Undenominational,"* on the other hand, is a term applied to those who oppose the denominational concept and who wish no denominations existed.

The two widely accepted major sub-divisions of *"Christians"* are Catholic and Protestant. This distinction would normally place such groups as the Roman Catholic and Greek Orthodox churches on the *"Catholic"* side while dividing Protestants into denominations such as Baptist, Methodist, Presbyterian, Episcopalian, and Pentecostal. The Catholic Church is not considered one of these denominations because it does not consider itself one among several equally valid types of churches as do Protestant churches.

This chapter takes the following position: (1) that the church Christ *"built"* was not a denomination, (2) that Christians should oppose the denominational concept, demonstrating, rather, the unity of believers in Christ and (3) that local congregations should teach the difference between the church of the New Testament and a denomination. We will approach these topics by considering four significant affirmations which local churches leaders, elders, and preachers should actively teach their local congregations in classes, from the pulpit, and in written materials, and which all congregations should practice.

Teach and Practice that the Church is One

The fundamental issue in the question of denominationalism deals with the nature of the church. Should we support as desirable the denominational concept of dividing believers in Christ into sects? Should we accept the denominational concept as undesirable but inevitable? Should we oppose the concept of denominational as un-biblical?

The church, as it began in the First Century, did not have denominational divisions. When distinctions began to arise that might have led in that direction, Paul firmly opposed them. When Christians in Corinth were beginning to *"denominate"* themselves according to the preacher who baptized them, Paul forcefully

200

condemned such a practice. *"Is Christ divided?"* he asked. *"Let there be no divisions among you - speak the same thing,"* he urged (I Corinthians 1: 10).

Two simple drawings will contrast the denominational view and the biblical view of the nature of the church.

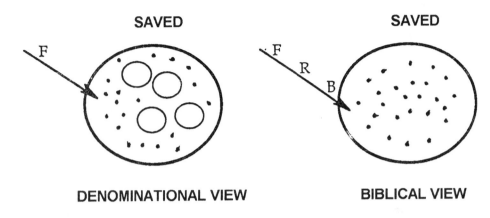

The typical view among denominational churches is that one becomes a member of the *"church universal"* at the moment of belief. Thus, by *"faith only"* one becomes a Christian, a member of Christ's universal body. This is represented by the arrow and the "F." By faith one enters the circle of the saved. The dots inside the big circle but outside any small circle represent believers who have been saved, but who have not, as yet, entered any of the small circles representing denominations. This concept suggests that since these persons are saved, they are not required to enter any small circle to be saved. Thus, one already saved by faith is told to *"join the church of his choice."* He is already saved but is not yet part of a denominational church. Those persons who have been saved and have chosen to join a denomination are represented by the *"dots"* inside small circles.

Since this view holds that one is saved before joining any denomination, obviously being in a denominational church is not essential for salvation. So we often hear the statement, *"one does not have to be in a church (denomination) to be saved."* Each denomination sets sits own requires for membership. One *"church"* may accept any "saved" person into fellowship while another may require baptism by immersion or by sprinkling. Another may require a religious experience or acceptance of a particular creed. After all, this view holds, *"since being a member of our small circle has nothing to do with being saved we can set membership requirements as we choose."*

In this denominational approach, those in one small circle consider those in another small circle to be equally *"saved."* All are seen as heavenbound, just following different roads. The person was saved before he *"joined"* any of the denominations and stayed saved after he joined. So, salvation is not exclusive to any of the small circles and one may change from one denomination to another without affecting his saved state.

The second large circle demonstrates a different concept. It, likewise, has a circle representing all who have been saved. The arrow indicating entrance into the circle, however, not only has an "F" for faith but an "R" for repentance and a "B" for baptism. While this chapter cannot pursue such matters at length, the scriptures teach that both repentance and baptism precede *"forgiveness of sins,"* admission into the body, or acceptance into Christ. Galatians 3:27, for example, teaches that a person is *"baptized into Christ,"* indicating that one remains outside of Christ and His body until the time of baptism. In Acts 2:38, Peter tells his convicted audience that they should *"repent and be baptized for remission of sins."* Later in the same chapter, verse 47, Luke records that those being saved each day were added to the existing body of believers. God added them when they confessed their faith and they obeyed in repentance and baptism.

As Paul tells the story of his own conversion in Acts 22:16, he says Christ sent a preacher who told him to be baptized to *"wash away"* his sins. He had believed while on the road and had repented as evidenced by his fasting and praying for three days. So, in Paul's case, and all others, past sins are not forgiven at the moment of belief but at the point of baptism. In I Corinthians 12:13, Paul reminds the Corinthians that they were *"baptized into one body."* Baptism was the final step in their being added to the saved. Finally, Paul reminds the Romans that their new life in Christ started as they had been raised in baptism (Romans 6:4) The line of demarcation between saved and lost in all these cases is the baptism that makes one part of the body of Christ.

These and many other passages suggest we should not consider ourselves or others to have completed the process of being added to the circle of the saved until we have confessed our faith in Christ, repented of past sins, and submitted to baptism for remission of sins. At this point, the scriptures teach, God adds us to the body of the saved, putting us inside the circle. The first difference between the circle on the right and the one on the left, then, concerns the actions one takes to be saved, to be added to the body of Christ, to be in the circle of the saved.

The second difference concerns the small circles inside the large circle. The denominational concept suggests believers may be divided into sub-groups, each holding somewhat different beliefs, and each with somewhat different requirements for entering their small circle. The Bible, of course, opposes such a view. Paul rebukes the Corinthians for starting in such a direction by commanding them all to teach the same thing and not to call themselves by different names. Paul also speaks of *"one body"* in I Corinthians 12:12 and Ephesians 4:4, and condemns *"factions, divisions, and parties"* in Galatians 5:20.

But Jesus gives the strongest statement urging unity among believers when, on the night of his betrayal, He prays that His follows will possess the same degree of unity He and God share. Thus, Christ disapproves of any view of His church which condones dividing it into competing, differing factions. This admonition speaks, of course, (1) to those who hold the denominational view as a desirable feature among believers, (2) to those who prefer that such divisions not exist but who continue to support and promote denominations, and (3) to those in Christ 's body who create divisions among believers. The Bible teaches that one is saved by God's grace as he/she obeys the conditions God established for acceptance of His grace: faith, repentance, and baptism for remission of sins. The Bible also teaches that those in Christ's body should not divide believers into sects and parties.

Therefore, those who follow Christ today must affirm and practice what the scriptures say about <u>becoming a Christian</u> and <u>uniting believers in one body</u>. Christ's followers should condemn the concept of denominationalism which teaches both the wrong way to enter the body of Christ and the wrong view of the church. Certainly a major reason why many Christians today do not see the distinction between Christ's conception of the church and a denomination is that they have lacked sufficient teaching on these points.

Care, of course, must be exercised in doing such teaching. A hundred years ago, society allowed a more direct, controversial approach to religious differences. Specific comparison of beliefs and mentioned church names was common. Even then, of course, harsh or unkind statements were not appropriate. Today, society is different. Tolerance is the watchword. To many, this means not only that one should tolerate the views of another by respecting the right to differ, but that all views are equally valid or acceptable. This sense of tolerance has affected the church as well. Today many hesitate to teach on matters of doctrine lest someone take offense. To disagree publicly with others on such matters as denominationalism and baptism is to violate the code of *"political correctness"* that has become so common.

So, in this age of tolerance, how can we be undenominational in a denominational world? We must take a biblical stance on the nature of Christ's church but we must teach this concept in a different manner than we might have in an earlier time. We must always be kind and never judgmental. We must never ridicule the view of others. Unfortunately, many have chosen to avoid these issues, resulting in a lack of understanding and even a lack of concern among us on many key issues.

We should, rather, teach and practice Biblical doctrines both on how to become a Christian and how to be unified. Church leaders should teach their congregations about Christ's church and its undenominational nature. And they should lead in the practice of harmony even when differences of opinion arise about matters the Bible does not declare essential. This work on unity alone, however, will not keep the church of our time undenominational. Other related themes must be taught and practiced to give the full picture and to keep a proper balance.

Teach and Practice that Christ is Lord

Teaching about the church can be misleading. We are not to convert the world to an organization but to a person. It is Jesus who saves, not the church.

The church, however, is the *"assembly"* of the saved, the fellowship of baptized believers. It is the body containing Christ's disciples. The Bible provides a plan for the organization of the church and for the collective work of Christians through the church. Through their congregations, Christian join themselves for worship, fellowship, benevolence, evangelism and nurture. So we should teach about the church and how Christ has told us to work in and through His body. At the same time, we must always emphasize Christ and our relationship to Him. Jesus is our savior and we must keep a strong personal tie with Him. While we have loyalty to the church as an institution, we need to feel a strong connection with Christ personally. He is *"my everything"*; I should have a strong commitment to Him.

The key here is *"balance."* Some would preach only Christ and ignore the biblical teaching on the church. Others give the structure and work of congregations such prominence that they seem to ignore our relationship to Christ. Thus, the question has been asked, *"Do you preach the man or the plan?"* Obviously the answer must be <u>both</u>.

Others ask whether we have emphasized the epistles to the exclusion of the gospels. As LaGard Smith observed in *The Cultural Church*, the concern of 19th century preachers in our fellowship was to identify those issues where they felt denominations had gone astray. These issues did not focus so much on matters of Christ's life and teaching on how to live as on how one responds to Him and how Christians were to live and work together in the church. This early emphasis on matters pertaining to *"the church"* has sometimes caused us to give less attention to Christ and our relationship to Him (p. 49).

We must, of course, teach the epistles, letters written to teach, command, direct, rebuke, and encourage those who were already Christians. We must, however, also teach the gospels so we can be filled with the teaching and example of Christ. <u>Neither the epistles nor the gospels is a complete diet of spiritual food without the other</u>. Why should anyone recommend that we teach one part of God's message above another part? The gospels and the epistles are not at war with each other - they are complementary.

Early Christians called Jesus their <u>*"Lord."*</u> To them he was <u>ruler</u> and <u>king</u>. They obeyed Him because they loved Him. Whatever He taught them should be accepted and practiced. We need to keep this emphasis on Jesus as Lord, living daily under Christ as our King.

Christ is also our <u>brother</u> in God's family. This thought suggests a close fellowship with Him. We speak of *"sticking closer than a brother."* Christ wants more than just our intellectual agreement with doctrines, more than just our submission to His commands. Christ wants us to *"feel"* a close relationship with Him. Sometimes, some have made *"feelings"* the standard for deciding how to serve God. One is not right just because he feels right.

At the same time, just because some have abused *"feelings"* in one direction, we should not abuse them in another. <u>Christ wants us to sense a closeness with Him.</u> He wants us to be tied to Him emotionally. He wants us regularly to sense His presence with us and to let this closeness be a strength to us (Ephesians 3: 16-21). He is head and we are body. He is husband and we are bride. The tie is close and strong.

We will not win the war against denominationalism in our congregations, then, just by teaching the biblical view of the church. God made us to want relationships and offered us the opportunity to *"be one"* with Christ. Only by accepting this offer and feeling a close personal relationship with Christ can we experience a faith strong enough to resist the temptation to make the church what it is not.

So let us enjoy our relationship with Christ, living daily with Him as Lord, and teaching our congregations how to be one with Christ.

Teach and Practice that the Word is the Seed

In Matthew 13, Jesus taught the parable of the sower. In it, a farmer sows seed by the *"broadcast"* method -- scattering seed by hand. The seed produces different results depending on the state of the soil in which it falls. When Jesus interprets the parable, He says that the seed is *"the word of the kingdom."* This word, sown in good hearts, produces fruit -- that is, makes disciples.

From this parable, from the great commission, and from first-century Christian practice, it is evident that <u>the gospel message can be preached in any nation and produce the same result</u> -- individuals are saved and thus are added to the church. Peter preaches this word in Jerusalem and simultaneously three thousand respond in repentance and baptism (Acts 2:37-41). Philip, in Samara, proclaims *"the good tidings concerning the kingdom of God,"* and many believe and are baptized (Acts 8:12). This same Philip, in a chariot, could *"preach Jesus"* to one man who would ask, *"Look, here is water. Why can't I be baptized?"* (Acts 8:36). Christ Himself tells Paul on the Damascus road that someone will tell him *"what he must do,"* and later Ananias comes urging him to *"wash away his sins"* (Acts 9:6, 10-18; 22:16). Peter goes to Caesarea to speak *"words"* whereby Cornelius and his household *could be saved"* (Acts 11:14). Paul, on his missionary journeys, preaches this same message around the world. He calls it *"the gospel "* which he received from Christ (Galatians 1:7-12), *"the truth"* (Ephesians 4:14), *"sound doctrine"* (II Timothy 4:3), and "the *faith"* (I Timothy 4:1). Jude also speaks of *"the faith, once for all delivered unto the saints"* (Jude 3).

Clearly, in the minds of these inspired prophets of the first century, the Holy Spirit had come, as Jesus had promised, *"to guide them into all truth"* (John 16:13). They had received *"the truth,"* a body of teaching which told of the life of Christ, His death for all mankind, and His resurrection as a demonstration of how all will someday be raised. This inspired message also gave instructions for how to demonstrate one's faith by repentance, confession, and baptism, and how Christ wanted His disciples to work as a body in worship, evangelizing, nurturing, and showing benevolence to others. This gospel gave hope for the time when those who obeyed could enter the mansions Christ had prepared for them.

Paul, John, Jesus and others in the New Testament forbid anyone to change or vary from this teaching. Jesus warned of false teachers and spoke of those in judgment who thought they were His but would be turned away because he *"never knew them"* (Matthew 7:15-23). Paul condemned those who taught the Galatians a *"different gospel"* than the one he had received *"through revelation of Jesus Christ"* (Galatians 1:6-12). Paul warned the Corinthian church it was risking *"damnation"* by changing the manner of observing the Lord's Supper which he had *"delivered unto them"* as he *"received it of the Lord"* (I Corinthians 11:23-29). John taught that those who *"abide not in the teaching of Christ"* do not have God (II John 9). Jude tells of those who are condemned because they *"deny our only Master and Lord, Jesus Christ"* (Jude 4). And these are but a few of the encouragements to *"contend earnestly for the faith, once for all delivered to the saints"* (Jude 3).

New Testament writers also <u>predicted a departure</u> from the teaching of the apostles. Paul warned the Ephesian elders to *"take heed"* unto themselves and their flock because from among their own ranks men would arise *"speaking perverse things, to draw away the disciples after them"* (Acts 20:29). Paul also predicted apostasy as he wrote to Timothy: *"But the Spirit saith expressly that in later times some shall fall away from the faith"* I Timothy 4:1).

From these scriptures, a number of conclusions are evident. (1) Salvation is promised <u>only</u> to those who follow the true gospel not a distorted one. (2) The seed of the gospel, pure from contamination by false teachers, can be planted in any geographical location or in any century, and the result will be true disciples for Christ. (3) Since *"falling away"* is clearly identified as wrong, those coming after such apostasy must restore the true teaching because the *"different gospel"* has no power to save.

If, then, we would be true disciples of Christ, we must allow the seed of the gospel to be planted in our hearts and must share it with others. Our salvation is too precious to rely on a distorted gospel. If we would be undenominational in a denominational world, we must follow the teachings of those who received *"the truth"* by inspiration, not the changes made later as Paul predicted. If it was wrong to make the changes, it is wrong to perpetuate them.

We must plant the *"word of God"* as a seed in hearts today just as it was nearly two thousand years ago. Those who receive it can be blessed even as were those who heard it in the first century. In this way, we go back beyond denominationalism, back before the apostasy, back to original ground.

But is it possible to do this? Can we know the original way? Are we too separated in time and culture to follow the plan revealed in the first century? The answer to that comes from two directions. The first is from the word itself. Jude said *"the faith"* was delivered *"once for all"* -- one time for all times (Jude 3). If Paul said that a departure from *"the faith," "the truth," "the gospel,"* was a bad thing, then the intent of God must have been that the original continue. If not, then there was nothing wrong with a departure. But if the departure was against God's desire, then surely returning to the *" pre-departure"* gospel is God's wish.

But there is a second way we can tell whether it is possible to practice first century faith today. If there are cases from all over the world and from all through the centuries of those taking just the scriptures and independently coming to the same understanding of the original faith, that would demonstrate that the seed can be planted in later times. Has such taken place?

Indeed it has. Many documented cases tell of those with only a Bible who have come to a very similar practice of the gospel. While we in American churches of Christ are more familiar with the efforts of Thomas and Alexander Campbell, Barton Stone, and Walter Scott, these are but a few of those who have followed the scriptures to first century practice. Cases could be cited of many others in America, Scotland, France, Ethiopia, India, Spain, German, Italy, Poland, and Nigeria.

It is not unusual for missionaries today to find those who have said, *"I have been looking for someone who taught as you do because these are the conclusions to which I have already come from a study of the scriptures."* Reports have come even from those behind the *"iron curtain"* who, with a Bible and nothing else have come to a belief similar to that of American churches of Christ. Denominations have no such reports. Who, for example, just from reading the words, would practice Christianity as any denomination does? Who, from scripture alone, would conclude that salvation is by *"faith only"* without baptism, that there should be a church hierarchy, that Christians should call themselves by a denominational name or that baptism is by sprinkling?

One of the most striking cases recently came from inside the El Reno Federal Prison in Oklahoma. Here a group of inmates, with only the Bible as their guide, came to an understanding of the gospel that led them to establish a thriving congregation of Christianity as they understood it just from scripture. Only later did they find that they had many brothers in the outside world among churches of Christ who had reached the same understanding.

Some have recently said that our fellowship has been too much affected by the *"logical"* approach of John Locke. Certainly some who helped us find our way to original grounds were influenced by him. But the conclusions we have drawn about the essentials of the Christian faith have also been reached by others who never heard of John Locke or Alexander Campbell. True, some have pushed emotion too far out of the picture, and some have carried reasoning to the point of legalism. This, however, should not be taken to mean either that we should not use reason in the proper way or that re-producing the essentials of first century Christianity in our day is either an impossibility or undesirable.

The seed of the word is still here. It still convicts and converts. Those who will receive the seed, as presented in the scripture, can still let that seed grow in their hearts where it produces the same fruit it did twenty centuries ago. We must have faith that *"the word"* still provides *"all things that pertain to life and godliness"* (II Peter 1:3). We must use the terms of scripture to describe spiritual concepts, and we must treat as essentials only what the scriptures declare as affecting our eternal salvation.

To be undenominational in a denominational world, then, we must study the word carefully to learn God's message for us and practice it as revealed. Such is not only possible, it is happening all over the world.

Teach and Practice that We are Teachers Not Judges

One reason why we have difficulty reaching the world with the undenominational message and why we sometimes lose members to a denomination is because some consider us harsh and judgmental. There is a fine line to walk here, but it is one we must recognize.

As we have seen, there is the true gospel and there are perversions of this gospel. The true gospel has the promise of salvation, the perverted gospel does not. In preaching the gospel we will, of course, have to contrast it with where others have missed the mark. We will have to teach it is better to follow the gospel as revealed than to follow man-made changes. All of this

209

we are under the charge of scripture to do. We are, then, to <u>judge</u> whether a teaching is in harmony with the scripture.

At the same time, it is <u>not our role to be the judges of the souls</u> of those around us, to pass judgment on the eternal destiny of others. Romans 14:4 states: *"Who art thou that judgest the servant of another? to his own lord he standeth or falleth."* While we must judge whether a teaching or practice is in accord with the scripture, we do not have to predict anyone's eternal destiny. There is much we do not know about the Lord's judgment and much we do not know about the heart of another. God shall judge the secrets of men, according to the gospel Paul preached (Romans 2:16).

So what is the connection between not judging the destiny of others and being undenominational? Some in the church today feel we should not teach against the doctrines or practices of denominations because to do so is being judgmental and harsh. Others are confused about how to deal with the question of what will happen eternally to the member of a denomination who is *"honestly"* wrong about a doctrine like baptism or instrumental music but who is a believer in Jesus and a good person morally. Such concerns are causing us to say less and less about the evil of denominationalism and about the errors in doctrines by denominations. So we teach less about such matters because more are troubled when we do. Less teaching on this topic means even more will be concerned when we do teach on it. And so the cycle proceeds.

The answer to this problem lies in <u>teaching</u> on the right issues and <u>judging</u> on the right issues. We do not have to condemn to hell someone we believe is wrong about an essential doctrine. We should teach what the Bible says on the point and should, in an appropriate way, contrast it with false teaching on that point. But we should never ridicule the beliefs of others and/or predict the eternal destiny of those who believe it. Of course, if the Bible says those who practice or do not practice certain actions have a specific destiny awaiting them, we must teach that passage.

<u>So let us teach all that the scripture teaches</u>. Let us teach what the Bible says on those points where we differ with our religious neighbors. Let us even teach that certain doctrines held by others are wrong. But let us balance such teaching with the positive teachings about love and the lordship of Christ. Let us never teach harshly but *"speak the truth in love"* (Ephesians 4:15). Yet, let us not flinch from *"exhorting in the sound doctrine"* and *"convicting the gainsayer"* (Titus 1:9). Let us *"teach, reprove,*

correct, and instruct" as Paul taught Timothy (II Timothy 3:17). If we fail to do so, we will fail to stem the tide of denominationalism. We will have fewer and fewer among us who understand the difference, and we will become more and more like the denominations in belief and practice.

The Old Testament applies the word *"remnant"* to the faithful among the Israelites who made it possible to continue God's covenant with the nation (Isaiah 10:20-22). Thus a relatively small number can make a significant impact by remaining true to the covenant.

Churches of Christ today can serve in that same role. We can be God's remnant in our age: (1) by committing ourselves to teaching Christ and the church as taught by inspired writers of the New Testament, (2) by demonstrating to the world how these truths can be practiced today, and (3) by calling on all others -- whether believers in Christ or non-believers -- to join us in this effort. We <u>can</u> understand the essentials of *"the faith, once for all delivered to the saints."* We <u>can</u> practice these essentials as first century Christians did in following *"the apostles' doctrine."* We <u>can</u> have and have had an effect on denominations around us to bring them closer to these teachings and practice.

To do this we do not have to predict God's final judgment on those who do not understand or practice as we do. This is God's work, not ours. We do have to teach the truth. We do have to teach that what one believes and practices does make a difference to God. And we do have to teach what the Bible says will save or condemn in the final judgment. But we judge whether a teaching is scriptural, not what someone's eternal destiny will be.

It will help us to be undenominational, then, to clarify our role as <u>teacher</u> and <u>example</u> but <u>not judge</u>. In this way we can *"speak the truth in love,"* proclaiming the full gospel, showing mistakes in views that contradict the scripture, and exemplifying the life and worship of the early church.

Conclusion

Jesus said, *"I will build my church"* (Matthew 16:18). Christ *"loved the church, and gave himself up for it"* (Ephesians 5:25). All the saved have been added to this body, this family, this kingdom. The same response to God that saves also adds one to the body of the saved.

Can one be saved outside of the church? The answer is *"no"* if we use church, as the Bible does, to mean the body which includes all the saved. If all the saved are added to it, then none are saved outside of it.

Does one have to be a member of the *"church of Christ"* to be saved? If we use *"church of Christ"* as do the scriptures, to mean all whom Christ has saved, then the answer is *"yes,"* for the saved are the church and the church is the saved. In giving this answer, however, we must be sure that neither the speaker nor the hearer is thinking of *"Church of Christ"* in denominational terms.

We live at a time when pressure is strong to conform to common beliefs. The typical belief of those around us who profess to believe in Christ is that one is saved by *"faith only,"* and then he/she may join the denomination of his/her choice.

It is always difficult to change people's minds concerning a commonly held view, but we must believe and teach that, even twenty centuries later, one can still be in the church Jesus built and none other by doing the same thing to be in it those in the first century did. We can be the brethren of first century Christians when they were guided by inspired leaders. We can teach and practice that the church is one, that Jesus is Lord, that the Word is the seed, and that we are teachers not judges. If we will commit ourselves to these truths, we can remain undenominational and lead others out of that error.

Questions

1. Should churches of Christ seek to be distinctive from denominations?
2. To what scriptures would you refer in explaining that the church is not a denomination?
3. How can we more effectively communicate to our own members the undenominational concept?
4. How can we more effectively communicate to others the undenominational concept?
5. Should we join with denominational churches in joint efforts such as a ministerial alliance or a community benevolence event?

6. Will only the church of Christ be saved?
7. Can one join the church?
8. Can we know the original plan for being saved and living as the saved sufficiently to go back to it?
9. Why should we seek to go back to the original plan?
10. How should you answer if someone asks:
    a. What denominations are you a member of?
    b. What church are you a member of?
    c. What does your church teach about "x"?

16. Who's in the Fellowship?

Carl Mitchell

Questions about fellowship are varied and complex, and as shall be seen, may involve not only biblical truths, but also matters of conscience, as well as matters that are personal, emotional and subjective. Current controversies about fellowship among believers in Christ illustrate that while issues relating to fellowship are as old as human history, they must be dealt with anew in every age.

One of the most important of these controversies centers on a growing ecumenical spirit which holds that all those who believe in Christ should be fellowshipped regardless of denominational affiliation or doctrinal belief. If positions taken by some leading Protestant and Catholic theologians can be considered prophetic, pluralism will not be far behind![1] Other unsettling issues include controversies related to worship styles and content, male and female roles in the worship and work of the church, a re-evalutation of the place and meaning of baptism in the plan of salvation, and the nature and purpose of the church. All churches may not yet be affected by these developments, but history tells us they eventually will be.

While a study of the biblical nature of fellowship may not necessarily resolve the above mentioned areas of controversy to everyone's satisfaction, hopefully it will lead to a careful restudy of the points at issue and a desire to sincerely follow God's will. Even a cursory analysis of the contemporary scene will show that what we are experiencing in the church is a reflection of what is happening in our culture. The rejection of absolutes, the subjective centering upon experience and feeling, the upheaval of public views relative to traditional male/female distinctions, the glorification of a youth-culture, and a growing trend toward personal and social isolation all find their counterparts in the church. Perhaps those who militantly reject any effort to force a first century culture on the twentieth century would do well to remember that it is equally untenable to force our twentieth century culture on the Bible! If we believe the Bible to be the inspired word of God, then we must believe that God's word stands above culture. is intended to be a change agent wherever cultures deviate from divine standards, and ultimately sits in judgment on all cultures which reject biblical norms.

In the following paragraphs, attention will first be given to a definition of the biblical meaning of the words translated "fellowship" in both the Hebrew and the Greek texts of the Bible. Then attitudes and principles related to fellowship as they were acted out in early Jewish and Christian cultures will be examined. Next, a study of biblical principles related to fellowship will be given. Finally, an effort will be made to draw some conclusions on the basis of the above three areas of study as they apply to our contemporary scene.

Fellowship Defined

Perhaps it would be best to begin with an English definition of fellowship. According to *Webster's College Dictionary*, fellowship connotes:

> 1. the condition or relation of belonging to the same class or group, the fellowship of humanity. 2. friendly relationship; companionship; camaraderie: the fellowship among old friends. 3. community of interest, feeling, etc. 4. friendliness. 5. an association of persons having similar interests, occupations, enterprises, etc.[2]

The word "fellowship" in the English New Testament is usually a translation of the Greek term *koinonia*, or an alternate form of the *koinon* group.[3] According to Vine, *koinonia* means "communion, fellowship, sharing in common (from *koinos,* common)..."[4] Kittel says it "denotes participation, fellowship, especially with a close bond.... As with *Koinoneo,* emphasis may be on either the giving or the receiving. It thus means 1. participation, 2. impartation, 3. fellowship." He further states, "The *koinon* group is most common in Paul, for whom it has a directly religious content. Paul uses *koinonia* for the religious fellowship (participation) of the believer in Christ and Christian blessings, and for the mutual fellowship of believers."[5]

A second Greek term for fellowship which is used less frequently in the New Testament than *koinonia* is *metoche*.[6] Vine says this term means "partnership, (and) is translated 'fellowship' in II Corinthians 6:14.... The word seems to have a more restricted sense than *koinonia*."[7] Kittel explains,

> *Metoche* is used in II Corinthians 6:14 not so much in the sense of participation as in that of fellowship . . . . It is thus a synonym of *koinonia*, though elsewhere there is a distinction of meaning, since it is a common participation in a third which establishes mutual fellowship (*koinonia*).[8]

A third Greek term for fellowship is *kallao*,[9] which Vine says means "to join fast together, to glue, to cement...." It is also used "in the sense of becoming associated with a person so as to company with him,. or be on his side...."[10] Kittel states that it means" to glue together, to join together, to bind, or to cleave to."[11]

While the concept of fellowship is central to Old Testament content, Kittel says the *koinon* word group has no precise equivalent there. The Hebrew term *chabar*[12] is probably the closest, and means to bind, to string together, to unite, to hold in common, to associate with, along with ideas that relate to companionship.[13]

Fellowship In The Old Testament

The great stories of the Old Testament illustrate repeatedly that to be called of God always includes some degree of separation from those who do not accept God's call. When Paul told the Corinthians to avoid "unequal yokes" with unbelievers, to form "no partnership" with unrighteousness, and to avoid "fellowship" with darkness, he did so on the authority of God's statement in Isaiah (II Corinthians 6:14). Therefore, they were to "come out from their midst and be separate," says the Lord, "and do not touch what is unclean; and I will welcome you" (II Corinthians 6:17; Isaiah 52:11).

Because Noah walked with God, he was designated "righteous" and "blameless" in the midst of a perverse generation (Genesis 6:9). By building the ark, he separated himself from his contemporaries, and condemned their sinful life (Hebrews 11:7).

Abram was called by God to separate himself from both his country and his kin in order to follow God's leading to a new country (Canaan) and to the formation of a new family (Israel), (Genesis 12:1-2). Once established in the new land, "he lived as an allien....as in a foreign land" and joined his voice with others who answered the call of God, testifying that "they were strangers and exiles on the earth" (Hebrews 11:9,13).

When the great deliverer Moses led Israel to the promised land, he ordered Israel to make no covenants with the local inhabitants, to not join in their sacrificial meals, and to refuse to allow their children to intermarry with them. They were, in fact, ordered to destroy the dispossessed nations so that they would not become a snare to Israel. God also gave the reason: they were a people whom He, because of His love, had chosen to be His own possession (Exodus 34:11-16; Deuteronomy 7:1-6).

Sadly God's people did not share His vision of life in the "land of promise." The Canaanites were not destroyed, and both religious and social alliances were made with them. When the Israelites became more evil than their contemporaries, God's wrath was displayed in the Assyrian and Babylonian captivities (II Chronicles 36:11-21).

When some of the Israelites were finally restored to the land of promise, they found themselves surrounded by "foreigners" who had been brought in by Assyria to repopulate Palestine at the time of the exile. As the Jews began the reconstruction of the temple, the "locals" offered to help. They, being syncretistic, said they too served the God of the Hebrews having added Him to their pagan gods (II Kings 17:24-41). Israel refused their offer, saying "You have nothing in common with us in building a house to our God" (Ezra 4:3). Pluralists would do well to ponder Christ's statement about the Samaritan descendants of these people, "You worship that which you do not know, we worship that which we know, for salvation is from the Jews" (John 4: 22).

However, once more the Jews chose to have social and spiritual fellowship with the local people, including intermarriage and giving temple privileges. When these conditions were brought to the attention of Ezra and Nehemiah, the temple was cleansed of foreign intrusion (Nehemiah 13:4-9). The Jews who had foreign wives and children were ordered to send them away (Ezra 9:1-10:4; Nehemiah 13:23-31).

In the intertestamental period during the reign of Antiochus Epiphanes, Jewish efforts to remain separated from their pagan environment were frustrated by great pressure exerted on the Jews to Hellenize. It became unlawful to circumcise, to keep the Sabbath, and to offer the appointed sacrifices to Jehovah. Anyone who possessed a copy of the books of the law was killed, and the books were destroyed by fire. Eventually, Antiochus profaned the temple, dedicating it to Zeus, and offered a swine on the holy altar. Many Jews accepted death, rather than compromise their faith (II Maccabees 1:41-64). However, other Jews joined fellowship with the new culture.

The two Jewish sects most influential in Palestine at the time of Christ were the Sadducees and the Pharisees (separated ones). Some scholars think that both of these find their roots in the developments related to Antiochus.[14] It is possible that the Sadducees grew out of those Jews who agreed to have fellowship with the Syrian Hellenistic policies., From the time of John Hyrcanus, the Sadducees grew in favor with the Hasmonian rulers, and at the time of Christ they were the aristocracy of Israel. They also exercised great power in the Sanhedrin, and high priests were elected from their number. Materialistic in philosophy, they did not believe in a bodily resurrection, in spirit beings, nor in angels (Acts 23:8).

The Pharisees may have evolved from the "hasidim" or "godly people" who chose death at the time of Antiochus rather than violate God's law. As is often the case, when persecution passed, their faithfulness changed into legalism and self-righteousness.

Fellowship Among Jews In New Testament Times

The Pharisees became separatists to an extreme, developing as signs of their righteousness such strict dietary and purification traditions that they could no longer even eat with fellow Jews, let alone with Gentiles.[15] As a result, the Pharisees were frequent targets of some of Jesus' most scathing rebukes. When they criticized Him for eating with tax-collectors and sinners, He said that He had come to heal the sick, and not the well (perhaps those who thought they were well!!!), and to call sinners, and not the righteous (perhaps the self-righteous, see Luke 16:15). He then told them that compassion ranked above offering sacrifices (Matthew 9: 9-13).

It was the Pharisees whom he warned not to commit the ultimate sin of blasphemy against the Holy Spirit (Matthew 12:22-32). On one occasion he compared the prayers of a Pharisee and a tax-collector, saying a tax-collector with a humble spirit was more acceptable to God than a self-righteous Pharisee (Luke 18:9-14). It was the Pharisees who were warned that they and their traditions represented a plant not planted by the Lord that would be rooted up (Matthew 15:1-14). He also said to them, "You serpents, you brood of vipers, how shall you escape the sentence of hell" (Matthew 23:34)....And they killed Him! Especially in the Pharisees we see that a self-righteous, legalistic spirit can force the drawing of lines of fellowship never intended by God. While taking it upon themselves to become judge and jury even of Jesus, the Son of God, they only ended up disenfranchising themselves from the kingdom of God.

Fellowship In The Early Church

Given God's record of calling men and women to Himself (and consequently to each other), and away from any entanglements that might interfere with that process, it is not strange that He chose the word "church" to designate His people (Matthew 16:18). The Greek term is *ekklesia,* meaning "that which is called out."[16] As is clearly visible in the New Testament, not only are we fully informed as to that to which we are called, we are also informed as to those things from which we are to be separated.

The call of God is always a call into community, into fellowship with others who are similarly called of God. In fact, Christ said the "brand mark" which would prove our discipleship is the love that we have for each other (John 13:35). As demonstrated by the famous triangle illustration, those who are drawn closer to God are also drawn closer to each other. The earliest descriptive statement about the first Christians was that they continued steadfastly in "fellowship" (Acts 2:42). So rich was their love that no one had need, as those who were more financially capable shared with those who were not (Acts 2:44-45; 4:32). This was a trait which quickly attracted the attention and the admiration of their Jewish contemporaries (Acts 2:47; 5:13). This love also held the church steady in times of stress, and led to peaceful solutions which allowed the church to continue to give its attention to the chief matter at hand, the saving of the lost (Acts 6:1-7).

An analysis of the manner in which the first Christians went about practicing fellowship reveals some very interesting facts. First of all, it was a matter of great concern that one has been truly admitted into the family of God. Jesus Himself had set the criteria when he said, "unless one is born again, he cannot see the kingdom of God" (John 3:3). He then gave a fuller explanation to the puzzled Nicodemus, "Truly, truly, I say to you, unless one is born of water and the Spirit, he cannot enter the kingdom of God" (John 3: 5).

In the prologue of John it is revealed that only God can effect this "spiritual birth." "But as many as receive Him, to them He gave the right to become children of God, even to those who believe in His name, who were born not of blood, nor of the will of the flesh, nor of the will of men, but of God" (John 1:12-13). Peter confirms this saying, "Blessed be the God and Father of our Lord Jesus Christ, who according to His great mercy has caused us to be born again to a living hope through the resurrection of Jesus Christ from the dead" (I Peter 1:3). He then adds that the impregnating element which brings about this spiritual birth is the word of God: "you have been born again not of seed which is perishable but imperishable, that is, through the living and abiding word of God" (I Peter 1:23). Lest someone think we are talking here about an esoteric inner experience, Peter adds, "And this is the word which was preached to you" (I Peter 1:25). Verses commenting on the "new birth" stress believing (I John 5: 1), turning away from sin (I John 3:9; 5:18), baptism (John 3:3-8), loving (I John 4:7), working righteousness (I John 2:29), and overcoming the world (I John 5:4).

Except to those who are limited by the doctrinal views of their churches, it is clear that this "new birth" which God effects, includes the believer's baptism. Even a casual survey of the Book of Acts will demonstrate this. It is through baptism that Peter says the forgiveness of sins and the gift of the Holy Spirit are given (Acts 2:38). It was those who were baptized who were added to the church or the number of the saved (Acts 2:41,47). In fact, each illustration of conversion in Acts includes baptism (Acts 2:1-47; 8:1-3; 8:25-39;10:1-48;16:14-16;16:22-34;18:1-8; 19:1-7; 22:1-16). While Rudolf Bultmann is far from being a religious conservative, he is able to exegete objectively the New Testament doctrine of baptism:

> What is expected as the effect of baptism....is first: **Purification from one's sins**, and it is several times expressly said, from one's sins committed in the past (II Peter 1:9 Herm. mand. IV 3, 1, Justin Ap. 61:10). Paul undoubtedly means purification by baptism when after

describing the sinful heathen past of the readers he continues: "But you were washed, but you were made holy, but you were made righteous in the name of the Lord Jesus Christ and the Spirit of our God" (I Corinthians 6:11). All three verbs describe the sacramental bath of purification; and in this series "made righteous" is not meant in the specific sense of Paul's doctrine of justification, but, corresponding to "made holy," is meant in the general-Christian sense: cancellation of sin...........The related passages also show that Paul is here presenting the general Christian view of baptism. In the deutero-Pauline literature such passages include: Ephesians 5:26, where the purpose of Christ's work of salvation is "that he might make her (the Church) holy, having cleansed her by the washing of water with the word"; or I Peter 3:21, where baptism is interpreted as "not the removal of dirt from the body," i.e. the bath of baptism is no external purification, but creates the possibility (by cleansing the believer of his sins) of "calling upon God" with the consciousness of purity (cf. Hebrews 9:14; 10:2,22). Similar passages occur in literature nearly or entirely independent of Paul. Since baptism takes place "for the forgiveness of sins" (Acts 2:38), Saul-Paul is commanded to "rise and be baptized and wash away your sins, calling upon his name" (Acts 22:16). According to Hebrews 10:22 we, as Christians, have "our hearts sprinkled clean from an evil conscience and our bodies washed with pure water" in which "body" is separated from "heart" only for the sake of the rhetorical parallelism of members; for the washing is, of course, not limited to the "body," but applies just as much to the "heart." The "cleansing from one's old sins," II Peter 1:9. is, of course the cleansing received in baptism. According to Barnabas II:II "we go down into the water full of sins and foulness, and we come up bearing the fruit of fear in our hearts and having hope on Jesus in the Spirit"; and according to 16:8f, we become a temple of God by "the remission of sins" (received in baptism). When we went down into the water, Hermas said (mand. IV 3,I), "we received remission of our former sins" (cf. Justin Ap. 61:10).[17]

The New Testament insists that one enters the body of Christ through believer's baptism (*baptizo,* immersion): "For all of you who were baptized into Christ have clothed yourselves with Christ" (Galatians 3:27), and "By one Spirit we were all baptized into one body" (I Corinthians 12:13). Therefore, attention was given as to whether or not persons claiming to be brothers and sisters in Christ had actually experienced this spiritual rebirth. When Paul came into contact with believers in Ephesus, and learned they had not yet received the Holy Spirit, he immediately asked about their baptism. When he learned they had received the baptism of John rather than that of Christ, he commanded baptism in the name of the Lord Jesus (Acts 19:1-7). When Peter crossed over the Jewish-Gentile line and baptized Cornelius and his relatives into the one body, he was immediately called into question by Jewish Christians in Jerusalem. Only after they were convinced that the Lord had worked supernaturally to bring this about did they praise God for granting salvation to the Gentiles (Acts 10:1-11:18).

When the biblical case for baptism is thus set forth, some accuse those who believe it of holding to water salvation. Nothing could be farther from the truth! Never does scripture suggest that water suddenly possesses some kind of magical power. It only states that God has chosen this medium through which to do His work. Paul writes to the Colossians that one who is buried with Christ in baptism is "raised up with Him through faith in the working of God" (Colossians 2:12). When God healed Naaman the leper, he required that he dip himself seven times in the Jordan River. The water of the Jordan River had no power to cure leprosy, but God who did have the power, chose this medium. If Naaman had refused to follow God's way, he would not have been healed (II Kings 5:1-19). The man born blind who was told by Jesus to wash his eyes in the pool of Siloam did so, and "came back seeing" (John 9:1-34). He later said to the Pharisees, "you do not know where He is from and yet He opened my eyes" (v.30). The water of the pool had no power to cure blindness, but the Lord chose this medium. In the same manner, the Lord has ordered that all believers be baptized (Matthew 28:18-20; Mark 16:16). God has chosen the medium of baptism in water to save the believer, not because water has the power to save, but because it is His will to save in this manner. Perhaps this is just another instance of His having chosen the "foolish things of the world," and "the things that are not" to "shame the wise" (I Corinthians 1:20-31).

When one gained entry into the household of God through the new birth, that person immediately began to receive wonderful blessings which flowed from the fellowship of the saints. As these are listed, one cannot help but notice the degree to which many of these outstanding components of fellowship have been lost! It may be that the most pressing issue related to fellowship is the need to experience again in our age the richness of fellowship shared in the family of God in the first century!

As already mentioned, members in physical need were aided by their brothers and sisters in Christ, whether Jew or Gentile (Acts 2:42; 4:32; 11:27-30; Romans 15:26-27; I Corinthians 16:1-2; II Corinthians 9:1-15). There was also an intimate emotional bond which resulted in their being able to feel and support each other's joys and sorrows (Romans 12:15; I Corinthians 12:26). Bound together as they were by love, they were able to defer to each other by giving rather than seeking honor (Romans 12:10), and by placing the good of others above the good of self (Romans 15:1-3). They were helped to understand that Christians are not in competition with one another, and that each is accountable to God only for what he or she has received (II Corinthians 10:12; 8:12). Giving hospitality was highly emphasized (Romans 12:13; I Peter 4:9). While Christians should do good to all men, they were especially challenged to do good to those of "the household of faith" (Galatians 6:10). As a general rule, they were to show Christ's love by bearing "one another's burdens" (Galatians 6:3). Their solidarity was to be so great that when fellow believers were imprisoned for the faith, the others felt as if they were in prison with them (Hebrews 13:3).

Spiritual Benefits of Christian Fellowship

The spiritual benefits of Christian fellowship were many. Believers were aided greatly by confessing their faults to one another and praying for one another (James 5:16). In the assembly, instead of seeking personal spiritual gain, everything was done to edify each other, even in the use of spiritual gifts (I Corinthians 14:12,26). In biblically neutral matters, individual freedom was never to be used in a way that was injurious to a fellow believer (I Corinthians 8:9-13). Members were never to be caustic and judgmental with each other, but rather were to allow their love to "cover a multitude of sins" (I Peter 4:8). When loving concern made it necessary to correct and even discipline a brother or sister guilty of sin, this was to be done with gentleness and personal soul-searching (Galatians 6:1-2). While this duty is not pleasant, God has ordained that Christians have the responsibility of discipling those within the church whose evil conduct brings reproach upon Christ and also threatens to spread to other church members (I Corinthians 5:9-13). However, even this was to be done with the best interest of the disciplined one in mind (I Corinthians 5:5; II Thessalonians 3:15).

In addition to the vertical dimension of worship (person to God), there was to be a horizontal dimension (person to person) (Ephesians 5:18-21). This occurred especially in the breaking of the bread and in the drinking of the fruit of the vine (I Corinthians 11:17-34). When member to member relationships were ignored, Paul warned that communion with God no longer existed (vs. 20,17), and spiritual sickness, and death resulted (v. 30). In the early church, this mutual spiritual upbuilding was considered most valuable. Therefore, as we "stimulate each other to love and good deeds," we also encourage each other not to forsake worshipping together (Hebrews 10:24-25).

Since fellowship is vital to the life of the church as she fulfills her tasks in the world, biblical principles relating to fellowship must be respected. Kingdom fellowship is given only to one who had entered the kingdom by the "new birth." The Bible gives no instance of kingdom fellowship being shared with anyone who had not been so born into God's spiritual family. Christians traveling from city to city even carried letters to identify themselves as church members in good standing (Acts 18:24-28; Romans 16:1-2; I Corinthians 4:17; 16:3; 16:10-11; II Corinthians 3:1; Colossians 4:10; III John 5-11).

The New Testament gives a number of reasons why a Christian brother or sister would be denied fellowship. Such was the case for anyone who insisted on living an immoral life (I Corinthians 5:11). Those who lived an unruly life or departed from the apostles' teachings were to be refused association and avoided (II Thessalonians 3:6,14). Factious (divisive) individuals were to be rejected after two warnings (Titus 3:9-11). Quarrelsome persons who caused others to stumble were to be "turned away from" (Romans 16:17-18). This was also the case for teachers of heretical doctrines (I Timothy 1:18-20; II Timothy 2:16-18). One who denied the incarnation of Christ was not to be greeted or shown hospitality (II John 6-11). Only those who walked in the light of God's word were to have fellowship with the Father and with one another (I John 1:5-7).

Biblical Principles Related To Fellowship

On the basis of this overview of fellowship as it was experienced by the "called out" of God in the Old and New Testaments, it is possible to draw some general guidelines.

(1) The call of God has always involved some degree of separation from persons and cultures which either had not been so called (in terms of a specific mandate as in the case of Abraham), or had chosen not to respond to God's call.

(2) However, this separation was never to be a withdrawal from the world, but rather a separation shown by lifestyle, and allegiance to God. Jesus prayed to God in behalf of his disciples, "I do not ask Thee to take them out of the world, but to keep them ⁓m the evil one. They are not of the world, even as I am not of ⁓vorld" (John 17:15-16).

(3) While the people of God were separated in mission, and obedience to the Father, they were at the same time their contemporaries as members of the human family

created in the image of God. This involved a kind of fellowship that was instrumental to their living together in this physical world. Aspects of this fellowship included friendship, hospitality, thoughtfulness in a particular way to strangers and to the poor, business relations, political or military pacts, and in some instances joint military ventures. It was always the purpose of God that His "chosen ones" showcase the uniqueness and excellence of the Lord as compared to all other gods.

(4) However, the "called of God" were to remain separate from their neighbors in their religious practices. In the Old Testament, they were to listen only to the Lord's voice, whether given orally through patriarchs or prophets, or in written form. In Christian times, in addition to the truths of the Old Testament, they were to be guided by Christ's teachings. Therefore, any move toward syncretism (mixing God's religion with pagan religions) was to be rejected. "Light" had no fellowship with "darkness." With the development of temple worship and later the synagogues, outsiders had only marginal access, unless they chose to become proselytes.

(5) The fact that one had been added to the kingdom through the "new birth" did not mean fellowship was always to be extended. As noted above, fellowship was withdrawn from the non-repentant over both moral and doctrinal issues, although this was done out of love, and only after all efforts at recall had failed. In addition, a door of reentry was always open when repentance occurred (II Corinthians 2:5-8).

Conclusions Regarding Fellowship

Believers share God's created world with all living things, but especially with fellow human beings because they too are created in the image of God. We are brothers and sisters in Adam and Eve, being equally descendants of our first parents. Therefore, Christians are not to seek to find some sheltered place isolated from the people of the world, but rather, are to love them, and serve them! Ultimately, it is God's will that all of these who are not in the spiritual family of the Lord, be given His invitation to become such (Matthew 28:18-20; II Peter 3:9). For this reason, all "the called of God" have a mission to those who have not yet heard or who have not yet responded to His call. This is to be fulfilled through preaching and teaching, but also through being light, salt and leaven by means of personal contact (Matthew 5:13-16; 13:33).

Our fellowship with those who are in the physical family of God, but not yet in His spiritual family, takes many forms. These people are numbered among our relatives, they are among our close personal friends, they are our companions at work, we make contracts with them, we serve with them in the military in times of external threat, and we unite with them in common causes which may be social, political, educational, or humanitarian. However, we cannot have kingdom fellowship with these people until they too choose to be "born again" into God's spiritual family. Further, we are warned in specific instances to break off even the above such physical alliances when we begin to see that in a given relationship, the spiritual effect on the Christian begins to be negative (II Corinthians 6:14-18).

As Christians interface with non-Christian religious groups, we are warned never to enter into any communion or contact that would suggest that they share in God's spiritual family (I Corinthians 10:14-21; Colossians 2:8-3:17). The New Testament claim is that salvation is to be obtained only through the death, burial and resurrection of Christ (I Corinthians 15:1-4). Christ is the one mediator between mankind and God (I Timothy 2:5), there is no other entry into God's salvation (John 14:6), and salvation is to be found only in His name (Acts 4:12).

It is more complex to decide questions of fellowship that relate to other believers in Christ who have not been "born again of water and of the Spirit." Evidence abounds to testify to the earnestness, dedication, love of Christ, strength of faith, and multiplicity of good works resident among many of these religious groups. However, the fact that they reject the gospel plan of salvation as it relates to the necessity of a penitent believer's baptism into Christ means, according to Christ, that they have not yet entered into the kingdom of God (John 3:3-9), and cannot therefore be given kingdom fellowship. In addition, many denominations have departed from the biblical teachings related to the church of the New Testament in matters having to do with organization (I Timothy 3:3-13; Titus 1:5-9), the Lord's Supper (Acts 20:7), acappella ("as in church") singing in worship to God (Ephesians 5:18-21), and the role of women in the public worship (I Corinthians 14:34-38; I Timothy 2: 8-15).

On the other hand, while granting that a great deal of diversity exists among the various churches claiming a relationship to Christ, we do share with most of them a common core of beliefs he Old and New Testaments, and a general allegiance to the nce of God and of mankind's ultimate answerability to Him. It seem that with many of the denominations, we are in a n comparable to that of Apollos and the twelve believers at

Ephesus, who precisely in relationship to Christian baptism needed to learn the way of the Lord more perfectly (Acts 18:24-19:7).

Having said that it is not possible to have kingdom fellowship with those who have not yet been added to the kingdom through the new birth of water and Spirit, there are many truths which we hold in common which may provide opportunity for common cause. The list goes beyond what will be detailed here, but I would mention promotion of the God-ordained family structure, resisting abortion, resisting same-sex marriage, promoting biblical moral and ethical standards, defending the uniqueness of the Godhead and of salvation only through Christ, defending God-ordained gender roles, and the translation and diffusion of scripture. The challenge in doing this is to find a way to promote common-cause activities in a manner that does not compromise biblical truths concerning the New Testament church. In the final analysis, such decisions will be made by local congregations or by individual Christians.

However, it must be stated that when religious division is denounced and the importance of returning to the church of the New Testament and the body of teachings committed to it is insisted upon (including the centrality of penitent believer's baptism), this often becomes a "turn off" to our denominational friends and a barrier to "common-cause" activities. In fact, it appears that some of our number have become so sensitive to this problem that they have decided to deal with it by turning away from their belief in the importance of the one non-denominational New Testament church, and by denying the essentiality for salvation of the new birth of water and the Spirit.

In defense of these changes, we hear those promoting them claiming that churches of Christ have become just as divided and sectarian as have the denominations. In addition, at least some have accepted the idea that those who insist that baptism is essential to salvation are promoting a "human-works" salvation.

In answer, I would say that our "so called" divisions are not true divisions in the denominational sense. The various exponents of the restoration movement do have points of difference which affect some aspects of fellowship, but do not equate to the organic divisions of the denominational world. They are not organically different churches. Typically, churches in the restoration movement have remained true to the basic tenets of scripture regarding the church (Ephesians 4:4-6). They recognize Jesus as the church's only head, that all Christians are to be unified in one church (neither mine nor yours but Christ's), that scripture is their only creed, local autonomy under the leadership of elders and deacons, the New Testament plan of salvation, and (with the

227

otion of some who have chosen to use instruments, or have
for unscriptural roles for women) worship after the New
nent order. The purpose of the restoration movement is not
ιo establish another denomination that is better than the others,
but rather a return to the one body of Christ to which, according to
New Testament teaching, the Lord adds those who are saved
(Acts 2:47).

The denial of Jesus' statement that entry into God's spiritual kingdom requires a spiritual birth of water and the Spirit
(baptism), seems to grow out of the Reformers' battle against the
idea that salvation comes through "works of merit." We need only
to be reminded that all the salvation work that occurs through
baptism is done by the Lord (Colossians 2:12; Ephesians 5:25-26).
More importantly, we should ask, "Does God have another plan by
which those who are not born again of water and of the Spirit can
be counted as having experienced the new birth?" If He does (and
only God can make that judgment), we will all rejoice; but until
Jesus comes, we are bound by what He has said, and we are led
to believe that His words will be the source of final judgment (John
12:48). It is a terrible and fearsome responsibility to reject clear
statements of Christ and the apostles about salvation (backed up
by much testimony from early church history), and illustrated by the
examples of conversion in the book of Acts. It is even worse to
teach the lost to ignore Christ's teachings about salvation. If the
fact that the Jews who rejected John the Baptizer's baptism meant
they rejected God's counsel, how much more does one reject
God's counsel by choosing to deny the essentiality of the baptism
commanded by Christ (Luke 7:29-30).

Kingdom Fellowship

All who have been "born again of water and of the Spirit"
have been added by the Lord to the family of God and are brothers
and sisters in Christ (Acts 2:36-41,47; Galatians 3:26-27). It is the
Lord who will settle the matter of final judgment, taking out of the
kingdom those who "offend and do iniquity" (Matthew 13:41-42); I
Corinthians 4:1-5; Hebrews 10:26-31). It is also the Lord who
decides when a church is no longer His church (Revelation 2:4-5).

The Lord is very concerned about the unity of His family.
Those who conduct themselves in "a manner worthy of their
calling" will make every effort to promote peace and unity in the
body (Ephesians 4:1-3). Unity enhances our ability to give glory to
the God and Father of our Lord Jesus Christ (Romans 15:5-7).

When love, joy, peace and unity reign in the church, then the followers of Christ become lights in the darkness of this world, and people come to the salvation that is in Christ (Philippians 2:12-18). Conversely, a warring, factious church will not be able to avoid planting the seeds of its own destruction (Galatians 5:13-15).

More than any other New Testament book, I Corinthians furnishes useful information related to fellowship within the kingdom. The Corinthians were dealing with many issues that were leading to division. It is interesting that right in the middle of his narration of these problems, Paul, perhaps in exasperation, said (my paraphrasing), "If you just had more love for each other, you would not have these problems" (see I Corinthians 13). It is love that brought Jesus to this earth, not to please Himself, but to please us and do that which would be useful to us (Romans 15:3; Philippians 2:1-11). It is love that does in fact cover "a multitude of sins" (James 5:19-20). It is love which causes us to put what is best for our brother or sister in Christ ahead of our own personal likes or dislikes (I Corinthians 10:23-24, 32-33; Romans 15:1-2). If our first and most impelling attitude toward our brothers and sisters in Christ is not love, then we lie against the truth of God's word (I John 3:10-24; 4:7-21).

There are some guidelines in I Corinthians which are intended to help the church avoid division: we are not to follow men (4:6-7; 3:21-23), we are to hold weaker members in special consideration (8:4-13), we are to do nothing that would be a hindrance to the Gospel (9:11-12), we are to identify with and seek the salvation of each other (9:12-23), in areas of freedom, we are not to use our freedom in a way that is destructive to others (10:23-24), we are to look critically first at our own spiritual condition before being critical of someone else (9:24-27....see also Matthew 7:3-5), we are to serve lovingly and try to please each other (10:23-24, 32-33), and everything in the assembly is to be done to edify or build each other up (14:12,23).

It should be noted that verses which caution against causing offense do not necessarily relate to every difference of view or opinion between believers, but rather, regard those individuals who are going to fall away from the faith, or be seriously damaged in their faith by a compromise of conscience as a result of the examples or actions of others (Matthew 18:1-7; I Corinthians 8:1-13; Romans 14:1-23). It is not the intent of the Holy Spirit that these verses about not offending others be used in a manipulative manner by those who claim "offense" in order to have their way.

It is never easy to decide that we have arrived at a point when fellowship with a congregation or an individual is no longer possible. The process is agonizing and disturbing, to say the least. Usually, according to scripture, the problems we face which lead to a withdrawal of fellowship have to do with salvation issues. However, other scriptures illustrate the withdrawal of at least some phases of fellowship may come due to difference of opinion or judgment, as in the case of Paul and Barnabas in a matter regarding John Mark (Acts 15:36-41). I do not believe that either Paul or Barnabas saw this as a salvation issue.

Since questions of fellowship are ultimately decided by individual Christians, three principles seem to be put forward in the New Testament. First of all, one cannot have fellowship with anyone in a matter which is clearly against the teaching of the Word of God (II Thessalonians 3:6; I Corinthians 14:36-38). Second, one cannot have fellowship in an activity which would involve a violation of conscience, even if it is a scruple derived from tradition or opinion and not specifically from the Word of God (Romans 14:13-23). In the third place one cannot have fellowship with others in an activity which may be "non-principle" to the spiritually strong, but which may become a stumbling block to the spiritually weak, causing them to sin when they follow the example of the spiritually strong (Romans 14:13-23; I Corinthians 8:4-13).

As painful as the process is, scripture does indicate that there are times to cut off fellowship from a brother or sister who insists on a direction which, whether in personal life or in church doctrine, is contrary to scripture (I Corinthians 5:1-13; 11:17-32; I Timothy 1:18-20; II Timothy 2:16-19; Titus 1:7-16; I John 2:7-11; III John 9-10;Revelation 2:2,14-16,20-23). First, however, a sincere and loving effort must be made to correct this deviation from God's Word (Galatians 6:1; Matthew 18:15-17; James 5:19-20). There are two reasons given for such corrective disciplinary actions: first, it is to promote repentance and salvation on the part of the errant believer (I Corinthians 5:4-5; I Timothy 1:18-20); secondly, it is to prevent the error from spreading throughout the congregation (I Corinthians 5:6-7).

The message that comes through loud and clear in the Corinthian letters is that we are to be very slow about cutting ourselves off from our brother and sister in Christ, even when there may eventually be valid scriptural reasons for doing so. God gives the model in frequent examples in His Old Testament dealings with Israel (Isaiah 65:2; I Corinthians10:11). It was always God's hope that repentance would come, and He gave Israel time to think, to study and to repent, as He repeatedly sent His prophets to call them back into the right way. This is still His attitude today (II Peter 3:9).

A perusal of I Corinthians shows that the following sins (including doctrinal departures) were present in the Corinthian church: division (1:11-13; 3:3-6), immorality (5:1-5; 6:15-20), lawsuits between brethren (6:1-8), marriage problems (chapter 7), idol worship (chapter 8), male and female role problems (11:1-16), Lord's supper problems (11:17-34), spiritual gifts problems (chapter 13 and 14), and problems related to whether or not there was a bodily resurrection (chapter 15). I have never been involved with a church that had either the number or the severity of these problems found in the Corinthian church. When we speak of restoring the New Testament church, we mean that we want to return to the teachings given to Christians in New Testament times and not to restore congregations such as the ones at Corinth, Ephesus, Rome, etc. Nor should we pretend that we have completed the work of restoration as the process by which imperfect followers seek to return to God's perfect way is never completed!

Now here is an amazing thing! Having seen all of the scriptural departures and violations that were in the Corinthian church, it would be easy to feel that the Lord (and Paul) would have just washed their hands of the whole congregation, but such is not the case. As God "all day long held out his hands to Israel" (Isaiah 65:2), so we see Him holding on to the Corinthian church pointing out their sins and asking them to repent. In the meantime, they are still called "the church of God," "the sanctified in Christ," "saints," and are to be "confirmed to the end blameless" (I Corinthians 1:1-9). It is however, to be understood that Paul expected them to respond to his exhortations by repenting, and if they did not, they would face God's judgment (I Corinthians 3:9-11; 3:16-17; 5:1-13; 6:11; 8:1-13; 10:1-2; 11:27-32; 13:1-3; 14:37-38; 15:34; 16:13-14,22). Of course, those in Corinth who had not participated in the sins here condemned would be like the innocent in Sardis, and would one day "walk with (the Lord) in white" (Revelation 3:4).

Questions

1. Describe the fellowship as shared by those individuals in the first century church.
2. Is there any sense in which a Christian may have fellowship with another fellow believer?
3. How does one determine when to withhold or withdraw fellowship?
4. How should a Christian regard a fellow Christian with whom he has doctrinal differences?
5. What part does baptism for the remission of sins play in the matter of fellowship? With Christ? With religious neighbors?
6. Are there any religious errors that would make fellowship impossible? Explain your answer.
7. The Pharisees went to extremes in being separatist. What are some of those extremes that should be avoided by Christians?
8. In the realm of fellowship, what does the word *ekklesia* (church) suggest?
9. What has always been God's warning to his people regarding interfacing with those who are not His people?
10. What standard is to be used in determining when and where fellowship should be extended?

APPENDIX

Introduction

Jack P. Lewis

Jack P. Lewis, professor of Bible at the Harding Graduate School of Religion in Memphis, Tennessee, has taught at that institution since 1954. He received his B. A. from Abilene Christian College, his M. A. from Sam Houston State Teachers, his S. T. B. from Harvard. He holds a Ph. D. from Harvard Divinity School and a Ph. D. from Hebrew Union College. He has preached in Throckmorton, and Huntsville, Texas, Providence, Rhode Island, Covington, Kentucky and Ripley, Tennessee.

He has written a number of books including: *Understanding Genesis, The Gospel According to Matthew, Leadership Questions Confronting the Church, Archaeology and the Bible, Archaeological Backgrounds to Bible People, The Minor Prophets, The Last Things,* and, co-authored, *The Instrumental Music Issue* with Everett Ferguson and Earl West.

Chapter 1

The State of the Church Today

Glover Shipp

Biography

Dr. Glover Shipp is the grandson and great grandson of elders and the son of a preacher and missionary. He has been a long-time preacher, an elder and a missionary in Brazil for eighteen years. He holds five college degrees.

For more than forty years he has been a prolific writer and presently serves as managing editor of the Christian Chronicle. He is on the editorial board and a staff writer for other church publications. He has authored a number of books in English, Portuguese and Spanish. He has written materials now in use in Russia and Eastern Europe.

He is a professor at Oklahoma Christian, an award winning artist, writer and distance runner. He is married to the former Margie Smith of Los Angeles, California, and they have nine grandchildren.

Bibliography

Anderson, Lynn, *Navigating the Winds of Change* (West Monroe: Howard Publishing, 1994).

Barna, George, *The Frog in the Kettle* (Glendale: Regal Books, 1990).

Chaldler, Russell, *Racing Toward 2001: The Forces Shaping America's Religious Future* (Grand Rapids: Zondervan, 1991).

Colson, Charles, *The Body: Being Light in Darkness* (Dallas: Word Publishing, 1992).

Foster, Douglas A., *Will the Cycle Be Unbroken? Churches of Christ Face the 21st Century* (Abilene: ACU Press, 1994).

Guiness, Os, *Dining With The Devil: The Megachurch Movement.* (Grand Rapids: Baker Book House, 1993).

Hall, Douglas John, *Has The Church A Future?* (Philadelphia: Westminister, 1980).

Johnson, Douglas W., *Growing Up Christian In The Twenty-First Century* (Valley Forge: Judson Press, 1984).

LaHaye, Tim, *The Race For The 21st Century* (Nashville: Thomas Nelson, 1986).

Luedtke, Luther., Ed. *Making America: The Society and Culture of the United States.* (Chapel Hill: The University of North Carolina Press, 1992).

McDowell, Josh and Bob Hostetler, *Right From Wrong* (Dallas: Word Publishing, 1994).

Niebuhr, H. Richard, *Christ and Culture* (New York: Harper and Row, 1951).

Raabe, Tom, *The Ultimate Church* (Grand Rapids: Zondervan, 1991).

Richards, Lawrence O, *A New Face For The Church* (Grand Rapids: Zondervan, 1970).

Roper, Randy, "Youth Survey". Edmond: Visitor, Jan 6, 1996.

Samuelson, Robert J., "Cheer Up, America: It's Not As Bad As You Think." *Newsweek*, Jan 6 1996, pp. 24-33.

Smith, F. LaGard, *The Cultural Church* (Nashville: 20th Century Christian, 1992).

Vinzant, Don, "Six Types of Community Churches and What They Need To Learn" (Unpublished Outline), 1995.

Vinzant, Gene, Ed., "Lessons from Willow Creek." *Ministry,* March-June, Garland: 1994.

Chapter 2

Hermeneutics, Culture, and Scripture

F. Furman Kearley

Biography:
Furman Kearley has served as Editor of the <u>Gospel Advocate</u> since 1985. He also serves as Dean of Magnolia Bible College in Kosciusko, Mississippi. He began preaching the gospel in 1950 and has proclaimed the Word for 48 years. He has preached for congregations in Montgomery and Ragland, Alabama, Covington, Kentucky; Lubbock, Burkett and Monahans, Texas. He has preached in approximately 500 congregations in our brotherhood in meetings, lectureship and workshops. He has lectured at all of the Christian colleges and a number of the Christian academies and many schools of preaching. He has preached in forty states ands ten foreign countries.

He has served as a faculty member of our Christian colleges for forty six years. He served as chairman of the Bible Department at Alabama Christian College, Dean of Alabama Christian School of Religion (now Southern Christian University), Chairman of the Bible Department at Lubbock Christian University, Director of Graduate Studies in Bible at Abilene Christian University. He has written over 500 articles and lectureship manuscripts.

Bibliography

Bush, L. Russ, et. al, editors, *The Proceedings of the Conference on Biblical Inerrancy* (Nashville: Broadman Press, 1987).

Carson, D. A., *Exegetical Fallacies* (Grand Rapids: Baker Book House, 1984).

Conn, Harvie M., editor, *Inerrancy and Hermeneutic* (Grand Rapids: Baker Book House, 1988).

Ensign, Grayson Harter, *You Can Understand The Bible.* (Joplin: College Press, 1978).

Fee, Gordon D. and Douglas Stuart, *How to Read The Bible for All Its Worth* (Grand Rapids: Zondervan, 1982).

Larkin, William J., Jr., *Culture and Biblical Hermeneutics* (Grand Rapids: Baker Book House, 1988).

Marshall, I. Howard, editor, *New Testament Interpretation* (Grand Rapids: William B. Eerdmans Publishing Company, 1977).

McKim, Donald K., editor, *A Guide to Contemporary Hermeneutics* (Grand Rapids: William B. Eerdmans Publishing Company, 1986).

Ramm, Bernard L., et. al., *Hermeneutics* (Grand Rapids, Baker Book House, 1977).

Thomas, J. D., *Harmonizing Hermeneutics* (Nashville: Gospel Advocate Company, 1991).

Chapter 3

The Role of Women In the Assembly of the Church

Nancy Ferguson

Biography:

Nancy Ferguson and her husband, Everett, have lived in Abilene, Texas for thirty six years, where they attend the Hillcrest Church of Christ. They have three children and five grandchildren.

Nancy graduated from Abilene Christian University in 1955 with a B. A. in Bible. She has written articles for *Power for Today, Gospel Advocate, and 20th Century Christian* and has written Vacation Bible School material for the Sweet Company. She has taught classes at Lectureships in Scotland and at both Pepperdine and Abilene Christian Universities. She has taught workshops on Teacher Training and Family Relationships in Texas, Michigan, England and South Africa. Nancy is currently writing a book entitled *Living A Worthy Life*.

Chapter 4

What Kind of Music Does God Want?

Milo Richard Hadwin

Biography:

Milo Hadwin is completing class work for the D. Min. degree from Harding Graduate School of Religion where he previously received an M. Div. He also has a B. A. from Harding University and an M. A. from Abilene Christian University. He is the author of *The Role of New Testament Examples as Related to Biblical Authority* and *The Overcomers: Sermons on Revelation*.

Hadwin was head of the Bible department at Northeaster Christian College and has worked full-time with churches in Wheeling, West Virginia; Kingston, Jamaica; Bellevue, Washington; Alamo, Tennessee; and Newberg, Oregon.

Recommended Books:

Bales, James D. *Instrumental Music and New Testament Worship* (Searcy; James D. Bales, 1973).

Ferguson, Everett. *A Cappella Music in the Public Worship of the Church*, (Revised Edition) (Abilene: Biblical Research Press, 1972).

Flatt, Bill. *The Instrumental Music Issue* (Nashville: Gospel Advocate Company, 1987)

Personal Note:

My research has led me to far more material that would support the conclusion reached than this chapter can contain. I would be glad to share this with any who would like the material. I can be reached at: Milo Hadwin, 2503 Haworth Avenue, Newberg, Oregon, 97132 (Phone: 503-538-4789)

Chapter 5

Are You on God's Praise Team?

Robert Oglesby, Sr.

Biography:
 Robert Oglesby has B. A. & M. A. degrees in Bible from Abilene Christian University and an honorary Doctor of Laws degree from York College. He has been the pulpit minister at the Waterview Church of Christ (a congregation of 1,350 members) in Richardson, Texas for thirty five years. He has taught more than three hundred fifty teacher training workshops at congregations across the United States and Canada, and on seven college and university campuses. He also teaches leadership training workshops with individual elderships. He has written twenty one Group Discussion books, including a handbook for teachers, entitled, *Group Dynamics in the Bible Class.* He is the narrator of a new evangelistic video series called, *The Story*, which was shot on location in the Bible lands. He is a member of the Board of Trustees for Abilene Christian University. He is President of *The Restoration Quarterly* corporation board.

Recommended Books:
Everett Ferguson, *A Cappella Music in the Public Worship of the Church*
 (Abilene: Biblical Research Press, 1972).
Everett Ferguson, *The Church of Christ*, (Grand Rapids: William B.
 Eerdmans, 1996).
Bill Flatt, *The Instrumental Music Question* (Nashville: Gospel Advocate
 Company, 1987).
F. LaGard Smith, *The Cultural Church* (Nashville: 20th Century Christian,
 1992).
F. Furman Kearley, Edward P. Myers, Timothy D. Hadley, Editors,
 Biblical Interpretation (Grand Rapids: Baker Book House, 1985).

Chapter 6

A Changing World, An Unchanging God

Allan McNicol

Biography:

Allan McNicol was born in Australia and came to America in 1962. He has degrees from Abilene Christian University, Yale and earned his Ph.D. at Vanderbilt. He married Patricia Burke in 1978. They have two children, Rob and Chris. Since 1972 he has taught at the Institute for Christian Studies in Austin. At present he is Dean of Students at the Institute and an elder of the University Church of Christ.

For the past decade McNicol has published a series of articles in various journals circulated among churches of Christ on the issue of maintaining and recovering our heritage within the Restoration Movement. McNicol considers that the principle of Restorationism is sound and finds great interest and acceptance of it among various cultures through the globe. Nevertheless, Restorationism is under assault in various quarters and it is necessary to think through and reclaim its basic tenets. The essay in this volume is a contribution to that end.

Footnotes on Chapter 6

1   Nils Dahl, *Jesus the Christ: The Historical Origins of Christological Doctrine* (Minneapolis: Fortress, 1991), pp 75-76 has discussed the importance of the theme of promise as the point of connection that ties together the theology of both the Old and New Testaments. Our task is a more modest one of using the theme of promise as a way of noting that for the people of God there are constants that remain in a world of great change.

2   B. S. Childs, *The Book of Exodus: A Critical Theological Commentary* (Philadelphia: Westminister Press, 1974) p 24 captures the paradox that the fulfillment of such a crucial promise rested on so fragile a set of circumstances with his comment "God seems to be taking such an enormous risk to let everything ride on two helpless midwives, a frail ark as protection from the sea, and a last minute flight to Egypt."

Thus, throughout the Old Testament this account of God's promises to bring salvation to the nations continues to be affirmed in stunning and unexpected ways. The temple is built and then destroyed. The people are taken into exile in a foreign land. But the promise remains in spite of great change. Finally, when the Messiah, the son of Abraham and David does appear among his people, in the greatest of all ironies, he becomes the vehicle of salvation to the nations by being handed over to them by his own to be put to death.

Surely, if we can learn anything from the biblical account of how God kept his promises to Abraham it is that the powers of the age and the varying fortunes and misfortunes of God's people will not ultimately hinder his will being accomplished in the world. Firm in the conviction that God does keep faith with the promises, no matter what the circumstances, the church ought not be overwhelmed and demoralized by the forces of change. The victory won by Christ remains the absolute that will abide in this century and for evermore (Matthew 16:18; 24:35). God has kept faith with his people. This is not the time to doubt but to keep faith in his promises.

3 J. H. Yoder, *The Fullness of Christ: Paul's Vision of Universal Ministry* (Elgin, Illinois: Brethren Press, 1987), pp. 86-91.

4 Ibid.

5 Ibid.

6 Ibid.

7 Carroll D. Osburn, *The Peaceable Kingdom: Essays Favoring Non-Sectarian Christianity* (Abilene: Restoration Perspectives, 1993) pp. 71-92 has documented the extremes to which some brethren have pushed this agenda. As Osburn notes, such methodology ultimately leads to absurd inner contradictions where some are prepared to "fellowship" those who differ on such issues as the use of multiple cups in communion and the validity of located preachers but must separate on issues such as the use of instrumental music in the assembly or a certain view of the millennium. Seemingly, it all depends on an arbitrary judgment as to what constitutes the constants. Osburn gives evidence that this is a far cry from the intention of 2 John 9-11. There John battles opponents who call into question the Word what had become truly flesh, and thus the means of salvation gained through the death of the flesh-and-blood Son of God was becoming endangered.

8 Allan J. McNicol, "Apostolicity and Holiness: The Basis for Christian Fellowship," *Mission* 18/7 (January, 1985) 3-7, 18/8 (February, 1985) 16-20; "The Lord's Supper as Hermeneutical Clue: A Proposal on Theological Method for Churches of Christ," *Christian Studies* 11/1 (Fall, 1990) 41-54: ("Scripture and Tradition: Two Essentials in the Search for the Ancient Order," *Christian Studies* 11:2 (Spring, 1991) 15-30.

Chapter 7

Church Growth: Nightmare or Dream?

Don Vinzant

Biography:

     Don E. Vinzant is the pulpit minister for the Edmond Church of Christ in Edmond, Oklahoma. He also is professor of Bible at Oklahoma Christian Science and Arts in Oklahoma City, Oklahoma. He was on the original Sao Paulo Mission Team, 1961-1982. He has served the Northside Church of Christ in Austin, Texas, the Village Church of Christ in Oklahoma City, the Church of Christ in Granbury, Texas.

     Don received his B. A. and M. A. degrees from Abilene Christian University. He received his D. Min. degree from Austin Presbyterian Theological Seminary.

Footnotes on Chapter 7

1   Carl George inherited the mantle of Peter Wagner as the "dean" of North American Church Growth. George popularized the "metachurch" which, through the use of small groups, intends to make possible unlimited growth of a local congregation.

2   Willow Creek was begun in 1975 by Bill Hybels, then professor at Wheaton. Located advantageously near innumerable evangelical parachurch organizations, it has grown dramatically to over 12,000 in attendance. Never a traditional congregation, Willow Creek now has its own connectional group. Willow Creek targets the unchurched. See also Ministry issue 13, 1994, p. 1, for some of Willow Creek's transferable and nontransferable concepts.

3   The Southern Baptist congregation, Saddlebrook Valley, California, does not carry the name "Baptist." Warren has also pioneered in seeking the unchurched.

4   Demographers and sociologists have spotlighted the Baby Boomer phenomena for over a decade. The boomer population bulge becomes evident when one constructs an age-sex pyramid. The number of live births in the US burgeoned nine months after VJ Day in 1945, and continued in a spectacular rate until 1964, when the birth rate slowed. For years advertisers have focused on this generation because of its unparalleled buying power. Church theorists have attempted to devise strategies to win Boomers, who appear as largely "unchurched" statistically. Tex Sample in *U. S. Lifestyles and Mainline churches: A Key to Reaching People in the 90's*, (Louisville: Westminister/John Knox, 1990) has shown that the "unchurched" condition of Boomers is probably much more complicated than some have seemed to realize.

5   The ambiance of southern California and suburban "Yuppie" Chicagoland is not at all analogous to that facing many congregations in the Southwest.

6   Leith Anderson in *Dying for Change* (Minneapolis: Bethany House, 1990) labors to make a strong case that a paradigm change has occurred; therefore churches need to change. To me it appears that some congregations (and ministers) are in the peril of dying <u>from</u> change. Forcing change that is unwanted to those who are unready can bring unnecessary decline and numerical and spiritual death to the congregation.

7   Gibbs, Eddie, *I Believe in Church Growth* (Grand Rapids: W. B. Eerdmans, 1981).

8   Humphries, Robert L, *A Proposed Plan of Group Mission Work in Sao Paulo, Brazil, Based on Indigenous Principles*, 1961 (A thesis toward the Master Science degree. Thesis is in the Abilene Christian University Library).

9   Pickett, a Methodist missionary in India is the man McGavran credits in the phrase, "My candle was lit at Pickett's fire." Pickett's significant book in this field is entitled, *Christian Mass Movements in India.*

10   Read, Williams, *New Patterns of Church Growth in Brazil* (Grand Rapids: W. B. Eerdmans, 1965).

11   It was later my privilege to spend pleasant hours discussing Church Growth with Professor Wendell Broom, missionary to Africa, student of McGavran, and to take a graduate course in "Church Growth" in 1974 at Abilene Christian University under Dr. Ed Matthews, former missionary to Guatemala, and student of Dr. McGavran.

12   McGavran, Donald, *Understanding Church Growth* (Grand Rapids: W. B. Eerdmans, 1970, reprinted 1980, revised and expanded, 1990).

13   <u>Ibid</u>.

14   <u>Ibid</u>.

15   Wagner, C. Peter, *Your Church Can Grow: Seven Vital Signs of A Healthy Church* (Glendale: Regal, 1976, pp.55-123).

16   Ibid., pp. 124-171. Wagner, who had always been highly complimentary of impressive numerical growth among Pentecostals in Latin America, finally seems to be in the charismatic camp, theologically.

17   Smith, Ebbie, *Balanced Church Growth* (Nashville: Broadman Press, 1984). <u>Definition</u>. CHURCH GROWTH - "Church growth is that body of discovered biblically appropriate and biblically based strategies that relate to the numerical increase and spiritual development of churches and Christians through fulfilling the mandates of evangelizing, disciplining, incorporating, and evaluating to ensure continued progress and ministry," see pp. 15-19.

18   North, Ira, *Balance: A Tried and Tested Formula for Church Growth* (Nashville: Gospel Advocate Company, 1983).

19   Davenport, Dewayne D., *The Bible Says Grow* (Williamstow: Church Growth, 1978).

20   Tippett, Alan R., *Verdict Theology and the Word of God* (Pasadena: William Carey Library, 1973).

21   Shenk, Wilbert R. (editor), *Exploring Church Growth* (Grand Rapids: W. B. Eerdmans, 1983).

22   Jarrell Waskom Pickett greatly influenced McGavran, especially with his early book *Christian Mass Movements in India,* published the year

McGavran arrived as a new missionary there. McGavran always stated his acknowledgment to Pickett.

23   McGavran, Donald, *Effective Evangelism: A Theological Mandate* (Philippsburg: Presbyterian and Reformed Publishing Company, 1988).

24   Zunkel, C.. Wayne, *Church Growth Under Fire* (Scottsdale: Herald Press, 1987).

25   Guiness, Os, *Sounding Out the Idols of Church Growth* (Fairfax: Hourglass Publishers, 1992).

26   Guiness, Os, with John Sell, *No God But God: Breaking With the Idols of Our Age* (Chicago: Moody Press, 1992).

27   Guiness, Os, *Dining With the Devil* (Grand Rapids: Baker Book House, 1994 - third printing).

28   Parro, Craig, "Church Growth's Two Faces," *Christianity Today,* June 24, 1991, p. 19.

29   Horton, Michael, "Foreword" in Robert Wenz's, *Room for God: A Worship Challenge for a Church-Growth and Marketing Era* (Grand Rapids: Baker Book House, 1994), pp.9-11.

30   Hemphill, Ken, *The Antioch Effect: 8 Characteristics of Highly Effective Churches* (Nashville: Broadman and Holman Publishers, 1994).

31   Op. cit., p. 10.

32   Op. cit., p. 11.

33   Op. cit., pp. 21-23.

34   Op. cit., p. 36.

35   Op. cit., p. 41.

36   Rainer, Thom S., *Eating The Elephant: Bite-Sized Steps to Achieve Long-Term Growth in Your Church* (Nashville: Broadman and Holman, 1994).

37   Hemphill, Op. cit., p. 44.

38   Op. cit., p. 48-49.

39   Rainer, Thom S., Op. cit., p. g calling attention to James Emery White's, *Opening the Front Door: Worship and Church Growth* (Nashville: Convention Press, 1992).

40   Ibid.

41   Ibid.

42   Hemphill, Ibid., pp. 73-101.

43   Ibid., pp. 103-128.

44   Ibid., pp. 129-135. The reminder of this chapter continues to draw heavily from Hemphill's, *The Antioch Effect*.

45   Andre Resner has a thoughtful article in *Restoration Quarterly,* Second Quarter, 1994, pp. 65-80, entitled, "To Worship or To Evangelize? Ecclesiology's Phantom Fork in the Road." See also Jeffrey Peterson's insightful article, "How Shall the Seeker Say Amen?" The "Seeker and the Service in First Corinthians," in *Christian Studies*, Number 13 (1993), pp. 22-31. This is a publication of the Institute for Christian Studies in Austin, Texas. Peterson observes that some in churches of Christ are arguing that "...worship must be refashioned so as to 'connect' with a new generation and serve more effectively as a means of evangelism. To attract the masses of the unchurched adrift in urban and suburban America, the public services of the church must be rethought with the tastes of these 'seekers' in mind". Peterson is talking about some who

write in *Wineskins*, who have advocated such an accommodation. As Peterson's article draws to a close, he trenchantly points out, "since the beginning of this century, conservatives have criticized mainline Protestantism for its accommodation of the church's faith to the assumptions of modern secular culture. Now, as the century draws to a close and liberal Protestants in increasing numbers call for an end of accommodation, it is the evangelicals who are taking the lead in fitting preaching and worship to the mold of modern culture.... The critical need in worship today is not for current tunes, celebrity testimonials, or increased outlets for self-expression and enjoyment; it is for clear affirmations of the fundamental convictions which unite the church."

Chapter 8

Human Opinion vs. Divine Doctrine

Howard Norton

Biography:

Howard Norton is a Bible professor and the executive-director of the Institute for Church and Family Resources at Harding University. He was chairman of the division of Bible at Oklahoma Christian University of Science and Arts for many years. He also was editor and publisher of the Christian Chronicle for many years. He worked from 1961 to 1977 as a missionary in Sao Paulo, Brazil. He is one of three directors of the Pan American Lectureship. He takes a campaign group to Brazil and conducts meetings there nearly every year.

Norton graduated from Abilene Christian University with his Bachelor of Arts degree in 1957, from the University of Houston with the Master of Arts degree in 1964, and from the Universidade de Sao Paulo with the Doctor of Human Sciences degree in 1981.

Chapter 9

The Mystery of Baptism - A Personal Odyssey

Prentice A. Meador, Jr.

Biography:

A native of Nashville, Tennessee, and a graduate of David Lipscomb College, Prentice A. Meador, Jr. holds the Ph.D. from the University of Illinois. He has taught communication at UCLA, the University of Washington in Seattle, Southwest Missouri State University, Springfield, Missouri, and is currently adjunct Professor for Abilene Christian University. He and his wife, Barbara, make their home in Dallas, Texas where he serves as Pulpit Minister for the Prestoncrest Church of Christ. Barbara is a registered nurse. The Meadors have three married children.

Meador serves on the Board of Trustees of Abilene Christian University and on the Chancellor's Council, Pepperdine University. He is Managing Editor of 21st Century Christian and assistant Editor of Power for Today. His most recent books include *Walk With Me*, co-authored with Bob Chisholm, which is a study of the Gospel of Mark, and *Genesis: "The Great Story."* In November 1994, Meador received David Lipscomb University's "Representative of the Decade" award.

Gospel vs. Epistles, Jesus vs. the Church - A Misplaced Debate

Michael Weed

Biography:

Michael R. Weed is Billy Gunn Hocott Professor of Theology and Ethics at the Institute for Christian Studies in Austin, Texas, where he also serves as Faculty Chairman. Weed is a graduate of Abilene Christian University, Austin Presbyterian Theological Seminary, and Emory University. Weed is author of the *Living Word Commentary on Ephesians, Colossians and Philemon.* He is also editor of <u>Christian Studies</u> and a member of the American Society of Christian Studies. Weed serves as an elder of the Brentwood Oaks Church of Christ in Austin, Texas.

Footnotes on Chapter 10

1   See James S. Woodroof, *The Church in Transition* (Searcy, Arkansas: The Bible House, 1990): "Plugging into any part of the Scripture, except the Gospels, expecting there to find power, is like plugging an electric motor into a reflection of a power outlet... A Christ -exalting restoration will plug our lives into the Gospel account first. Then, having been plugged into the life of Christ for our power, we can walk triumphantly through the rest of Scripture and through life, confident, we can do all things through Christ who strengthens us (Phil. 4: 13)"(34). Woodroof appears oblivious to the fact that the Gospels are written after most of the New Testament epistles. His point might better be made that Christian faith should center on the gospel, rather than the Gospels.

2   R. J. Banks, *Paul's Idea of Community* (Grand Rapids: Eerdmans, 1980).

3   Gerd Theissen, *Sociology of Early Palestinian Christianity* (Philadelphia: Fortress, 1978).

4   To my knowledge, contemporary revisionists within Churches of Christ have yet to make any serious call to turn from traditions such as expensive church buildings and well-paid ministerial staff.

5   Adolf Harnack, *What is Christianity?* (New York: Harper & Row, 1957; German original, 1900) 111.

6   Harnack, 187

7   Ernst Troeltsch, *The Social Teaching of the Christian Churches* (New York: Harper & Row, 1960, German original, 1911) 45.

8   In a sense, this whole theological movement represents in part the fruition of the Lutheran rejection of Roman Catholic ecclesiology and its own failure to develop an adequate alternative ecclesiology and concern for the shape and order of the church (see Harnack, 265f).

9   Cf. R. Newton, Flew, *Jesus and His Church* (
1938). This is a dated but still very helpful discussio
issues involved.   Also see Hans Kung, *The Chu*
Doubleday, 1976, German original, 1967) 69-144.

10   Ralph P. Martin, *The Four Gospels* (Grand Ra|
1975).   "It is true that Christians may well have desire
account of Jesus' earthly life and words, especially as moi
ers were dying. But it remains a conviction throughout the N
literature that the memory of Christ the Lord was a presen   , .v une
people who met to worship in his name, to break bread in remembrance
of him, and to realize the full extent and depth of his promise to be with
them (Matthew 18: 10)"(18).

11   Cf. Wayne A. Meeks, *The First Urban Christians: The Social
World of the Apostle Paul* (New Haven: Yale, 1983) 75f.

12   Contemporary concern for intimacy owes more to modern mass
culture and therapeutic models of the personal than it does to biblical
understandings of "fellowship" and the interpersonal.   See Michael R.
Weed, "Ethos and Authority: Then and Now," *Faculty Bulletin of the Institute for Christian Studies,* No. 7, Fall, 1986, 62-77.

13   The issue here is not *whether* Christian faith and the church are
relevant to   the wider political arena and particular political issues, but
how.

14   Lynn Anderson and Carey Garrett seem to approach this position
in their article "Getting Change into Your System," *Wineskins*, Volume 2,
Number 4, September/October, 1993: "....what happens if our security
rests in the church rather than in the Christ?.....How different our feelings
about change will be if we see Jesus (not the first-century church) as the
blueprint....."(34). Clearly Anderson and Garrett distinguish allegiance to
Jesus from allegiance to existing churches with practices they dislike.
Missing in this discussion are specific criteria, biblical and theological, that
guide and limit change. One wonders how (and whether) Anderson and
Garrett would defend innovative churches against those who reject even
their innovations as inhibiting and overly cautious. Presumably the incarnation and apostolic teaching and practice have some function in this
regard. When such criteria are not specified, however, "theology" inevitably becomes a shallow "theology of expediency."

15   I am not suggesting that churches of Christ are unique in this.
Our ambivalence regarding the relationship of the Gospels to the church,
however, may make our way of addressing the problem somewhat
unique.

The Ministry of the Spirit Among Us

Jimmy Jividen

Biography:
Jimmy Jividen preaches for the Oldham Road church of Christ in Abilene, Texas. He also speaks to some thirty congregations, lectureships and camps each year.

Jividen is the author of eight books and contributed chapters to ten books. Some of his writings have been translated into four languages. His books which discuss the Holy Spirit as: *Glossolalia, From God or man; Miracles, From God or Man; Miracles;* and *Alive in the Spirit.*

Footnotes on Chapter 11
1   The World *Only* operation of the Holy Spirit in the context of this chapter refers to the idea that the Holy Spirit does not *personally* dwell in a Christian but only works in and through the Word of God.

2   The *Charismatic* operation of the Holy Spirit in the context of this chapter is the idea that the Holy Spirit works in miraculous ways in the world today. This view is usually held by those who rely upon emotional experiences for religious authority. They believe their religious experiences are miracles - contrary to nature.

3   A full discussion of the present work of the Holy Spirit is found in my book *Alive in the Spirit, A Study of the Nature and Work of the Holy Spirit* (Nashville: Gospel Advocate Company, 1990).

4   I have documented and refuted these errors in two books: Jimmy Jividen, *Glossolalia, from God or Man?* (Fort Worth: Star Publishing Co., 1970); Jimmy Jividen, *Miracles, from God or Man* (Abilene, Texas; ACU Press, 1987).

Chapter 12

Boomergeist: The Spirit of the Age

Jim Baird

Biography:

Jim Baird has been an assistant professor in the College of Bible at Oklahoma Christian University of Science and Arts, since January, 1992. His areas of special interest are Christian Evidences and Philosophy of Religion. In December of 1991, he successfully defended his doctoral dissertation in Philosophy at Oxford University. His dissertation present a new argument that humans are created by God, based on Godel's theorems showing the incompleteness of all formal systems of mathematics. While studying at Oxford, Jim worked as a part time minister for the Oxford Church of Christ. From 1982 to 1988, Jim served as a minister of the church of Christ in Franklin, Indiana.

Baird received his Masters of Theology degree from Harding Graduate School of Religion in 1982. He received his B. A. in Bible and English from Oklahoma Christian College in 1978. Jim married Yolanda Gale Wyrick on January 5, 1979. They are proud parents of two boys: James and Taylor.

Footnotes on Chapter 12

1   See for instance, James Patterson and Peter Kim, *The Day America Told the Truth* (New York: Prentice Hall Press, 1991), p. 203.

2   The best recent analysis of our hyper-secularization is in Stephen L. Carter's, *The Culture of Disbelief: How American law and Politics Trivialize Religious Devotion* New York: Basic Books, 1993). Older works on this same topic which will be helpful are: Richard John Neuhaus, *The Naked Public Square: Religious and Democracy in America* (Grand Rapids, Michigan: Williams B. Eerdmans, 1984); Cal Thomas, *Book Burning* (Westchester, Illinois: Crossway Books, 1983) and Franky Schaeffer, *A Time for Anger: The Myth of Neutrality* (Westchester, Illinois: Crossway Books, 1982).

3   *Engel v. Vitale,* 370 U. S. 421 (1962).

4   Carter, p. 206.

5   Carter, p. 206 mentions growing evidence that the net effect of our current curriculum is actually hostile to religion. He recommends the bibliographical survey provided in Michael W. McConnell, "The Selective Funding Problem: Abortions and Religious Schools," *Harvard Law Review* 104 (1991): 1012-13 n. 75.

6   Philip Patterson, *The Electronic Millstone* (Joplin: College Press Publishing Company, 1992), pp. 18 & 19.

7   C. Leonard Allen, Richard T. Hughes and Michael R. Weed, *The Worldly Church* (Abilene: ACU Press, 1988), especially chapter two.

Recommended Reading:

Stephen L. Carter's. *The Culture of Disbelief: How American Law and Politics Trivialize Religious Devotion* (New York: Basic Books, 1993).

Richard John Neuhaus. *The Naked Public Square: Religion and Democracy in America* (Grand Rapids: William B. Eerdmans, 1984).

Cal Thomas. *Book Burning* (Westchester: Crossway Books, 1983).

Philip Patterson, *The Electronic Millstone* (Joplin: College Press, 1992).

C. Leonard Allen, Richard T. Hughes and Michael Weed. *The Worldly Church* (Abilene: ACU Press, 1988).

Chapter 13

Is The Bible Inerrant?

Edward P. Myers

Biography

Edward P. Myers was born in Crane, Texas. He began preaching in 1969 in Beaver, Oklahoma. He holds the B. A. degree from Berean Christian College, the M. A. degree from Cincinnati Christian Seminary, M. T. S & M.Th from Alabama Christian School of Religion, M. T. S., M.Th., D. Min. from the Harding Graduate School of Religion, M. A. R and Ph. D. from Drew University. Myers is now serving as professor or Bible and Christian doctrine in the College of Bible and Religion at Harding University in Searcy, Arkansas.

He has written books on *Angels, The Doctrine of the Godhead, The Problem of Evil and Suffering, Biblical Interpretation, and Letters to the Seven Churches of Asia.*

Footnotes on chapter 13

1   Earl D. Radmacher, Editor, *Can We Trust the Bible?* (Wheaton: Tyndale House Publishers, 1979), p. 9.
2   Everett F. Harrison, "The Phenomena of Scripture," in *Revelation and the Bible,* ed. Carl F. H. Henry (Grand Rapids: Baker Book House, 1958), p. 238.
3.   Davis, *The Debate About the Bible,* (Philadelphia: Westminister Press, 1977), p. 65.
4.   B. B. Warfield, *The Inspiration and Authority of the Bible,* p. 442.
5   Cottrell, *Solid: The Authority of God's Word,* pp. 31-32.
6   Each of these reasons could be developed into a chapter or an entire book. Some have been. Consult the books listed in these footnotes, and it will be evident that this is true.
7   Cf. James Montgomery Boice, *Does Inerrancy Matter?* (Oakland, California: International Council of Biblical Inerrancy, 1979), pp. 14-20.
8   Boice, p. 28.

Chapter 14

Trends in Chruch Leadership

Flavil Yeakley

Biography
Flavil R. Yeakley, Jr. is a Professor in the College of Bible and Religion at Harding University in Searcy, Arkansas. He started preaching in 1950 and spent almost twenty five years in full time local church work. Later he served as deacon and as and elder. He is the author of *Why Churches Grow, Church Leadership and Organization* and *The Discipling Dilemma*. He directs the Harding Center for Church Growth Studies. In this role he conducts research, does consulting work with churches, and conducts seminars on church growth, leadership and related topics. He is a former President of the American Society for Church Growth and presently serves on the Board of the Association of Statisticians of American Religious Bodies.

Footnotes on Chapter 14
1   Flavil R. Yeakley, Jr., *Church Leadership and Organization* (Nashville: Christian Communications, Inc., 1979), p. 30.   *Traditional/ Authoritarian Churches*
2   Flavil R. Yeakley, Jr. (ed.) with Howard Norton, Don Vinzant and Gene Vinzant, *The Discipling Dilemma* (Nashville: Gospel Advocate, 1988). See also: Jerry Jones, *What Does the Boston Movement Teach?* Volumes 1 & 2 (Bridgetown: Mid-America Tape and Book Sales, 1990); Ronald M. Enroth, *Churches That Abuse* (Grand Rapids: Zondervan, 1992); and, Steve Hassan, *Combating Cult Mind Control* (Rochester, Vermont: Park Street Press, 1988).
3   Leonard Allen and Richard Hughes, *Discovering Our Roots* (Abilene: ACU Press, 1988).
4   Gary L. McIntosh, "What's In A Name?" in *The McIntosh Church Growth Network,* Volume 3, Number 5 (May 1991).
5   William Strauss and Neil Howe, *Generations* (New York: Morrow, 1991).
6   J. R. P. French and B. Raven, "The Bases of Social Power," in D. Cartwright (ed.) *Studies in Social Power* (Ann Arbor: Institute for Social Research, University of Michigan, 1959), pp. 150-167.
7   G. Yukl and C. M. Falbe, "Importance of Difference Power Sources in Downward and Lateral Relations," *Journal of Applied Psychology,* Volume 76 (1991), pp. 416-423.
8   Tom Yokum, "A Word Study on Church Leadership," in Jerry Jones, *What Does the Boston Movement Teach?* Volume I, pp. 193-199.
9   Lyle Schaller, *Effective Church Planning* (Nashville: Abingdon, 1981), pp. 161-170.
10   Fred B. Craddock, *As One Without Authority* (Nashville: Abingdon, 1971).

Chapter 15

How to be Undenominational in a Denominational World

Stafford North

Biography:

Stafford North began preaching in 1948 and has served a number of churches since that time both as a regular preacher and in meetings. He has written several books and tracts. He writes regularly for the *Christian Chronicle* and *Power for Today.*

North has been associated with Oklahoma Christian University of Science and Arts since 1952. During all those years he has taught classes and for thirty eight years he held administrative posts. Now he teaches full time in the College of Biblical Studies. North is known especially for his work in Daniel and Revelation on which he lectures widely. He hold degrees from Abilene Christian University, Louisiana State University and the University of Florida

Chapter 16

Who's in the Fellowship?

Carl Mitchell

Biography:
Carl Mitchell is a preacher, teacher, missionary and college professor. He holds the B. A. & M. A. degrees from Pepperdine University, University of Florence, Italy, Ph.D. from the University of Southern California. He has preached in Los Angeles, San Francisco, Thousand Oaks in California, Cloverdale and Searcy in Arkansas. He served fourteen years as missionary in Italy. He was Professor of Religion at Pepperdine University for fifteen years and served four years as head of the Bible Department. He taught in the Bible Department at Harding for five years and was head of the Bible Department for many years. He continues to work with the mission work in Italy.

Footnotes on Chapter 16
1   Harold Netland, *Dissonant Voices: Religious Pluralism and The Question of Truth* (Grand Rapids: W. B. Eerdmans Publishing Company, 1991)
2   *Webster's College Dictionary,* (New York: Random House, 1991), p. 290.
3   Following are key passages which use some form of *Koinonia:* Acts 2:42; Romans 15:26 (contribution); I Corinthians 1:9; 10:16 (communion); II Corinthians 6:14;8:4 (participate); 9:13 (contribution); 13:14; Galatians 2:9; Ephesians 3:9; 5:13; Philippians 1:5 2:1; 3:10; 4:14 (share) I Timothy 6: 18 (share); Philemon 6; Hebrews 13:16 (share); I John 1: 3,6,7; Revelation 18:4 (participate).
4   W. E. Vine, *An Expository Dictionary of New Testament Words,* Volume II, (London: Oliphants Ltd., 1957).
5   Gerhard Kittel, *Theological Dictionary of the New Testament,* Volume III, (Grand Rapids: W. B. Eerdmans Publishing Company, 1974), p. 90.
6   Following are key passages which use some form of *Metoche:* Luke 5:7 (partners); II Corinthians 6:14; Hebrews 1:9 (companions); 3:1,14; 6:4;12:8 (partakers).
7   Vine, Vol. II, op. cit., p. 90.
8   Kittel, Vol. II, op. cit., pp. 822-823.
9.   Following are key passages which use some form of *Kollao* Acts 5: 13; 8:29; 9:26 (join); 10:28 (associate), 17:34 (join).
10.   Vine, Vol. I, op. cit., p. 90.
11   Kittel Vol. III, pp. 822-832.

12   Following are key passages which use *Chebar:* Judges 20: 11 (united); I Chronicles 20: 35 (allied; Job 34: 8 (to be in company with); Psalm 94: 20 (allied; Song of Solomon 1:7; 8:13 (companion); Daniel 2: 13 (friends); 11:23 (alliance).

13.   Kittel, Vol. III, op. cit., pp. 800-803.

14.   F. F. Bruce, *New Testament History* (New York: Anchor Books, 1972), p. 81.

15   Charles F. Pfeiffer, *Between the Testaments,* (Grand Rapids: Baker Book House, 1959), p. IIIf.

16   Vine, Vol. 1, op. cit., pp. 83-84.

17   Rudolf Bultmann, *Theology of the New Testament,* Volume I (New York: Charles Scribner's Sons, 1955), pp. 136-137).

MEET THE EDITORS

Jim Sheerer works with the Southern Oaks Church of Christ in Chickasha, Oklahoma. He was the pulpit preacher in Chickasha for thirty years and for the last two years has served as Involvement minister. He holds the B. A. and M. A. degrees from Abilene Christian University. He has preached on the island of Guam, Carbon, Llano and Austin, Texas, and Jamestown, New York. He and his wife, Nona Sue, have three daughters and six grandchildren.

Charles Williams serves an elder and preacher at the Oakcrest Church of Christ where he has served twenty two years. He was the pulpit preacher for the first sixteen years. He holds the B. A. and M. S. degrees from Abilene Christian University. He has preached in Van Horn, Mexia, Tomball, and Hurst, Texas and Jamestown, New York. He and his wife, Joyce, have three daughters and nine grandchildren.